Project Management for Flat Organizations

Cost Effective Steps to Achieving Successful Results

Laura Dallas Burford, M.A., PMP

J.ROSS PUBLISHING

ISBN-13: 978-1-60427-084-6

Printed and bound in the U.S.A. Printed on acid-free paper
10 9 8 7 6 5 4 3 2 1

Library of Congress Cataloging-in-Publication Data
Burford, Laura Dallas.
  Project management for flat organizations : cost effective steps to
achieving successful results / by Laura Dallas Burford.
     p. cm.
  Includes index.
  ISBN 978-1-60427-084-6 (hbk. : alk. paper) 1. Project management. 2.
Cost effectiveness. I. Title.
  HD69.P75B866 2012
  658.4'04--dc23

                                                    2012030920

Direct all inquiries to J. Ross Publishing, Inc., 300 S. Pine Island Road, Suite #305, Plantation, FL 33324.

Phone: (954) 727-9333
Fax: (561) 892-0700
Web: www.jrosspub.com

CONTENTS

SECTION 3: BUILDING THE ROADMAP

SECTION 7: CLOSING THE PROJECT

LIST OF ILLUSTRATIONS

SECTION 4: STILL MORE PLANNING

SECTION 6. MANAGING THE EFFORT

SECTION 7. CLOSING THE PROJECT

PREFACE

The idea to write this book developed over time and is based on experiences with client projects and project management seminars involving flat organizations. Client and seminar attendee question and discussion sessions always brought home the idea that, for these organizations and their staffs, the success of their projects was more important than whose methodology was being followed or what tools were being used for project management. Another striking common characteristic was that there was insufficient time to both train and work on a project, leaving them with an unattractive practical choice: either train when time permitted—and without purpose—or work on a project without the appropriate skills or knowledge. Back at the office, time and money, not to mention managerial appetite, were lacking for implementing lengthy formal processes and procedures. Consequentially, daily communication and control were informal.

The formal bureaucratic processes so characteristic of traditional hierarchical organizations undertaking large projects requiring dedicated (meaning full-time) project management and staff for implementation were not only beyond the reach of these organizations, but were also counter to their organizational culture. Nevertheless, there was a general recognition of the need, even a hunger, for a project management approach that would improve the chances of achieving project success. That was why clients were asking questions and people were coming to the seminars. This book resulted from the search for the right balance of formality and informality—control versus no control—that would prove practical and useful to flat organizations undertaking projects.

Authors always are indebted to their supporters and I am no exception. I need to thank the flat organizations that opened my eyes to a different project management approach after years of working with large corporate organizations with hierarchical structures. I am also indebted to colleagues and friends who encouraged and supported me as I wrote this book.

Seminars sponsored by the Nonprofit Resource Network (NRN), Millersville University, funded by grants from the Project Management Institute Educational Foundation (PMIEF), provided an additional forum for me to more fully understand project management outside of a large corporate environment. Thank you, Anne L. Gingerich, M.S.W., Director, and Victor S. DeSantis, Ph.D., Dean of the College of Graduate Studies and Professional Studies, for your confidence.

I also thank the Chester County Library System (Pennsylvania) for assistance in obtaining published works needed for background in writing this work; my publisher, Drew Gierman, for taking a chance on a new author writing about a niche topic; and my editor, Carolyn Lea, for her pertinent editing, suggestions, and guidance.

Perhaps most importantly, thanks to my husband and partner, Dave, who suffered through multiple drafts of a seemingly interminable topic. His thoughts on the brevity, clarity, and practicality of the ideas and instructions provided in this book were instrumental, if not essential, to completing this effort.

ABOUT THE AUTHOR

 Laura Dallas Burford has more than twenty-five years of domestic and international project management experience, working with organizations of various sizes, industries, and organizational structures. She has extensive experience with big four consulting organizations; was a managing director at a start-up international technology consulting organization; and currently is the owner and president of LAD Enterprizes. Over her career, she has worked for or provided consulting services to several Top 100 corporations. She has led numerous large information technology and business improvement programs, outsourcing efforts, start-up initiatives, and fundraising projects as well as project turnarounds. She also has assisted organizations with developing their own project management approach and methodology. Laura holds a Bachelor of Science in Commerce (B.S.C.) and a Masters of Arts (M.A.) from Rider University and is a Certified Project Management Professional (PMP®).

In addition to numerous speaking engagements and seminars, Laura has authored, facilitated, and taught several project management training programs, including a *Project Management Nonprofit Practicum*, for the Nonprofit Resource Network, Millersville University. As a practitioner, she focuses on coaching and advising flat organizations concerned with projects aligning strategy, processes, and information technology. Laura can be reached by email at LauraDBurford@ gmail.com.

Free value-added materials available from
the Download Resource Center at www.jrosspub.com

At J. Ross Publishing we are committed to providing today's professional with practical, hands-on tools that enhance the learning experience and give readers an opportunity to apply what they have learned. That is why we offer free ancillary materials available for download on this book and all participating Web Added Value™ publications. These online resources may include interactive versions of material that appears in the book or supplemental templates, worksheets, models, plans, case studies, proposals, spreadsheets and assessment tools, among other things. Whenever you see the WAV™ symbol in any of our publications it means bonus materials accompany the book and are available from the Web Added Value™ Download Resource Center at www.jrosspub.com.

Downloads available for *Project Management for Flat Organizations: Cost Effective Steps to Achieving Successful Results* consist of project management templates, an approach for selecting project management software, and steps for creating a standardized approach for managing projects:

Project Management Word Templates: The Word templates included in this download are referenced throughout the book. The templates are intended to be used as a starting point for a particular project or to assist with developing a project management methodology for an organization. They are to be modified to fit the needs of an organization. As noted in the book, templates that are unnecessary for your organization should not be used.

Selecting a Project Management Software Application—A Whitepaper: Successful projects require a project manager to plan, and then manage and control, a set of tasks that are required to create a unique and specific product or service. A project management (PM) software application is one tool that can assist with this effort, but deciding on the right PM software application is a project in itself. Expanding on the information included in this book, this whitepaper provides you with an approach for selecting the "best fit" PM software application.

Ten Steps to Create a Project Management Methodology—A Whitepaper: If an organization has enough projects, a standardized approach or what many people refer to as a Project Management Methodology (PMM) may be warranted because a PMM assists with providing consistency across projects and improves the likelihood of any particular project being successful. A PMM includes suggestions, guidelines, and other project aids for the project manager, sponsor, and team members. This whitepaper walks you through the steps for creating a PMM and augments information in the book.

INTRODUCTION

If you don't know where you're going, you might end up some place else.
—Yogi Berra

This book is aimed at helping people understand and implement project management by examining in some detail three project activities: defining the project outcome, developing a workable plan, and then executing that plan. The focus of the project management discipline has been on large projects undertaken by hierarchical organizations. Although the project management methodologies and frameworks are designed for projects of all sizes, the formal processes and controls are complex, cumbersome, and costly. By nature, project management is bureaucratic with detailed project plans and formal processes and controls that can take on a life of their own.

Simply put, these formal processes and controls involve too much overhead for organizations with a flat organizational structure, minimal bureaucracy, and informal processes and controls. As a result, people in flat organizations often just start working on a project, skipping the steps that help ensure success. In an effort move the project forward, requirements and expectations are not clearly defined. The ultimate result is delay, rework, increased cost, and frustration.

People working in flat organizations require enough formality to be successful, but not so much as to destroy the culture, creativity, and innovation found within the organization. They want project guidance and are looking to obtain skills or what some call "good old-fashioned know-how." They may never work on a very large project, they are not looking for a career in project management, nor are they interested in obtaining project management certification. Rather, they are looking to understand project management concepts so they can develop expertise that can be applied immediately. To obtain this expertise, they might attend a project management training seminar, take an online class, or read a book. They immediately apply what they learned, share their knowledge with others in the organization, and hopefully, successfully complete their project.

They want project management processes, tools, and techniques that fit their needs, enabling them to deliver projects efficiently, successfully, and with limited stress and minimal investment.

FLAT ORGANIZATIONAL CHARACTERISTICS

Flat organizational structures have few or no levels of management between senior management and the staff. The management environment tends to be open and informal. The staff are empowered and encouraged to collaborate. Teamwork is prevalent with open dialogue and consensus building dominating interpersonal relationships. Decisions are made collectively and, at times, staff work autonomously under a hands-off management approach. Reliance is placed on everyone "doing their job," being productive, and pitching in if a need arises. Communication is informal, resulting in quicker decision-making. The informality and lack of bureaucracy result in a flat organization being flexible and better able to adapt to change.

Even though there are large organizations with flat organizational structures, the majority of flat organizations are small- or medium-sized businesses, non-profits and associations, government agencies, or divisions of a larger business. They are manufacturing and distribution companies, software and hardware technology companies, professional services organizations, retail operations, construction companies, consulting organizations, training companies, smaller educational institutions, and more.

PROJECTS IN FLAT ORGANIZATIONS

A project initiated in a flat organization is generally a project of modest scale (of course, there are exceptions). The reason for the project is clear and easily defined with one or two project objectives and straightforward deliverables. A single decision-maker, the project's sponsor, is assigned to the project and takes an active role. A project manager is responsible for managing the effort and leading the team members. Sometimes the project sponsor and project manager are the same person. Team members often have day-to-day operational responsibilities as well as project responsibilities.

Projects of a modest scale can be easier to plan, manage, and execute than large projects. If planned and managed properly, these projects have a better chance of meeting expectations and finishing on time and on budget than large projects. The reasons vary, but the timeline is shorter, making it easier for key people to remain focused on the project, expectations, and work effort. Because the timeline is shorter, there are fewer changes to the project's requirements. Estimates are more accurate because many are based on historical information, industry standards, and relatively stable current conditions. Informal processes, controls, and communication result in timely reporting and quicker decision-making.

The key point is that project success is possible in flat organizations *if projects are planned and managed*—this requires debunking the belief that there is no simple way to implement a project management methodology because any approach is going to be too complex, too costly, and too formal or the project will require the purchase of expensive project management software. Simple, low-cost processes can be implemented and projects can be planned and managed without using expensive software.

THE PROJECT ENVIRONMENT IN FLAT ORGANIZATIONS

All projects need to be planned, managed, and executed, but flat organizations have unique characteristics that need to be considered.

The first characteristic is staff can rarely be devoted full time to projects. As a result, staff juggle their day-to-day operational and administrative responsibilities with their project responsibilities. If everyone involved is not careful, staff operational responsibilities and project tasks can easily become intermingled and the delineation between operations and the project can become blurred, impacting the project's completion and success. A project may also require lapse time to be built into the schedule to accommodate the day-to-day operational and administrative needs of the staff, resulting in an extended project timeline. Thus, the project takes longer to complete than a similar project in a hierarchical organization possessing team members whose only job is to work on the project.

A second characteristic is with a limited number of staff there tends to be a reliance on consultants to provide necessary expertise or vendors to augment internal staff and provide other project resources so that projects can be completed by the "required" date. This situation necessitates having a project manager with a solid understanding of procurement and vendor management.

A third characteristic is funds are comparatively modest for many flat organizations. Budget plans split these funds between day-to-day operations and new initiatives. Funds for training, project management software, or hiring vendors and consultants may be severely restricted for new initiatives. If a business emergency arises, the project may need to be postponed or "corners cut." The project may even need to be cancelled.

A fourth characteristic is communication tends to be informal, frequently consisting of conversations in a hallway or short emails. Formal documents confirming and memorializing the understandings reached are limited or do not exist. Under these conditions it is easy for miscommunication to occur or for decisions to be forgotten. In the meantime, the organization struggles to develop a simplified project management approach that has the right balance of informal and formal communication.

The fifth characteristic concerns project manager training and experience. Often the project manager role is assigned to a staff person who is not trained or is inexperienced in project management, which increases project risk. The organization as a whole also has limited training and instruction in project management and no standardized processes. The staff person assigned to the project manager role not only needs to figure out "what project management is," but also "what my role and responsibilities are" and "how to do the work." If an organization is fortunate enough to have a full-time experienced project manager, this project manager may be the only full-time person working on the project—and might also be responsible for training the team in project management skills.

THIS BOOK

This book has been written for:

- Individuals with little or no formal training in project management who are either working on or managing a modest-sized project in an organization with a flat hierarchy
- An organization with a flat hierarchy that is trying to develop their own project management approach and methodology

It applies to:

- New project managers, including an individual who is assigned the project manager role by organizational necessity or as a reward rather than a career path choice
- Project team members
- Experienced project managers looking for a quick refresher
- Business leaders, managers, and project sponsors

Why include business leaders, managers, and project sponsors on the list? Like living things, projects require care and feeding—things that only business leaders, managers, and project sponsors can provide. Three reasons for project failure are unrealistic expectations by management, lack of management support, and a disengaged project sponsor. Projects are team efforts that require business leaders, managers, and project sponsors to work together to achieve success.

This book describes a simple, no-nonsense, cost-effective approach to project management. Aimed at organizations with a flat organizational structure and informal communications, processes, and controls, the book assists an individual with managing or working on a project or an organization with creating a project management approach. It imparts knowledge of various project management concepts and provides an understanding of the purpose behind the processes, tools, and techniques so that the reader can analyze their organization's circumstances and synthesize an appropriate solution for their organization. Because time is a premium for many flat organizations, this book is targeted, not too long, not too wordy, and, where possible, visual. The book discusses three critical activities: the first key activity is the defining of the project outcome and the recording of that definition in a scope statement (or project definition); the second activity is to plan what needs to be done and create a project plan documenting what needs to occur to accomplish the outcome; and the third activity is to "work the plan," successfully delivering the outcome with the aid of a status report.

To do this, the book is divided into seven sections, starting with explaining the fundamentals of project management and then walking the reader through the entire project life cycle from management concept to completing the project. Sections and chapters are written so that a reader can grasp the points without digesting the entire work. To make it easier for the reader, the beginning of each section provides an overview of information to be covered, a brief explanation as to the importance of the section, and a description of each chapter.

Each chapter starts with a list of the subjects covered and ends with a review of key points. The theory of the subjects is introduced and then, using examples, visual aids, tools, and techniques, the chapter walks the reader through applying the theory. Reference is made to dedicated project management software applications, but Microsoft Office® Word and Excel, widely available and familiar productivity tools, are used to create tools and templates and to explain the techniques offered in this book. Included in the chapters are short stories, scenarios, suggestions, reference tables, questions to consider, and guidelines intended to illuminate the subject, issues, or skills. Except in Section 1, step-by-step instructions are provided at the end of each chapter for the reader to follow when working on a project or to incorporate into their organization's project management methodology.

This book is not a course or study guide to help the reader pass the PMP® exam, the PRINCE2™ exam, or any other project management certification. It does not extol the importance or the benefits of project management. It is not aimed at training the reader in how to be a "good" project manager or to teach a project manager leadership, management, or interpersonal skills.

HOW TO USE THIS BOOK

This book is designed to assist with planning and managing a project and to assist a flat organization with developing a standardized project management methodology. When using this book to assist with managing or working on a project, select a project and use each chapter to help plan and then execute the project. Not all chapters are applicable for every project nor is everything in every chapter applicable for any given project. Select what works for the project and the organization. Another option is to select a completed project and walk through each chapter, noting what worked and what could have been improved upon.

When using this book to create a project management methodology for managing projects within your organization, focus on the theory and the reasons for each of the processes. Adapt the material to fit the size and culture of your organization. The step-by-step instructions, tables, tools, and techniques are thorough and contain a lot of information, but they are designed to be used as guidelines. Edit them. Keep them simple. Make them work for you. Start with the minimum needed for your organization and add as warranted. A standardized approach or process enables a project team to remain focused on the project needs, to not overlook a needed step, and to have a consistent approach from one project to the next. Be careful not to implement formalized processes that are unsuitable. Doing so often leads to general frustration and noncompliance by the staff as well as the loss of motivation and creativity. One last point: having a standardized project management methodology is not a substitute for having a project manager. A project manager is still necessary for successful projects.

TAKING THE NEXT STEP

This book is a guide. The most successful projects are based on teamwork and people working together. In flat organizations, people understand teamwork, collaboration, and flexibility. Use the positive characteristics of your organization's culture when creating project plans or developing a project management approach. Lengthy, formal documents with elaborate processes and controls generally are not necessary, but for a project to be successful achieving a balance between formality and informality resulting in a modicum of control is required.

When planning and executing a project, do not get "wrapped around the axle" thinking that a certain process must be followed or a certain tool or technique must be used. Mistakes will happen, issues will need to be addressed, changes will occur, and some decisions will not be the best, but the goal is to make the best decisions possible based on what is known at the time. Many times, there are multiple ways of solving a problem. Use the skills of the team to solve problems. Some decisions will be based on the "gut feeling" of the project manager, the sponsor, and the team members. Learn to rely on that gut feeling, but base a decision on facts and judgment. Good project teams use processes and controls to assist them with a project and do not let the processes and controls dominate or manage them.

Managing a project does not need to be an enormous tedious bureaucratic controlling process-oriented production. It is possible to have fun. So have fun.

SECTION 1

SETTING THE STAGE

Projects come in all shapes and sizes, but the fundamental management processes are the same. Projects are defined and planned; executed; managed and controlled; and then closed when completed. A project approach that works in one organization, however, may not be feasible or realistic for another. A large, hierarchical organization that has multiple, complex, large-scale projects tends to also have a formal, complex project management control structure that includes many tools, techniques, and templates. A smaller, flatter organization with modest-sized projects, even if these projects are large for the organization, does not need nor necessarily want the same level of formality and complexity. Frequently a smaller, a flatter organization is unable to bear the large costs of a formal, complex project management effort. Regardless of organization size and structure, to optimize the likelihood of project success, every person working on a project needs to understand management project concepts and terms. Small differences in the definition of a concept or a term can influence how a project team works together and the success of the project. This section covers:

Chapter 1. The Fundamentals: Introduces fundamental project management concepts and terms that every member of a project team should understand

Chapter 2. The Project Process Flow: Describes a project life cycle, the differences between a project management plan and a methodology, and the usage of software tools to manage a project

Chapter 3. The Project Organization: Discusses a team versus a group, the common roles of team members, and different project team structures

CHAPTER 1

THE FUNDAMENTALS

Covered in this chapter:

- Definition of project management
- Linkage, impact, and influence of scope, time, and cost
- Characteristics of projects, programs, and portfolios
- Delineation between projects and operations

Children walk before they run; they learn how to add and subtract before they learn to multiply or divide; and they learn how to throw a ball before they learn how to play baseball. Project management is not any different. It is hard to plan and manage a project to successful completion with no training. Whether new to project management or looking to refresh your skills, the right place to start is at the beginning by mastering fundamental project management concepts and terms.

WHAT IS PROJECT MANAGEMENT?

Project management is an established approach for planning, managing, and controlling resources to achieve a particular goal. Project management focuses on the set of tasks that will create a unique and specific product or service within a specified timeframe. Management assigns the role of *project manager* to a person with management and leadership skills. The project manager has responsibility for ensuring that the project work is successfully completed on time and within budget.

A BRIEF HISTORY OF PROJECT MANAGEMENT

Project management is not a new discipline; it has been around for millennia. Can you image building the Egyptian pyramids at Giza or the Colosseum in Rome without a plan? How about an English castle or medieval cathedral?

Although project management is not new, the approach to projects has changed over time. The modern era of project management started in the 1950s when businesses and governmental agencies realized the need to strengthen and modify the ad hoc nature of projects. In the 1910s, *Gantt charts* (a project scheduling technique that highlighted project tasks) as well as other informal tools and techniques were in use, but they did not provide enough control to ensure completion of projects on time and on budget. Make no mistake, although quite common today, Gantt charts were considered revolutionary when introduced.

Two quantitative methods were introduced in the United States in the late 1950s; both methods continue to be used today. E. I. duPont de Nemours and Remington Rand Corporation (now part of Unisys) jointly developed the *Critical Path Method* or *CPM* to address plant maintenance projects. CPM focuses on the sequence of the activities (tasks) and determines how long a project takes to complete. During the same period, Booz Allen Hamilton in conjunction with the Lockheed Corporation developed the *Program Evaluation and Review Technique* or *PERT* as part of the U.S. Navy's Polaris missile submarine program. The emphasis of PERT was on major events and the use of probability to determine the estimates as to the length of time required to complete the project phases and tasks. CPM and PERT methods are still used today for planning and managing projects.

As new tools and techniques emerged, businesses, nonprofits, and governmental agencies started implementing their own project management approaches. Due to the lack of a standard project management approach, however, skill transference and agreement on fundamental project concepts and terms became issues as people moved from one organization to another. As the methods, tools, and techniques matured, a number of different project management approaches took hold. Two current approaches are

- The Project Management Institute's Project Management Standards promulgated in *A Guide to the Project Management Body of Knowledge* that is better known as the *PMBOK® Guide*
- The U.K. government process-based methodology, PRINCE2 or Projects in Controlled Environments promulgated in *Managing Successful Projects with PRINCE2™*

Each approach is generic in nature and provides a framework (*PMBOK Guide*) or a process (PRINCE2) that can be applied to any project regardless of size, industry, or location. The challenge for flat organizations is that these methodologies can be hard to follow and implement: the formal processes and controls are complex, cumbersome, and costly.

THE TRIPLE CONSTRAINTS

There is an old saying, "You can have it quick, cheap, or done right. Pick any two." Oh, by the way, do not forget we want quality, too. Every project, regardless of size, is impacted and influenced by three constraints that are closely linked: scope, time, and cost. *Scope* is the work that will or will not be performed to deliver a specific product or service; *time* is how long the project will take; and *cost* refers to the expenses for resources such as staff salaries, equipment, materials, vendors, and consultants. Although different methodologies and authors use different constraint labels, the three constraints are known as the *triple constraints*. The triple constraints also are referred to as *the project triangle* (Figure 1.1). The three constraints tie directly to delivering a specific product or service within an agreed upon timeframe and budget.

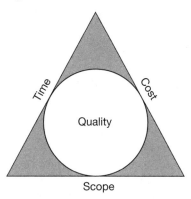

Figure 1.1. The project triangle.

In an ideal world, the scope, time, and cost of a project are agreed upon and do not change as a project progresses—they remain constant over the life of the project. In reality, change occurs in all three constraint dimensions. Because they are interdependent, if any one of the constraints changes, at least one of the other constraints will be impacted. If the work or scope is increased, typically there is an increase in time and costs. If the amount of money available or costs are decreased, typically there is a mandated decrease in the scope or an increase in time. A time constraint change could result in a decrease in scope and, depending on the project, a reduction or increase in overall cost.

The quality of the product or service is an outcome of the interaction among the constraints and is a subjective assessment of how close the product or service meets its requirements. Quality, too, is impacted by changes to any one of the constraints. If the full impact of a constraint change is not considered, then the result is a deliverable, a product or service, which may not meet the original quality requirements. Think about what would happen if, for an event, instead of the 100 invitations being printed, 200 invitations are now required, but there are no additional funds. Instead of color invitations, the invitations must now be printed in black and white or on a lower-quality grade of paper. The result is the original quality of the invitations was sacrificed to accommodate the scope change.

Most of us unconsciously deal with the triple constraints in our daily lives. Consider the real-life project of remodeling a home kitchen. The requirements (or scope) are new cabinets, counter tops, appliances, and floor. The kitchen is to be entirely updated. The targeted completed date (or time) is mid-December so the project will be finished in time for the annual family holiday party. The budget (or cost) is $25,000 for the entire project. Three different vendors provide quotes, but as the quotes are reviewed, it becomes apparent that some hard decisions need to be made:

- Vendor 1's quote is $25,500, but the job will not be completed in time for the party.
- Vendor 2's quote is $30,000 and the job will completed in time for the party.
- Vendor 3's quote is $21,000 and the job will completed in time for the party, but there is a catch. The requirements have been modified to install a lower-grade floor so that the project remains within the requested budget and timeframe.

Vendor 1 could not meet the time constraint; Vendor 2 could not meet the cost constraint; and Vendor 3 could not meet the scope constraint. Which vendor should be hired for the job? Should additional quotes be obtained? Should one of the constraints be changed allowing for more flexibility? Every project runs into similar situations.

At times one or two of the constraints are fixed, even before the project manager starts planning the project. For example, the cost cannot exceed a certain dollar limit. In this situation, the organization's business leaders and project manager need to work together to develop a solution that benefits the organization, but still results in a successful project. At other times, the project manager is informed during the project's execution of a change to one of the constraints, such as the project needs to be completed two months sooner than originally planned. Again, the project manager needs to work with business leaders to either add more people to the project team (increasing costs) or to decrease the scope of work. In these circumstances, if more money is not available or the scope cannot be decreased, the project often is setup for failure.

Project management is the art of juggling work and understanding trade-offs—it can be messy and painful. Keeping the triple constraints in balance while still delivering a quality product that meets expectations and requirements can be difficult, but it is possible. How well a project manager manages and controls a project based on the scope, time, and cost factors is a measurement of success.

Suggestion: Use acronyms and buzzwords. Every discipline has its own set of acronyms and buzzwords. The project management discipline is no different. Depending on the methodology a team member has been trained in, the industry the team member is working in, and even the experiences of the team members, concepts and term definitions can vary. Over 100 project management terms are used in this book. Organizations that have a limited understanding of project management concepts and terms or that are in the process of creating a project management methodology should consider creating a glossary of terms to assist with eliminating confusion, frustration, and miscommunication. The glossary might only have 10 or 25 key concepts and terms. Keep it simple. The goal is to ensure that the same definitions are used by everyone from executive management and vendors to staff and volunteers. To assist in the creation of a list of key concepts and terms, refer to the Glossary at the end of this book.

PROJECTS, PROGRAMS, AND PORTFOLIOS

Within the project management discipline, there is a project management hierarchy that groups collections of work, with the lowest level being the project and the highest level being a portfolio.

Projects

A *project* is temporary work with a defined beginning and end that results in the creation of a unique and specific product or service (Figure 1.2). The reason for the project is clear and easily defined with one or two project objectives. Projects differ in size and complexity and each has an associated degree of risk and uncertainty. In a project, there is a single decision-maker, a *project sponsor*, who champions the project and supports the project manager and team.

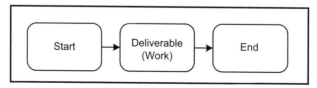

Figure 1.2. A project.

Many organizations with flat organizational structures are smaller organizations. Most of their projects are also smaller. Smaller projects normally are less than six months from start to finish. Seldom are they over a year in duration. Team members many times have *dual responsibilities*, taking care of their day-to-day operational responsibilities as well as their project tasks. The project manager may be the only full-time project person, and he or she could also have dual responsibilities.

An example of a small project could be the development of a new website. The reason for the project could be the business updated its image last year by modernizing its logo and creating new marketing literature, but the website had not been changed or "spruced up." The business wants to have the same logo and relay a similar message as in the paper marketing literature. The project sponsor is the person responsible for sales and marketing and the project duration is five months. The deliverable is a new website.

Programs

A *program* is a group of related projects with a common objective (Figure 1.3). Projects that are part of a program are closely linked, are often dependent on one another, and, by managing them together, a benefit to the organization is realized. An organization considering expanding and moving into another regional area could create a program to determine the effort's viability. The projects could include market research to establish market demand for services, finding a funding source, or investigating potential new space. All the projects combined together are called a program.

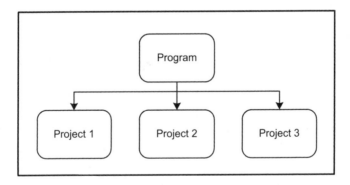

Figure 1.3. A program.

Sometimes, when all of the projects associated with the program are complete, a program's final products or services are moved into day-to-day operations. For a business, it may be a new service or product while for a nonprofit or a governmental agency it may be a new "program" (an example of a term with multiple meanings depending on context).

Portfolios

A *portfolio* is a collection of programs and projects that are linked together because they support the overall strategic business objectives of the organization (Figure 1.4). The programs and projects in a portfolio may or may not be interdependent, but by grouping them together, management has a better view of how the programs and projects are meeting overall organizational goals at a macro level.

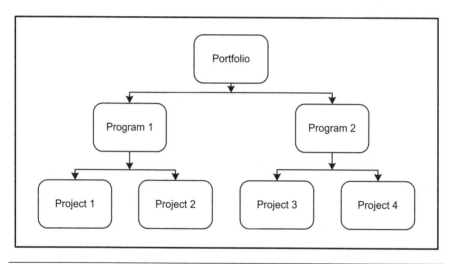

Figure 1.4. A portfolio.

Consider a flat medium-sized service organization with informal communications and ten people reporting to the president, located in four different small facilities. During a strategic planning session, management and the advisory board decide on two initiatives: one initiative is to raze a facility and replace it with another slightly larger but more modern facility and the second initiative is to upgrade the computer network infrastructure for the entire operation. Each initiative within the portfolio is a program with a number of projects.

SEQUENTIAL VERSUS OVERLAPPING PROJECTS

Some projects consist of a number of smaller projects or what can be referred to as *phases* or *subprojects* of a larger project. In theory, a phase ends and the deliverable is approved before the next phase begins—and thus is sequential. Often, however, phases or subprojects are not sequential. In reality, some of the phases overlap with one another. *Sequential and overlapping phases* are illustrated in Figure 1.5.

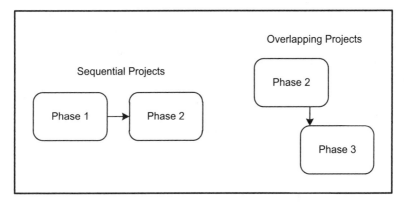

Figure 1.5. Sequential versus overlapping projects.

Project risk, such as project rework, can increase when the phases overlap, yet overlapping projects might be the right approach because overlapping enables team members to work independently on different parts of an overall or larger project. One team member could be working on the project completing a deliverable while another team member could be concurrently reviewing the requirements for the next project phase.

Also possible is having both sequential and overlapping projects. For example, the management team of a professional services business authorizes a "project" or a program to select and implement a midmarket customer relationship management (CRM) system. The "project" or program includes phases—subprojects such as requirements gathering, software selection, software implementation, data conversion, and training. The first subproject is the requirements gathering project. The output or deliverable from the project is used as input into the vendor selection subproject. The projects are sequential, each with their own unique project plan. The software implementation subproject and the data conversion subproject might overlap. Again, each subproject has its own unique project plan.

PROJECTS VERSUS OPERATIONS

Projects and *operations* complement one another so that an organization can continually achieve their goals and objectives (Figure 1.6). Operational tasks sustain the business and frequently generate income while projects have a specific objective and may only have costs. An outcome or result of a project can become a part of operations upon completion.

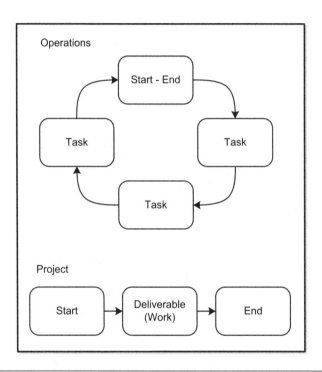

Figure 1.6. Operations work versus project work.

Operations includes tasks that are repeatable, cyclical, and ongoing. Projects have a defined start and end date, are temporary, and provide a unique product or service. A project can be recurring, such as an annual dinner in which the annual dinner is temporary and unique for that particular year. Here are a few examples:

- Daily accounts receivable and payable processing is operations, but selecting a new accounting system is a project.
- Selling clothes every day at a retail store is operations, but developing a new product line is a project.

- Handling customer call center service calls is operations, but developing a new customer service script to support the new product line is a project.
- Maintaining computers and the network infrastructure in the businesses is operations, but implementing a new computer network is a project.

In flat organizations with informal processes and controls, and where staff work on projects and operational tasks concurrently, intermixing project and operational tasks can easily occur. An unintended result might be a project that never ends and repetitive work that never migrates into an operational mode.

IN REVIEW

- Project management is an established approach for planning, managing, and controlling resources to achieve a particular goal. It is a discipline with its own concepts and terms. Planning and managing a project is difficult unless everyone working on a project has the same understanding of project management fundamentals and uses the same terminology.
- Scope, time, and cost are project constraints that are interdependent. If any one of the constraints is changed, at least one of the other constraints is impacted. The quality of the final product or service is a function of the interaction of the three constraints. Project managers monitor, from beginning to end, changes and impacts to a project's scope, time, and cost and the impact on a final product's or service's quality.
- A project is temporary work, with a defined beginning and end, which creates a unique product or service. Operations are repeatable and ongoing work. The result of a project can become an operational activity.
- In a flat organization, where staff works on projects as well as on operational tasks, intermixing projects and operations can easily occur. The result can be a project that never ends.

CHAPTER 2

THE PROJECT PROCESS FLOW

Covered in this chapter:

- Phases or logical divisions of project work and project processes
- Definition and characteristics of a project management methodology
- Definition and characteristics a project management plan
- Using software tools to manage a project

When constructing a custom home, the builder starts with a focused project plan that follows a specific process, ensuring that the house meets the agreed-upon requirements and is completed by the contractual date. The custom home project plan is unique to that particular project and has a beginning and end. The custom home project plan employs basic project concepts and follows the organization's approach to planning and managing projects. Before creating a project plan, the project manager needs to understand project planning concepts and terms.

WHAT IS A PROJECT LIFE CYCLE?

A traditional *project life cycle* has four *phases* or logical divisions of work: *initiate, plan, execute,* and *close* (Figure 2.1). In theory, one phase ends before the next phase begins, and the output of one phase is the input for the next phase. A traditional project life cycle also has five components or *processes: initiating, planning, executing, closing,* and *monitoring and controlling.* Monitoring and controlling occurs throughout the project.

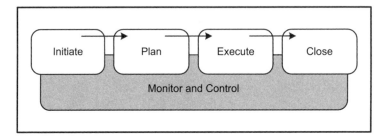

Figure 2.1. Project life cycle phases.

Different project management approaches have different phases or divisions of work. Some approaches have three phases, such as initiate and plan, execute and control, and close, while other approaches have five, seven, or even ten phases. The term for each phase and the work included in each phase can vary based on the approach and industry. All project management approaches, however, have a beginning (an initiation) and an end (a close) because a project is temporary work with a defined beginning and end.

Initiating. Initiating starts the project and clarifies the delivered product or service. The project manager visualizes the end deliverable. The *stakeholders* (the beneficiaries of the project) are identified, the requirements are determined, the project scope is defined and clarified, and success criteria are articulated. (Chapters 4 through 7 cover initiating the project.)

Planning. Planning defines the course of action for the project and includes the plans for the triple constraints, scope, time, and cost:

- Scope (or *work*) defines the work to be performed and the final product or service. The scope is based on having a clear understanding of the project requirements.
- Time (or *schedule*) comprises the dates for starting and ending the work and the hours required to create the final product or service and to manage the project.
- Cost (or *budget*) is the amount of money allocated to the project to perform the work and to deliver the final product or service based on the scope and schedule.

Depending on project needs, plans may be required to address:

- Risk (or unknown, unplanned, or unexpected events)
- Purchasing (or procurement)

- Communications
- Quality control
- Staff (human resources)
- Industry or project-specific requirements

(Chapters 8 through 17 cover planning the project.)

Executing. Executing starts when team members are added and the work necessary to create the product or service begins. (Chapters 18 through 19 cover executing the project.)

Closing. Closing completes the project, hopefully successfully, and celebrates success. Project documents are archived for future reference, lessons learned are written, and, if applicable, the final product or the service is moved into operations. (Chapter 23 covers closing the project.)

Monitoring and controlling. Monitoring and controlling, known as "keeping an eye on the work," includes tracking, analyzing, and adjusting the project's work, schedule, and budget, and then reporting on the progress of the project. (Chapters 20 through 22 cover monitoring and controlling the project.)

To explain the project life cycle further, envision a small garden project. The project's deliverable is fresh homegrown vegetables. The reason for the project could be a gourmet restaurant needs fresh vegetables for its daily meal preparation, a social service nonprofit has a program educating children in healthy lifestyles, or a family just wants homegrown produce in their diet.

Initiate. The first step is to initiate the project. Clarify the purpose (or need) and define the requirements. Ask questions such as:

- What is the goal of the vegetable garden?
- What vegetables are needed?
- Who decides on the vegetables to be planted?

Plan. Next, project plans are developed, balancing the triple constraints of scope, time, and cost. The team develops plans to manage risk, assist with communications, manage quality control, educate staff, purchase resources, and prepare plans that are unique to the project. Potential questions the project manager may ask:

- Will we plant tomatoes, lettuce, green beans, squash, carrots, peppers, and onions? (Scope)
- What other vegetables will we plant? (Scope)

- Do we have a spring and fall planting? (Scope)
- When do we start? (Time)
- How long will it take to build a raised vegetable bed? (Time)
- Who is going to build the raised garden bed, cultivate the soil, and plant the seeds? (Staff or Human Resources)
- How much is it going to cost? (Cost)
- Do we need to add enhanced garden and vegetable soil? (Quality)
- How do we tell our friends and family that we have extra vegetables? (Communication)
- What do we do if we do not get enough rain? (Risk)
- What can we do to prevent animals from eating our vegetables? (Risk)
- What local farm do we use to purchase seeds and plants? (Purchasing or Procurement)
- Do we need to a permit for a shed to store our equipment? (Unique to the Project)

Execute. Execute the plan:

- Purchase the seeds and equipment.
- Recruit and educate additional team members.
- Build and plant the garden.

Monitor and control. The team members start watching, keeping an eye on the garden. They monitor and control to see if:

- The plants are growing properly.
- The plants need more water.
- Insects or small animals are eating the plants.
- The vegetables are ready for picking.

A successful harvest occurs, dead plant matter is tilled back into the soil, and the lessons learned are documented. The project is successfully complete and it is time to celebrate.

As much as a project life cycle appears to be sequential, it does not necessarily need to be. In the garden project example, the project scope was to plant vegetables. After planting the vegetables, if the team decides they should have planted herbs in addition to the vegetables, they can revisit the project plan and modify it accordingly.

Consider an example in which a team is building a new product for global distribution. As management discusses the new product with potential distributors, management determines that sales could increase by 30% by adding an additional small feature. They then initiate a *change request* (a request to expand or reduce the project scope or another aspect of the project plan) for approval. After approval of the change request, they modify the project plan accordingly.

THE DISTINCTION BETWEEN A METHODOLOGY AND A PLAN

Project management methodology is not the same as a project management plan. A *project management methodology* is a standardized approach that all projects within the organization follow to ensure project management consistency; it is the starting point for every project. A *project management plan* is unique to a particular project; it is the anticipated course of action for that project and answers questions specific to that project. The format of the project management plan is part of the organization's methodology.

THE PROJECT MANAGEMENT METHODOLOGY IN MORE DETAIL

The project management methodology is the standardized approach, the guidelines—the *tools, techniques,* and *templates*—that ensure consistency across all projects. For clarification purposes, a *tool* is something tangible that team members use to perform the project work, such as a software application; a *technique* is a procedure employed by a team member; and a *template* is a document in a predefined format used to collect, organize, and present information and data. The project management methodology includes guidelines for all the plans that are included in the project management plan, plus more. The project management methodology provides the guidelines for the five project processes: initiating, planning, executing, closing, and monitoring and controlling.

The most successful methodologies are those that are created for the organization by the organization. Just as projects are unique, so are organizations, each with their own personality and culture. Some organizations try to leverage another organization's methodology. A methodology that works for one organization, however, does not necessarily work for another due to each organization's uniqueness. In other words, a best practice for one organization is not necessarily a best practice for another organization. Some organizations purchase a project management software application, expecting the application, which is a tool, to provide the project management methodology. A project management software application does not provide a project management methodology: it is assumed that people understand the fundamentals of project management and all that they require is training in the software application.

Most flat organizations need an approach that is flexible and strikes a balance between formal and informal procedures. The methodology could be as simple as one or two pages of suggestions or guidelines to follow for every project or only for projects over a certain dollar amount. The suggestions and guidelines do not need to be complex, detailed, formal, or rigid, but they do need to be specific enough to provide consistency and keep frustration to a minimum when there are multiple project managers or first-time project managers. There needs to be enough consistency so that it is possible to compare projects from one year to the next and have historical project documentation.

Creating a methodology does not require an excessive amount of time or money, but it does require:

- The support of management
- An understanding of the culture and people
- An awareness of the organization's project management maturity

Management support. Having the support of management means management clearly articulates that, although a project is an ad hoc event, the project is as important as the daily operations. Management and project managers in the organization work together by agreeing on project guidelines and standards. Periodically, management meets to review the project methodology to ensure it still supports the needs of the organization and to modify it accordingly.

Culture and people. Understanding the culture and people in an organization acknowledges that an organization with informal communication and limited controls and processes may struggle if a project management methodology with formal communications and rigid controls and processes is implemented. For example, if the team members are accustomed to being able to resolve their own problems and are told to be innovative when performing their day-to-day responsibilities, they may find project work difficult if they are provided very detailed and mandatory step-by-step project instructions.

Project management maturity. Project management maturity refers to the project management knowledge of the staff and organization. Is the staff and organization new to the concept of project management? If so, has the staff received some training or is a mentor working with them? How many projects have followed a "formal" approach? How many projects has the project manager managed? If the project manager has managed projects, how sophisticated and complex were the projects? Answers to these questions indicate the project management maturity of the staff and organization.

When creating a methodology, focus on the theory and the reasons behind the numerous processes. Determine if the organization needs the process or if the process only applies in certain situations such as when the project budget is over a certain dollar amount or requires a significant time constraint. Not every process, tool, technique, and template fits every organization and every project.

The project management methodology and day-to-day operations need to complement one another even though there are differences. Strike a balance between operations and projects. The last thing a methodology should do is cause a project manager or team member to be so frustrated that they ignore any or all of the methodology.

The step-by-step instructions, tools, techniques, and templates provided in this book can be used create an organizational project management methodology. Use them as guidelines. Use them in conjunction with a project. Decide what works and what does not work for your organization. Above all, for a flat organization, keep it simple.

Suggestion: Create a table listing the project management documents. Consider creating a table that lists the organization's standard documents as illustrated in Table 2.1 (A Project Management Methodology Table). This table is a chart that provides a list of the organization's project management documents, states the reason or purpose for the document, and indicates if the document is required or optional. An example of required or optional documents: an organization has twelve recommended project documents listed in their table, but in an effort to provide some management consistency in the various projects in the organization and to provide historical information for comparison purposes, management requires or mandates creating only three documents for all projects:

- Scope statement: a formal signed document that provides an official description of the project
- Project management plan: the scope, schedule, and related budget data
- Status report: a snapshot of the project's progress as of a point in time

The other nine documents are optional or discretionary based on the project and the project manager's judgment as to each document's project value. (Some of the documents discussed in this book are the requirements document, scope statement, stakeholder list, project plan, risk register, issue log, change request log, status report, and lessons learned.) Table 2.1 is a project aid for the project manager and team members. Modify the table so that it works for the organization. For example, add columns that are categories or a group, such as projects under three months in duration or projects over three months; technical or nontechnical projects; fundraising projects; or operational projects. Alternatively, expand the table so that it includes not only documents, but also tools, techniques, and templates.

Table 2.1. Project Management Methodology Table

Project Management Methodology		
Document	**Purpose**	**Required/ Optional**
Scope Document	Provides description of the project, the project objectives, requirements, and deliverables; high-lights what the project will and will not accomplish	Required
Project Plan	Provides the work to be completed, the project schedule, and project budget; used to manage the project and to report the project status	Required
Estimating Worksheet	Used to collect duration, level of effort, resource needs, cost estimates, and any potential risk for each task	Optional
...	...	...
Status Report	Provides a snapshot of project performance as of a point in time; report frequency depends on project, but for most projects, report should be created weekly	Required
...	...	...

THE PROJECT MANAGEMENT PLAN IN MORE DETAIL

The project management plan is created during the planning phase of the project life cycle, but it is not one plan. Rather, the project management plan includes (or refers to) all of the planning documents needed to execute and manage the project. The project management plan is a living document requiring periodic updates and sponsor sign-off.

A plan is a method or approach for doing something, but there is no requirement stating that a plan needs to be in writing. In a flat organization, some plans that are part of the project management plan are formal and written while others are informal and verbal. The balance between formal and informal varies greatly for each plan based on the type and size of project, the organization, and the project manager and sponsor. Prior to a project starting, the project manager and sponsor should review, discuss, and agree upon which plans need to be created, the level of formality, and the sign-off process by the sponsor.

What is included in a project management plan depends on the project, but at a minimum, a project management plan should provide a clear, realistic, concise understanding of the project scope (work), time (schedule), and cost (budget). In this book, the combination of the work, schedule, and budget is referred to as the *project plan*. Additional plans that might be included in the project management plan are risk, procurement, communications, quality, human resources, and an industry- or project-specific plan.

A project management plan can be as simple, complex, or detailed as the project and organization wants or needs. Include enough detail for a project manager to manage the project. Complexity or more detail does not mean the plan is "better." If a project management plan is unnecessarily complex, too formal, or too detailed, the project team may ignore it because it might be too hard to follow. Another way to think about the level of detail: if the project manager leaves, would there be enough detail and formality for the new project manager to understand the plan of action for the project? Having a good project management plan does not mean a project manager will not make some mistakes or need to ask questions. A good project management plan just means that there is enough detail for a person to understand what constitutes success.

USING SOFTWARE TO MANAGE THE PROJECT MANAGEMENT PLAN

The decision to use a project management software package versus using productivity tools such as Microsoft® Word and Excel to aid in project management depends on a number of parameters that can be easily measured and quantified. These parameters include the size of the project, how much money is available to purchase a product, and the time required to train people in the application.

Large, complex projects with full-time team members tend to use a project management software package and various collaboration tools because the software package and the tools are robust and they provide the team members with features and functionality that assist them with more efficiently and effectively planning and managing a project. The frequent use by the team members and management enables them to achieve a level of comfort and proficiency with the software package and tools. If the project is smaller, team members are not familiar with a software package, only work part-time on projects, or only occasionally work a project, using productivity tools such as Microsoft® Word and Excel might be a better option.

Consider this story about an inexperienced project manager at a professional service company who was struggling with a project that was behind schedule and costing more than budgeted. Management needed to get the project back on track, so they hired an experienced project manager to assess the project's status and provide the project team advice.

During an initial meeting to discuss the project's status, one of the team members commented, "There's a project plan, but we're only somewhat following it." As the discussion progressed, the project manager learned that a project management software package had been purchased to assist with the project and a project plan had been created using the package. The team and management thought they needed a software package to manage the project, but they found the software package was too difficult to use and update. One team member commented that the software "seems to have a mind of its own." Due to the size of the project, and in an effort to move the project forward, the project manager exported the project plan from the software package into an Excel spreadsheet. For the remainder of the project, management and control of the project occurred using the project plan in Excel.

The project manager then explained to the team (and management) that the project plan had not been set up properly in the software package, and the plan had not been completed or optimized. There were other issues: the project manager and the staff were not versed in project management concepts and terms, and no money or time had been allocated for training in project management, let alone the software package. Consequentially, the software package purchased was too complicated and complex for them. Additionally, the organization had no standardized project management methodology or approach. The project manager continued by highlighting a few points:

- Determining how to manage a project, including how the organization is going to approach project management, is important because once those decisions are made the appropriate automated and manual tools and techniques required to support the organization's approach can be selected.
- Project management software packages are tools that assist with managing and controlling a project. Using a tool does not mean mistakes will not be made during the planning effort. If the wrong estimate data is entered, the project plan created will be wrong. Before a person obtains training in a particular tool, he or she needs to have a solid understanding of the concepts. The person should be in a position to ask questions about the answers provided by the software, such as "Does the completion date make sense and is it realistic? Have all tasks, durations, and relationships properly entered? Has anything been missed?"
- Selecting a project management software package is a project in itself. A package that works for one organization might not be the right package for another. Base the tool (or a combination of tools) needed to be "right" for the project or organization on the type of project, size of the project, and the culture and structure of the organization.
- Regardless of the tool selected, time to implement the tool and time to train the team needs to be factored into the project plan.

Although flat organizations with modest-sized projects can and do plan and manage projects successfully with productivity tools such as Excel and Word, the above story does not mean a flat organization cannot or should not use a project management software package. Additionally, it does not mean an organization cannot start a project using Excel and then decide to use a software package, particularly because many of software packages make importing Excel files easy. If the decision is to use a software package, follow a selection approach to determine the right software package. The software selection approach can be simple. It does not need to be the complex, drawn-out approach followed by a large hierarchical organization. It just needs to be thorough and the project management software application needs to fit the organization.

Remember: If a great project plan is developed, but then not followed when executing the work, it does not matter whether a project management software package or productivity tools such as Microsoft® Word and Excel is used to manage the project because the project will be executed haphazardly impacting potential project success. Using a tool does not make a project successful; a tool is only an aid that helps a project manager be successful.

IN REVIEW

- All projects have four phases or logical divisions of work: initiating, planning, executing, and closing. All projects have five processes: initiating, planning, executing, closing, and monitoring and controlling.
- A project management plan is a project roadmap. It is unique to a specific project. A project management plan is a collection of a number of plans that are required to execute and manage the project. A project management plan is a living document: modify and update it throughout the project life cycle.
- A project management methodology is a standardized approach that is unique to a particular organization. If an organization does not have a methodology, but undertakes projects, consider creating a methodology even if it is only a one- or two-page document with general project guidelines. Most flat organizations with informal communication, processes, and controls need to develop an approach that is flexible and informal enough to fit their culture and organizational structure, but still maintains enough formality and control to ensure project success.

- Using project management software tools is optional. Project management software tools are not a substitute for understanding fundamental project management concepts and terms. They do not guarantee a successful project.

CHAPTER 3

THE PROJECT ORGANIZATION

Covered in this chapter:

- Definition of a group, team, and teamwork
- Description of the different roles of staff on a team
- Different project team structures

Effective project teams are thoughtfully assembled, ensuring the right persons with the right technical or industry expertise are selected. As soon as management authorizes a project, the project manager and sponsor begin to discuss the project team roles and organizational structure necessary for the project to be successful. This discussion requires an understanding of project management concepts and terms pertaining to teams, key team roles, and project team structures.

WHAT IS A PROJECT TEAM?

A common fault found in organizations is that individuals are unclear and do not understand the differences between a *group* and a *team*. A group of people is not a team, yet a team is a group of people. So what distinguishes a group from a team? A group is a collection of people who make few formal demands on each other. A team is a group of people who demand interaction and performance from each other and who are bound together with a common purpose. Teamwork is the process of working together to achieve the common goal.

A team is a group of people with complementary skills and expertise who work together for the good of the group. Effective teams:

- Have a clear and well-defined common goal
- Need each other's skills and experience to attain the goal

- Believe working together and supporting one another is more effective than working individually
- Share responsibility and accountably for success

Teams work best when everyone contributes and everyone benefits. Team members put aside their own wants and needs for the good of the group.

PROJECT TEAM ROLES

The project team roles required by a project depend on the type and size of the project. All projects have leadership roles and work-oriented roles. All projects have people who fill the generic roles of project sponsor, project manager, team members, and stakeholders. Some projects have specific roles such as a business analyst or a part-time subject matter expert because of the type of project. On some projects, particularly a smaller project, one person might fill multiple roles. For example, the sponsor may also be the project manager.

Project sponsor. The project sponsor (referred to as *sponsor* in this book) is the executive or manager who is committed to ensuring that the project outcome meets the requirements; normally has a personal stake in a project's success or failure; and is a vocal, visible champion of the project. He or she supports the project manager by removing obstacles, such as staffing conflicts, by ensuring that the funds required are available; by assisting with the resolution of major issues and problems; by being an active participant with the planning; and by signing-off on appropriate deliverables. The sponsor is the point person responsible for communicating with management and ensuring management understands the reasons for the various decisions. If the organization's priorities change and impact the project, it is the sponsor's responsibility to work with the project manager to modify the project accordingly. In general, the sponsor is responsible to ensure overall viability of the project and to remove roadblocks.

Project manager. The project manager is the person responsible and accountable for ensuring that the project delivers a specific product or service on time and within budget. A successful project manager is multifaceted: a manager, leader, administrator, entrepreneur, facilitator, arbitrator, mediator, liaison, and coordinator. A project manager is knowledgeable in project management concepts such as the triple constraints of scope, time, and cost and knows how to develop a project management plan and then manage its execution. Although there are traditional management responsibilities such as managing the budget, assigning tasks, and tracking the work, a good project manager must do more than manage. A good project manager leads by focusing on the big picture, not just the project details. He or she understands how the project fits within the organization's strategy. As a leader, a good project manager motivates team members, negotiates with other managers, resolves project conflicts, manages project risk, provides project status, and respects the culture of the organization as well as the team's culture. A project manager rarely works alone and realizes it is acceptable to ask others for assistance. A good project manager does not presume to know everything, but he or she does know their own strengths and weaknesses. Decisions are often the result of the project manager working and collaborating with the sponsor and team members.

Suggestion: Select the "right" project manager. Often management assigns a person to the project manager role because of their subject matter expertise or their strong technical skills. It is not uncommon, however, for a person with subject matter expertise or strong technical skills and no or limited project management training to struggle as the project progresses. They find delegating work difficult or they become stressed when confronted with a conflict situation. Their frustration can result in a sponsor removing them as the project manager or worse yet, they resign from the organization. As the project management profession has matured, the skills necessary and the understanding of what it takes to successfully manage and lead a project has changed. Many projects no longer need an expert in a particular subject area. They only need a general manager. A project manager has moved from being a hands-on technician or subject matter expert to a person who is more of a generalist with an understanding of business and management. Effective project managers understand the business. They know how to plan and manage projects, including motivating teams. Subject matter experts or persons with strong technical skills should only become project managers if that is what they really want to do and understand what managing a project means. Ensure they have the necessary training (or receive it) and the skills to be successful. To assist first-time project managers, consider having them work with an experienced project manager, someone who can coach and give advice.

Team members. In theory, anyone who contributes or has some sort of role in assisting with achieving the project goals and the overall success of the project is considered to be a member of the project team. (In this book, when the term *team member* is used, it means the people, the staff, who are directly working on the project.) Each team member is responsible for completing assigned tasks on time, but they also are responsible for knowing when to ask for help. Concerns need to be communicated and team members need to provide support to everyone working on the project, from the sponsor to the client. Choosing a good team, particularly in a flat organization, can be difficult because staff may be limited, the skills needed to get the job done may not be available internally, and team members might have *dual responsibilities*, day-to-day operational responsibilities as well as project responsibilities. More explicit and detailed team member roles, such as the role of a subject matter expert, start to be determined and individuals are "assigned" to a project by the sponsor and project manager as soon as management authorizes the project and the project starts being defined, the initiation phase. Some of these team members start working on the project shortly after the project manager and play the role of *core team member* (or key team member). Core team members normally are involved in more than one project life cycle phase and perform a significant amount of the project work. They are an integral part of the team, know exactly what is going on, and understand the implications and impacts of decisions. The number of core team members varies by project, but on a smaller project, there may be only one to two core team members.

Stakeholders. Stakeholders normally are beneficiaries of the project. A potential stakeholder is anyone who has an interest in the project, takes the time to understand the project, has a degree of commitment to the project, or is willing to assist with the project. Stakeholders can be positive, wanting the project to succeed, or negative, hoping for a negative project result or a failed project. Stakeholders are senior management, team members, customers, vendors, third-party consultants, volunteers, event sponsors, board members, and advisory board members.

THE ORGANIZATIONAL STRUCTURE OF A TEAM

A flat organization has few or no levels of management between executive management and the staff. Although there are three basic project organizational structures, *functional*, *project*, and *matrix*, each with advantages and disadvantages, the majority of projects within flat organizations follow what is known as a matrix project structure. Functional and project organizational structures are found in flat organizations, but they tend to be used less frequently.

Functional Structure

Think of a classic organization that is divided into departments. Each department has its own specific function, such as accounting, marketing and sales, or customer service. Under this structure, the department with the appropriate expertise takes responsibility for the project. The project manager is the department or functional manager or a staff person who reports to the manager (the term *manager* as used in this book refers to the department or functional manager). If the project manager is a staff person who reports to the manager, the majority of, if not all, decisions are cleared through the manager. Although the department with the appropriate expertise is responsible for the project, staff from other departments can be assigned to work part-time on the project.

An advantage of the functional organizational structure is that team members already know how to work together. Normally they have the necessary skills, knowledge, and expertise required for the project. A disadvantage for the project manager as well as team members is the ease of intermingling operational and project work, resulting in unclear lines of distinction between project and operational work. This intermingling of operational and project work could result in missed project deadlines.

Project Structure

A project organizational structure is the easiest type of structure to understand. It is commonly reserved for larger projects. In a project organizational structure, the project manager and the team members are assigned exclusively to the project. They have one goal: to complete the project. The project manager has complete authority over the time and work assignments of team members.

An advantage of a project organizational structure is that the project manager and team members are focused on a single project with a single goal. A disadvantage is that, unless the organization is large, the project manager and team members may only be hired for a specific project. (In a larger organization with multiple projects, however, the project manager and team members can be assigned to another project.) Another disadvantage is project managers and team members can lose touch with the daily operation needs of the parent organization.

Matrix Structure

The majority of flat organizations have projects that follow a matrix organizational structure. The matrix organizational structure combines the characteristics of the functional and project organizational structures (Figure 3.1). Think of a matrix organizational structure as a dotted- or broken-line relationship because individual team members report to two different managers: the project manager and their functional manager (manager).

Matrix organizational structures are classified as *weak matrix* (close to the functional organizational structure), *strong matrix* (close to the project organizational structure), or *balanced matrix*. In a balanced matrix, the project manager and managers are equals, requiring each manager to collaborate, compromise, negotiate, and work together for the good of the organization. They rely on each other's expertise. Team members work on projects when their knowledge, skills,

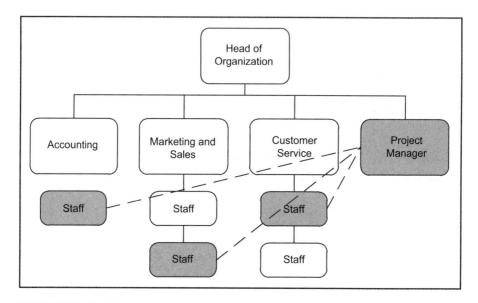

Figure 3.1. An organizational structure in a flat organization.

and expertise are needed and continue to have dual responsibilities: their day-to-day operational responsibilities and their project responsibilities.

An advantage of a matrix organizational structure in a flat organization is that the project structure can be similar to the daily operational structure, emphasizing collaboration, consensus, and open dialogue. A disadvantage is that team members can have two bosses: the project manager and a functional manager (manager). This situation might result in communication challenges and authority conflicts. If not quickly resolved, these challenges can jeopardize the project.

Suggestion: How to deal with different matrix structure scenarios. Various matrix structure scenarios can occur within a flat organization. Two common scenarios are

- The project manager becomes a working member of the team because the project is falling behind schedule and the completion date is in jeopardy. One reason could be that an operational emergency has occurred that requires a team member to focus on his or her daily operational responsibilities rather than project work and there is no one else in the organization available to work on the project. In an effort to prevent slippage as well as to prevent any impact on other team members, the project manager rolls up his or her sleeves and completes the work of the team member who can no longer work on the project. In the meantime, the project manager ignores his or her own project management-related responsibilities, hoping the project takes care of itself. It rarely does.

- The project manager works part-time on the project and also supports his or her daily operational responsibilities. Within a 40-hour workweek, if day-to-day operational responsibilities take 30 hours a week and project responsibilities take 25 hours, how best should a project manager spend his or her time? The same situation can occur for team members. The project manager and manager are required to work together to find a solution.

There are no simple answers to resolving the challenges in either of these scenarios.

Even when management places the same priority on daily operational and project needs, there will be staffing and time commitment conflicts. Some ideas to consider:

- Implement an "emergency" policy that necessitates contacting the sponsor to assist with resolving conflicts.
- Permit a project manager to be a working team member only if the team is under five members. Make this a matter of policy.
- Assign a project manager responsibility for a number of smaller projects and eliminate involvement in day-to-day operational tasks.

All of this is theory. In real life, there are all sorts of variations to the three project organizational structures. It is up to an organization to structure a project team based on the organization's staff, budget, and culture. Each project within an organization can even have its own project-specific structure. What is necessary is to:

- Understand the advantages and disadvantages of a particular structure
- Decide on a structure that works best for a particular project
- Implement appropriate processes and procedures to ensure project success

IN REVIEW

- Flat organizations are accustomed to the concept of teamwork. Effective teams are bound together with clear and common goals. Team members believe that by working together, supporting one another, and sharing responsibility, projects can be successful.

- The project sponsor is management's spokesperson and works with the project manager to ensure that the project meets the required outcome. The sponsor is the final project decision-maker.
- The project manager is the day-to-day person responsible for ensuring that the project delivers a specific product or service on time and within budget.
- Core team members are integral to the success of the project. They are normally involved in more than one phase of a project. Typically, core team members start working on the project shortly after the project manager. They assist the project manager with project planning.
- The three basic project organizational structures are functional, project, and matrix. Flat organizations usually follow a matrix structure, or dotted-line relationship, with a project manager, managers, and team members working together to ensure project success and making decisions based on what is best for the organization.

SECTION 2

GETTING STARTED

Starting a project is like starting a new job. The more you know about the organization and what is expected, the more likely you are to succeed. The same is true with a project. The better a project is defined, the better the chance of success. Defining a project is an iterative process beginning with management stating the need; ensuring that the effort is aligned with the organization's business strategy or that it is solving a problem; and authorizing the project. Expectations are articulated and understood; objectives are defined and specified; the timeframe is identified; and funding is set aside. Agreement occurs among the project manager, sponsor, and stakeholders on the outcome of the project—the final product or service to be delivered and what constitutes project success. Most important, even though a flat organization has informal communications, processes, and controls, the understanding is memorialized in a formal written document, a scope statement—the contract between the sponsor (management), stakeholders, and the project manager (project team). This section covers:

Chapter 4. Authorize the Project: Discusses why projects occur, how projects are linked to an organization's business strategy, and the authorization process, including the hand-off of pertinent information to the project manager by the sponsor

Chapter 5. Identify the Stakeholders: Focuses on identifying the people or groups who have a vested interest in the project—the stakeholders—and each stakeholder's role and expectations

Chapter 6. Determine the Requirements: Discusses the need to understand the requirements so that a determination can be made as to what is included in the project, how big the project is, and the amount of time, resources, and funding required to complete the project

Chapter 7. Define the Project Scope: Focuses on the importance of defining the project in a clear, concisely written, agreed-upon scope statement that highlights what the project will and will not accomplish, by when, and at what anticipated cost

CHAPTER 4

AUTHORIZE THE PROJECT

Covered in this chapter:

- Understanding the reasons for projects
- Determining what the project is to accomplish
- Understanding why a project is important
- Writing a project objective
- Prioritizing and tracking projects
- Assigning a project manager

How management defines the organization's strategy varies by organization, but in all organizations, it is management's responsibility to determine the strategy, authorize a project based on that strategy, and then *hand-off* the project by assigning a project manager. Hand-off to a project manager is the start of the project. The sponsor explains to the project manager the reason, justification, and objectives of the project. They have a discussion and clarify questions about the final product or service, time requirements, and cost estimates.

WHAT ARE THE REASONS FOR PROJECTS?

Projects occur for two reasons:

- To meet a planned strategic or operational business need
- To resolve an unplanned business opportunity or problem

A Planned Strategic or Operational Business Need

Normally management decides on strategic projects (projects that provide a competitive advantage or enhance profitability) or operational projects during a planning process. Each strategic or operational project supports a need and is justified based on business drivers such as:

- A *market demand*, such as an increased need or demand to manufacture clothing for K-6 school children
- An *internal organizational need*, such a need to upgrade a network infrastructure due to the age of the current hardware
- A *customer or client request*, such as a request to establish a satellite medical office for an underserved community
- A *technical advancement*, such as a need to develop mobile training applications for field employees in compliance with a governmental mandate.

Because the projects are decided on during a planning process and each project involves time and requires resources to complete, management also determines, estimates, and documents the preliminary expected project constraints—scope, time, and cost—for each project.

An Unplanned Business Opportunity or Problem

An unplanned business opportunity or a problem normally is addressed by an organization immediately. If the situation is an opportunity, the timeframe for acting on it could be short. A problem can be an emergency that is impacting day-to-day operations. Regardless of whether the situation is a business opportunity or a problem, the reason for the project and the scope are already known.

Examples of unplanned business opportunities are

- A competitor that provides a slightly different service decides to retire and lists the business for sale. Because the competitor's service would augment the current business services and expand the service area, the business decides to take advantage of the opportunity.
- A software vendor offers a significant financial incentive to upgrade to a new version before the end of the year. Upgrading the software is a project scheduled for next year, but the financial incentive justifies taking advantage of the opportunity this year.

Examples of unplanned business problems are

- A fire in a restaurant's kitchen destroyed part of the floor, ceiling, and walls, resulting in closing the restaurant until repairs are completed.

- An office building inspection revealed serious code violations that if not immediately corrected would result in the office building being shut down.

As with strategic and operational projects, the scope, time, and cost constraints of unplanned business opportunities and problems need to be managed. An organization may have emergency reserves that can be used for unplanned business opportunities or problems, but it is also possible the funds are exceptionally limited or there are no reserve funds at all. Funds that have been allocated for another project might need to be reallocated, postponing that project to a later date or cancelling it completely. Alternatively, funds may need to be obtained from a third party.

When working on an unplanned project, it is easy (and may be necessary) to skip project management steps, but the tradeoff or the impact to the scope, time, and cost of skipping project management steps needs to be understood. Skipping steps can make it easy to overlook an important requirement or make a mistake when performing the project work, resulting in project rework at a later point in time.

EVALUATE AND JUSTIFY THE PROJECT

Evaluation is determining what the project is to accomplish; estimating the time and cost required; understanding potential risks; determining if there are alternatives; and ensuring that the funding is available or can be obtained. *Justification* is the understanding of why a project is important and should be undertaken. Many people think project justification needs to be financial, but it does not. A new regulation, a safety requirement, and a market demand represent valid project justification.

Some organizations may require a formal project evaluation and justification. A written business case, a feasibility study, and a cost-benefit analysis are formal processes whose outcome is used to determine if the project should proceed, follow an alternative course of action, or be dropped. In some cases, because there is a formal requirement, the evaluation and justification efforts are projects or subprojects of a much larger project.

Note the word *may* in the previous paragraph. For many flat organizations with informal communications, detailed studies and formal analysis reports created to justify a project are not necessary unless a financial institution, investor, or foundation, or other funding source requests them. Having no request for a formal analysis report, however, does *not* mean a potential project should not be evaluated and justified. It just means only an *informal* evaluation and justification will be performed. For example, management decides a major network infra-structure upgrade, an operational requirement, is needed. The reason and justifi-cation is the organization has already extended the useful life of servers, routers, and some of the other network hardware. Management realizes a business down situation would have a financial impact and that there is no need to spend money creating formal documentation.

A good approach for evaluating and justifying a project is to create a stan-dardized list of questions. Some questions to consider include:

Justification or Business Reason:

- Will this project result in a solution to a market demand, an organiza-tional need, a customer or client request, or a technical advancement?
- How well will the project meet our priorities?
- Can the project be started and completed in time to meet the business need?
- Are the expectations realistic based on our organization's culture?
- Are stakeholders willing to make a commitment to the project's suc-cess?

Cost and Time:

- Is it possible to estimate the cost or the time needed to complete this project?
- How realistic are the estimated cost and time?
- Are funds available so that the whole project can be delivered?
- If needed, can funding be obtained from third-party sources?
- Can the project be achieved with the current staff and other resources?

Risk:

- What can go wrong with the project?
- What are the consequences if the project fails?
- Will working on this project impact the daily operations?
- What is the risk of doing nothing about the problem or opportunity?

Alternatives:

- Have other options been explored?
- What have other organizations done to solve a similar problem?

Suggestion: Consider proposed ideas. Employees, clients, board members, advisors, volunteers, or anyone else affiliated with the organization could have a great idea for a project, but the idea has not been vetted. So, instead of ignoring an idea or commenting, "Right now is not the time. We have too many things going on," ask for help in evaluating and justifying the idea. The easiest way is to ask the person submitting the idea to answer questions such as: "What market demand or an organizational need will this project solve? How much time do you think the project will take? What are our competitors doing?"

If the idea is accepted, the person will feel good about contributing to the organization. If, however, the idea does not tie to the organization's strategy and goals, the timing is not right, or funds are not available, the person suggesting the idea will at least have been part of the evaluation process, will understand why the suggestion was not adopted, and hopefully, will not be afraid to provide suggestions in the future.

WRITE THE PROJECT OBJECTIVE

After management evaluates and justifies the organization's projects, each project's objective(s) is determined. Every project has at least one objective. Objectives are statements describing what the project is trying to achieve and are written so that they are understandable by everyone. The objectives tie to the organization's strategy and operational needs and should be written by management.

Project objectives are expressed in terms of the triple constraints: scope, time, and cost. Project objectives are specific in terms of the work to be achieved; quantifiable or measurable in terms of time and cost; and are realistic and attainable. Objectives use strong action verbs, such as apply, write, produce, select, and develop, and should be written following *SMART* (*Specific, Measurable, Attainable, Realistic,* and *Timely*) logic:

- *Specific*: Be precise about the target and the intended outcome. There should be one outcome per objective. Ask: "Is it attainable? What are we trying to accomplish? What needs to be achieved?"
- *Measurable*: Quantify the objectives. Use measurements or metrics to indicate project success.
- *Attainable (achievable, accomplishable)*: Align the objectives with the needs of management, the sponsor, and other stakeholders. The results of the objectives need to be able to be defined.
- *Realistic*: An objective needs to be reasonable based on project constraints. Ask: "Do we have the people, money, or other resources needed? Is a ten percent increase realistic and attainable if last year's increase was two percent?"
- *Timely*: Provide a timeframe as to when the objective will be met.

For example, a possible objective for an annual fundraising project could be:

Objective: Increase our under-the-age-of-thirty donors from four percent to at least five percent within the next six months.

Objectives not only need to be measurable, but they also need to be realistic and therefore attainable.

Using the fundraising example again, last year's percentage of donors that were under the age of thirty was four percent. Ask: "Is it realistic and attainable to have five percent of our donor base composed of people under the age of thirty?" The answer: "Probably yes." Management and the project manager can perceive how increasing the percentage from four percent to five percent is realistic and achievable and is a goal that is workable for the project team. If the percentage had been increased from four percent to ten percent, a *stretch goal* in management's opinion, the project manager might consider the goal a realistic try, but not achievable based on a number of factors (including prior experience). This objective could be counterproductive, resulting in the team not being motivated, particularly if the team members feel there is no chance to succeed.

DETERMINE PROJECT PRIORITIES

After all projects have been evaluated, justified, and the objectives written, it is possible and likely that there are more projects than the organization can afford in terms of money as well as time. Additionally, it is easy to start too many projects or to have too many projects occurring at the same time. Such a situation can result in frustration, the staff being overcommitted, and project failures as highlighted in the following story.

The fifth annual golf outing was a huge success with no major catastrophes. Tom, Sarah, and Rachel met to recap the event by documenting what they had done right and what they should improve upon for next year. Comments were made such as: "We had the right number of people working the event" and "The buffet lunch worked much better than the sit-down lunch the year before." These comments were noted. The three continued until Sarah said, "Next year could we please not have any other major projects during the same month as the golf outing? I'm exhausted. I realize the money was donated for the new marketing brochure, but by working on the brochure and the golf outing at the same time, I've fallen behind with my day-to-day work." Rachel piped up with, "I agree. I've been working with the consultant on the new website. I need to review the test website he created for us. I was supposed to complete that last week, but I've not even started. Why didn't we work on the new website last quarter when there were no other projects?"

To avoid overcommitment of staff, money, and time, prioritize projects. This can be as simple as assigning projects a high, medium, or low rating or prioritizing them based on strategic criteria, such as "enhances customer service" or "an operational necessity." Then rank the projects based on the importance of each strategic criteria. Strategic criteria are identified by management during the strategic planning process. Based on the priorities and factors, such as each project's scope, the estimated costs versus funding available, and project timing requirements, management can make project-related decisions and identify which project can occur immediately, in two months, or next quarter. Prioritizing is an iterative process and there will be tradeoffs. For example, it is possible that a medium-priority project is placed on hold while two low-priority projects are authorized and completed. The reason can be as simple as funding was not available for the medium-priority project or a staffing conflict with another project made the higher-priority project unworkable.

For many flat organizations, simply prioritizing the projects is adequate. Occasionally a more sophisticated approach is necessary. In that case, consider using a tool such as a *Decision Matrix*. A Decision Matrix applies a different weight to each strategic criterion, ranks the potential projects based on the criteria, and calculates a score. This score is the basis for deciding if the organization should proceed or not proceed with a project.

TRACK THE PROJECTS

The intent of a project tracking report is to assist with managing project status. A project tracking report can be a formal, detailed document, such as a Word document with a summary page of all projects and then a detail page for each project, or an informal summarized list, such as a simple Excel spreadsheet. The level of detail as well as the information captured depends on the organization. For example, Table 4.1 (Project Tracking Report) includes the project, the description and justification, the deliverable, the estimated budget, the estimated schedule (start and end dates), and the project sponsor of the annual fundraising effort.

Table 4.1. Project Tracking Report

Prepared by: Chris Date: January						
Project	**Description and Justification**	**Deliverable**	**Estimated Budget**	**Estimated Schedule**		**Project Sponsor**
				Start	**End**	
Network Infrastructure Upgrade	Network hardware past useful life will be replaced	Upgraded network	$60,000	January	July	James
Annual Fundraising	Annual fund drive	Donations of $150,000	$10,000	June	Nov	Kathy

Modify and expand the project tracking report illustrated in Table 4.1 as needed by the organization. For example, some organizations add a column with the project objective(s) in SMART format or just provide the project description with no justification. Projects also take longer than anticipated, funding disappears, and unplanned projects occur. There can be project dependencies, such a project needs to wait for funding from a financial institution to be received before it can begin or a project is dependent on another project's completion, so a dependency or comment column might be added. The report is to assist with managing and tracking *all* of the organization's projects—the report should be modified to support the project life cycle. The tracking report in Table 4.1 can be modified by adding project manager, actual start date, and actual completion date columns to the report (Table 4.2) or two separate reports can be created: one with potential or pending projects and another that reports current projects.

Table 4.2. Expanded Project Tracking Report

Prepared by: Chris Date: January							
	Other Table 4.1 Columns Hidden	Estimated Schedule		Project Sponsor	Project Manager	Actual Schedule	
Project		**Start**	**End**			**Start**	**End**
Network Infrastructure Upgrade		Jan	July	James	Joe	Jan 15	May 1 (A)*
Annual Fundraising		June	Nov	Kathy	Kathy		

*(A) indicates anticipated completion date.

THE HAND-OFF

The authorization hand-off occurs when management authorizes a project and assigns a project manager. The project manager and sponsor meet to discuss the reason and justification for the project, the objective(s), the final product or service (deliverable), the targeted costs, and the estimated schedule (start and end date). The project manager documents the conversation. They discuss what needs to occur so that the project is a success and how potential project concerns will be resolved. This discussion is a two-way conversation, with the project manager and sponsor asking each other questions.

The project manager asks the sponsor for any pertinent documentation. If there is a business case or feasibility study, the project manager asks for a copy. The project manager also asks for any project-related correspondence memos, emails, studies, procurement documents, or regulatory requirements. The project manager and sponsor review similar past projects, including the project plan and any lessons learned. It is possible that prior project documentation is not available, but the project manager or people who worked on the project might be available to provide insight. It is the project manager's responsibility to understand the "why" of the project before proceeding.

Additionally, the project manager and sponsor spend time gaining an understanding of the expectations of each other. The most successful projects have a sponsor and project manager who take the time to explain their needs and wants to each other. The project manager makes it a point to ask what he or she needs to do to be successful and make the sponsor successful. They figure out how to work together and communicate with one another. They talk about project logistics, potential core team members, resource needs, and facility requirements. They are comfortable asking each other tough questions. Nothing, as it relates to the project, is off limits.

There will be exceptions to this authorization approach. Some flat organizations require the creation of a formal document by management known as a *project charter* or *project authorization form*. If such a document is a requirement of the organization, follow the organization's formal approach and use the document during the meeting. A mistake some organizations make is thinking that a formal document takes the place of the meeting—it does not. Formal documents only memorialize human interaction. Human interaction makes the project successful.

IN REVIEW

- Projects occur for two reasons: to support a planned strategic or operational business need or to resolve an unplanned business opportunity or problem.
- Management evaluates and justifies potential projects. Evaluation is the determination of what the project is to accomplish and a preliminary estimate of potential time and costs, risks, and alternatives. Justification is the understanding of why the project is important.
- Objectives are statements written to describe what the project is trying to achieve. Objectives are expressed in terms of the triple constraints: scope, time, and cost and should be written following SMART logic (Specific, Measurable, Attainable, Realistic, and Timely)
- Prioritize projects based on strategic criteria or operational necessity and then track each project's start and progress.

- Authorization of the project begins with the assigning of a project manager and a sponsor providing project-related information to the project manager.

STEP-BY-STEP INSTRUCTIONS

Management begins the authorization process when they:

1. Determine, evaluate, and justify the organization's projects for the year or for some other specified timeframe.
2. Write objectives for a project that are expressed in terms of the triple constraints of scope, time, and cost. The objectives follow SMART logic:
   - Specific
   - Measurable or quantifiable
   - Attainable
   - Realistic
   - Timely
3. Determine the priority for each project and make project tradeoffs, particularly if staff, funding, or time is restricted.
4. Create a project tracking report to assist with managing the organization's projects. Although level of detail varies by organization, consider including:
   - Project name
   - Description and justification
   - Targeted costs
   - Estimated schedule (start and end dates)
   - Sponsor
5. Authorize each project and assign a project manager. The project manager and sponsor meet to:
   - Discuss the reason and justification, project objective(s), product or service being delivered, estimated cost, and estimated schedule (start and end date)
   - Resolve any questions
   - Discuss project logistics

CHAPTER 5

IDENTIFY THE STAKEHOLDERS

Covered in this chapter:

- Identifying stakeholders
- Determining stakeholder roles and expectations
- Understanding each stakeholder's power and interest
- Creating a stakeholder list

Engaging the people or the groups who have a vested interest throughout the life of a project is key to, although not a guarantee of, a project's success. These people or groups are the stakeholders, each with their own expectations and reasons why a particular project is important to them. By involving them early in the project's life cycle, ideas are expressed, knowledge is shared, project expectations are confirmed, requirements are made known, and risks are identified. By keeping stakeholders involved throughout the project, interest and support are gained.

WHO IS A STAKEHOLDER?

It is easy to miss identifying a stakeholder, but overlooking a stakeholder, whether they have a major or minor role in the project, can delay or derail a project. A change late in a project can impact not only the completion date, but also the scope and cost, placing the overall success of the project at risk. Although the project manager is responsible for identifying the stakeholders, the identification process is not performed in isolation.

Start the stakeholder identification process by reviewing project-related documentation. Next, ask the sponsor, core team, and experts in the organization to identify potential stakeholders. The aim is to develop a list of potential stakeholders and then to ask questions in an effort to narrow the list down or in some cases increase it. Potential questions to ask and obtain answers to are

- Who will be directly or indirectly impacted by this project?
- What will change when this project is complete?
- Who will benefit from the success of the project?
- Who will lose something with the success of the project?
- Who has the skill(s) or expertise required by the project?

Stakeholders are not just people or departments internal to the organization, such as accounting, human resources, or sales. Stakeholders can be customers, volunteers, the board of directors or advisory groups, nonprofit or professional associations, regulatory agencies, vendors or contractors, and outsourced providers.

STAKEHOLDER EXPECTATIONS

After the potential stakeholders are identified, interview each one. Determine their role with or in the organization as well as their involvement, or what they think their involvement is, with the project. For example, a stakeholder could be the accounting advisor the project team needs or a key end user who is necessary for testing a software application. Ask stakeholders questions such as:

- How will you know success has been achieved?
- Do you have project success measurements?
- Are there a few things that you feel need to be done well?
- Why is this project important to you?
- How involved do you want to be in the project?
- What do you need from the project team?
- What is the preferred way to communicate with you?
- How often do you need to be briefed on the project?
- Is there someone else who is a stakeholder that we have missed?

Recap and confirm each stakeholder's expectations and any other comments that might be pertinent to the project. Recapping is a simple, but important step because it confirms what was heard. The best method for recapping is *in writing*, but the recap does not need to be elaborate. A short email to the stakeholder may be all that is necessary to confirm an understanding.

Depending on the stakeholder, their answers and expectations of the project could be ambiguous and unclear. Comments could have hidden meanings, so it is important to listen closely. A statement such as, "I do not expect our daily operations to be impacted" could mean "I do not anticipate you using people in my department to assist with testing the new application." A comment such as, "I anticipate the new application system will improve our productivity" might mean "I am expecting the application's workflow to work flawlessly and that there will be fewer workflow process steps to complete an accounting entry."

Stakeholder roles can change as a project progresses. Be prepared to periodically review each stakeholder's interest in the project. A person can be promoted to new position or leave the organization, with a new person joining and taking his or her place. For example, the CFO, who is a stakeholder, resigns. A new CFO joins the organization halfway through a project to select new accounting software. The new CFO becomes a new project stakeholder. Although the new person is in the same role and continues to be a stakeholder, his or her expectations as well as level of interest in the project may differ.

STAKEHOLDER ANALYSIS

Understanding each stakeholder's power and level of interest assists with managing and communicating with each stakeholder. *Power* refers to the amount of influence the stakeholder has in the organization. *Interest* is subjective and refers to a person's attention to and concern about a project's success (or failure). Interest can be difficult to gauge. For example, a CEO or owner has power, but the project might be a maintenance-type project for which he or she has little interest. If the project is the introduction of a new product line, the CEO or owner might have a high interest level in addition to his or her power.

An important point: all stakeholders matter. All stakeholders need information about the project. The difference is the level of communication and frequency required, which can depend on the project and the stakeholder.

A way to evaluate a stakeholder's power and interest in a project is to use a *power-interest grid* (Figure 5.1). The grid shows four boxes with four possible combinations. Each stakeholder falls into one of the four boxes and is rated with high or low power and high or low interest. The power-interest grid is a "keep-it-simple" analytical technique.

High power/high interest. Stakeholders in the upper right corner with high power and high interest are called *key stakeholders*. These are the stakeholders with significant influence and the most to gain or lose from the project. They can also be the most resistant to change, whether positive or negative. Engage with and consult with these stakeholders on a regular basis. Consider brainstorming and discussing new project strategies with them before deciding to implement a strategy. Involve them in the project's decision-making process. These are the

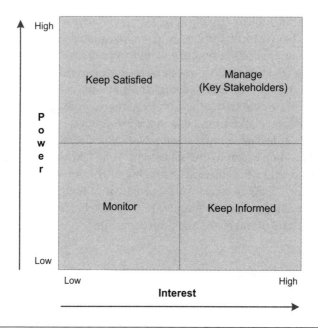

Figure 5.1. Power-interest grid.

people who can make or break a project and are important to the success of the project.

Low power/low interest. Stakeholders that fall in the bottom left have low levels of power and interest in the project. They are the easiest group to keep informed and the least important to the project. Monitor this group for changes in either their power or interest.

High power/low interest. Stakeholders with high power and low interest can be passive. They do not get involved with the project until an event occurs that changes their interest level, making them key stakeholders. Engage and consult with these stakeholders. Strive to keep them satisfied, meet their needs, and keep them informed.

Low power/high interest. Stakeholders with low power and high interest are project supporters or project ambassadors. Keep them involved in and informed about the project. Consult with them on topics and issues that involve their particular interest area. Although they have low power, this group can influence the key stakeholders.

Consider the following story in which a power-interest grid was used by an association with a volunteer committee of twenty small business owners. During their annual planning meeting, the committee decided on four breakfast programs, each being a "project" with a different start and end date highlighting a different small business topic. A project manager and one staff person from the association were assigned to work part-time on all four breakfast projects. The remainder of the team members needed for each breakfast project would be different small business owners.

The project manager reviewed the twenty small business owners and determined each stakeholder's fit in the power-interest grid for each project. The result was each breakfast project had different key stakeholders. This required the project manager to work in a slightly different manner on each project to ensure the expectations of the stakeholders were met.

Suggestion: Start communicating now. Some people think a project manager should wait until a project plan is complete before they start communicating with the stakeholders. The challenge to this thinking is there is momentum and interest now, at the beginning of the project. For the project manager, there is a need to keep this momentum going so that the interest and support required for the project to be a success will be maintained throughout the project. What should you do? One idea is to set up a meeting and introduce the internal and external stakeholders to each other. There still is a lot of planning that needs to occur, but it is good for stakeholders to know who the players are early in the project's life cycle. Let the stakeholders share ideas, expectations, and requirements with one another.

STAKEHOLDER LIST

As the stakeholders are identified and analyzed, a *stakeholder list* may be necessary (Table 5.1). The intent of a stakeholder list is to capture pertinent information to assist the project manager and core team with managing each stakeholder's expectations. Although not every project needs this document, a stakeholder list is a particularly useful tool for projects with many stakeholders.

If the project manager decides a list is necessary, customize the document to meet organizational and project needs. Consider including each stakeholder's name, organizational position, project role, power and interest, expectations, and preferred communication method. The primary reason for listing a stakeholder's preferred communication method is for use in the planning process. During the planning process, the project manager and core team will determine the best

Table 5.1. Stakeholder List

Prepared by: CRM Software Selection						
Date: March						
Name	Category	Position	Project Role	Method	Power and Interest Class	Expectations
John	Mgmt	CEO	Steering Cmte	Status Reports Phone Calls	Key Stakeholder *(High/High)*	John expects project to be completed on time, but would prefer to see it be completed ahead of schedule. John wants to be kept informed about actual cost versus budget.
Dave	Mgmt	CFO	Steering Cmte	Status Reports Email	Keep Satisfied *(High/Low)*	Dave expects project to adhere to budget.
Mary	End User	Sales	Team Member	Status Reports Project Documents	Keep Informed *(Low/High)*	Based on feedback from competitors, Mary hopes new software tracks potential clients better than current software, making meeting sales quotas easier.
Joe	Team Member	IT Support	Team Member	Status Reports Project Documents	Monitor *(Low/Low)*	Joe expects to be given ample time to work with the vendor to implement the software and make any necessary network infrastructure changes.

approaches and methods for keeping everyone informed. Some potential customizations include:

- Develop a list of stakeholder categories, as shown in Table 5.1, that are pertinent for the project. Stakeholders in the same category tend to have the same or similar expectations and requirements of a project as well as the same communication needs. For example, a fundraising project might have the following categories: team members, board of directors, and volunteers. Other potential categories might be end users, volunteers, the board of directors, vendors, and contractors.

- Add an "Information of Interest" column. The project manager might want to know that a stakeholder has been a project manager and is an ally of the project. When adding subjective information of interest, be careful. Why? The stakeholder list is a document that should be available to all team members. It will be in the hands of many. Ensure that there are no negative comments or any comments that might damage either a person or the project.

IN REVIEW

- Identify the stakeholders and each stakeholder's role and expectations early in a project's life cycle. Changes later in the project due to missed expectations and requirements place the overall success of the project at risk.
- A power-interest grid is one tool that assists with evaluating a stakeholder's power and interest in a project. Power in a project refers to how much influence the stakeholder has within the organization while interest in a project is subjective and refers to a stakeholder's attention to and concern about a project's success or failure.
- Understanding a stakeholder's expectations and power and interest classification in a project assists the project manager and core team with developing an approach to satisfy each stakeholder's needs and concerns and to provide the preferred communication method for keeping them informed.

STEP-BY-STEP INSTRUCTIONS

When identifying stakeholders:

1. Review project documentation to identify stakeholders. Look for names of people and groups who may have an interest in the project. Project documentation includes:
   - The project justification
   - The business case and feasibility study

- Correspondence
- Procurement documents
- Regulatory documents
- Historical documents from prior projects

2. Brainstorm to determine if there are additional potential stakeholders.

3. Perform stakeholder interviews to:
   - Determine roles and expectations
   - Develop a sense of each stakeholder's power and interest in the project
   - Determine the preferred communication method

4. Recap each stakeholder's interview to confirm his or her expectations, interest, and preferred communication method.

5. Determine if a stakeholder list is necessary. If so, consider including stakeholder name, stakeholder categories, organizational position, project role, preferred communication method, power and interest classification, and expectations.

6. Review the identified stakeholders with the sponsor. Modify the list accordingly.

CHAPTER 6

DETERMINE THE REQUIREMENTS

Covered in this chapter:

- Definition of a requirement
- Determining the project and product or service requirements
- Documenting and prioritizing requirements
- Determining and using the appropriate data-gathering techniques

Just about every project manager has heard a stakeholder say, "I don't know what I want or need, but I'll know it when I see it." A project manager and core team, however, need to be able to understand and clearly and concisely articulate the requirements so that they know what the project will and will not need to accomplish. Understanding the requirements assists with determining: how big the project is; the amount of time and resources required; and the amount of money necessary for completion.

WHAT ARE REQUIREMENTS?

Requirements are something wanted, needed, or expected to satisfy a condition, contract, or standard expressed by management, the sponsor, or other stakeholders. Without well-defined requirements, the project manager and core team cannot plan a project—they are unsure what the deliverable should be, and there is no way to confirm that the final product or service satisfies the needs of the organization. Projects have two different types of requirements:

- Project requirements: the business and project management requirements of the project, such as contractual requirements stipulating that the project is to be completed in three months

- Product or service requirements: the must-have features and functionality of the final product or service, such as the sales force application must be accessible from any location in the world by all sales employees

THE REQUIREMENTS PROCESS

The requirements process is the defining and documenting of the high-level or key requirements needed to meet the project objectives. The project manager and core team start the process by reviewing and discussing the information provided by the sponsor during the hand-off meeting and the stakeholder comments received when the stakeholders were identified. The project manager and core team discuss the known requirements and determine the best approaches for clarifying and obtaining additional requirements. After additional requirements are obtained and any necessary clarification has occurred, the requirements are documented. The requirements are then used to create a scope statement, a formal document defining the project, and (again) to articulate the work required to complete the project.

When the stakeholders were identified, they explained their project expectations, but some stakeholders might not have realized that the project team needed to understand project and product or service requirements. Other stakeholders, because of daily responsibilities, have only limited amounts of time to devote to the project and do not have time to meet again. These situations require the project manager and core team to be creative when clarifying and gathering additional requirements. Begin with *not* assuming that every stakeholder needs to be involved in the requirements gathering effort—they do not. For example, if the stakeholders have been categorized, interviewing one or two from each category may be sufficient to provide input for the entire group, particularly if similar requirements will be received from every stakeholder in the category and there are time constraints. Consider the following story. It describes how a confused and frustrated project manager realized that the requirements gathering approach the team was following needed to be modified.

Sarah, the project manager, walked out of the CFO's office confused and frustrated. She had just had a very unpleasant conversation with the CFO, a key stakeholder, regarding gathering requirements for the project. Sarah thought she was being sensitive to the CFO's time, but instead, the CFO asked why she was wasting his time. He thought that he had provided the requirements when they spoke earlier: he expected the project to be completed within six months. The CFO did not realize that he had provided a project requirement, but no product (or service) requirements.

As Sarah analyzed what had occurred, she realized she had not articulated what was needed from the stakeholders nor had she explained how the team was going to gather the requirements from the stakeholders. As a result, Sarah and the core team met and agreed on an approach for gathering the requirements. An email was created informing the stakeholders that the next step in the project was to clarify and gather the project and product (or service) requirements. To eliminate confusion, definitions and examples were provided of potential project and product (or service) requirements. The email went on to explain that:

- When the stakeholders were identified, their project expectations were obtained. Some stakeholders had provided requirements, but the project team needed to interview some stakeholders to clarify a few points as well as to gather additional project and product (or service) requirements. Not every stakeholder would be interviewed, but the final requirements list would be available to everyone for review and comment.
- Prior to each interview, an agenda that included four or five discussion points would be sent.
- Two core team members would be assigned to interview each stakeholder: one would ask pertinent questions while the other would be responsible for taking notes. The core team members would listen closely and recap the project and product (or service) requirements that they heard expressed.
- A verbal recap by the core team members would occur at the end of the interview. If there were any points that still required clarification, the stakeholder and core team members would agree on action items and dates.
- An email recapping the core team member's interview notes would be sent within three days. The stakeholder would be asked to confirm the notes and requirements. If the stakeholder did not get back within a week with comments, the assumption would be that the interview notes were acceptable. (In a flat organization with informal communications and processes, using email to communicate instead of creating formal document with a write-up for each interview may be adequate and appropriate.)

This story highlights two important points:

- For all projects it is important to communicate and to be very clear as to the project team's expectations and requirements of stakeholders. Stakeholders need to understand what is expected and required of them, how much time they need to commit, and what that means for them as well as the project's success.

- It is the project manager's responsibility to sort through the information received during the hand-off meeting with the sponsor and the information received when stakeholders are identified. It is common to receive not only a stakeholder's expectations, but also some requirements during stakeholder identification conversations. It is the project manager's responsibility, working with the core team, to determine the expectations and requirements and then determine the best approach for clarifying and collecting additional requirements.

DATA-GATHERING TECHNIQUES

Not every requirements gathering technique is effective for every stakeholder, every organization, or every project. Based on the stakeholders identified, determine the right data gathering technique. Although there are a number of techniques, common, frequently used data-gathering techniques include interviews, brainstorming, observations, questionnaires and surveys, facilitated workshops, and prototypes (Table 6.1). For example, consider:

- An individual interview if confidential information needs to be discussed
- A brainstorming session if a number of people will use the project's product, such as a specific software application
- Observation if a person is not able to describe what they do, but he or she realizes that the process is not working properly
- A questionnaire or survey if there are number of volunteers who need to provide input, but are rarely available at the same time
- A facilitated workshop if the project manager and the core team should be part of the discussion, thus requiring an objective third party's assistance
- A prototype to provide a model or sample (such as a website) that has working links, but does not have any design elements (images or content displayed) on the pages

The time required to collect requirements varies by project and requirements evolve over time for all projects. There will be changes. The goal is to minimize changes after the requirements are gathered. Early in the project, gather requirements so that enough information is available and understood to properly define and plan a project.

If detailed requirements are needed to properly determine the scope, time, and cost of a project, a separate project plan with its own project life cycle should be created to define the detailed requirements. Then, after the requirements

Table 6.1. Common Data-Gathering Techniques

Technique	Description
Interview	An interview normally is a one-on-one discussion held with a stakeholder to outline and clarify requirements.
Brainstorming	Brainstorming is a common way to collect requirements by gathering groups of people to identify and share ideas and solutions.
Observation	Observation involves watching how the work is accomplished. Diagramming the process flow is good way to confirm the current process, develop ideas for solving problems, and note requirements people forgot to mention. Some people refer to this process as "as is" to "to be" diagrams.
Questionnaire or Survey	A questionnaire or survey involves distributing a series of questions for the purpose of soliciting feedback and gathering information. A questionnaire is a good technique to use when there are too many people to interview or include in a brainstorming session.
Facilitated Workshop	A facilitated workshop is a structured group session facilitated by a moderator in which cross-functional requirements of the various stakeholders are defined. Issues can be reconciled and quickly resolved because all applicable stakeholders are in the workshop together.
Prototypes	A prototype is a model of the final product based on the requirements.

gathering project is complete, a second project can be authorized to deliver the final product or service. For example, a manufacturing company has a strategic initiative that requires designing a new product. In this case, the manufacturing company would have a separate project that defines the detailed requirements for the new product. A second project would then be authorized designing the new product based on the detailed requirements. Consider another story that highlights how easy it is to spend time gathering requirements and lose focus.

A project manager and two core team members were in week five of collecting the project requirements. The sponsor was becoming concerned because management had anticipated that the project, which involved selecting and implementing a new sales management system, would take no more than six to seven months from start to finish. The sponsor thought it was taking too long to gather the requirements and was concerned that the project was getting off-track. He also realized this was the first time the project manager was in a project management role. Additionally, the sponsor was new to project management and had limited knowledge of the project management process.

The sponsor hired an experienced project manager to work part-time assisting and coaching the project manager. The experienced project manager reviewed the project's status and explained that although the project was to select and implement a new sales management system, this was not one project. Rather, it was a number of smaller projects, each with its own project life cycle: software requirements gathering, software selection, software implementation, data conversion, and training. The project manager and core team were trying to gather all the project and product requirements for all the smaller projects.

The outcome of the review was the experienced project manager worked with the project team to sort the collected requirements into each smaller project and then worked with the project team to determine the high-level or key requirements for the software requirements gathering project. The final deliverable of the software requirements-gathering project was the detailed software requirements that were to be used by the next project, which was the software selection. The experienced project manager also explained that if requirements gathering were becoming too complicated, it is possible that there is more than one project. Take a step back and objectively evaluate the work that is being performed.

DOCUMENT AND PRIORITIZE THE REQUIREMENTS

Capture gathered requirements in a written document. The format of the requirements document can range from a simple document that lists the requirements by stakeholder or by stakeholder group to a very formal, elaborate report with an executive summary, detailed descriptions, and matrix comparing each key stakeholder's requirements to another stakeholder. There is no right format, but the format needs to work for a particular project. For example, for the project that was to select new software, the requirements document might be divided into three sections:

- Business requirements, such as requiring a new system to track all of potential and current customers
- Functional requirements, such as needing to generate sales forecast reports on demand
- Technical requirements, such as runs on a Microsoft® platform

It is important for a project manager to be able to delve into the requirements gathered and keep asking questions. Why? Not all requirements have the same priorities for every stakeholder. A top requirement for one key stakeholder might not be a requirement for another key stakeholder.

The challenge for the project manager is that key stakeholders need to agree on the requirements. Determining the requirements is an iterative process. The project manager, sponsor, and stakeholders need to come to consensus, agreeing on which requirements, if not met, would constitute project failure.

Another reason for prioritizing requirements ties to the triple constraints. Only so much time, so many resources, and so much money are available. If too much work needs to be accomplished in a specified timeframe or too much money needs to be spent to complete the entire project, the project might need to have the scope reduced. Understanding the priorities and having agreement on the priorities can eliminate frustration late in the project if delays or reduced funding require features and functionality to be removed from the project's final product or service.

Suggestion: Use a requirements document for smaller projects. An approach that works well for flat organizations with smaller projects is to create a document that categorizes the requirements into needs, wants, and nice-to-haves, as shown in Table 6.2 (Requirements Document). Categorizing requirements as wants and nice-to-haves does not mean that the wants and nice-to-haves are not important—they are. What this categorizing does is to assist with classifying requirements by sorting them into three categories so that if features or functionality do need to be removed during planning or execution, there is a starting point for discussion. Additionally, this list assists the project manager during the execution process. If the project falls behind schedule, there are cost concerns, or the project needs to be completed sooner than originally planned, the project manager and sponsor have a starting point for discussion and decision-making purposes.

Table 6.2. Requirements Document

Project Name: CRM Software Selection
Prepared by: Anna
Date: March
Interviewee: John (Sales Manager)
Needs: Sales tracking including opportunity management, contact management, proposal review, and account management
Wants: Smartphone integration
Nice-to-Have: Customer satisfaction surveys

IN REVIEW

- The high-level requirements process defines the project and the product or service necessary to meet the project objective(s). Project requirements are the business and project management requirements of the project while product or service requirements are the must-have features and functionality of the final project or service delivered by the project.
- Frequently used data-gathering techniques include interviews, brain-storming, questionnaires or surveys, facilitated workshops, and prototypes. These techniques can be used individually or in combination, but not every technique works for every stakeholder, organization, or project.
- Document the requirements, either informally or formally. The requirements gathered are used to create a scope statement and to determine the work required to produce the final deliverable.

STEP-BY-STEP INSTRUCTIONS

When gathering requirements, the project manager and core team:

1. Review project documentation for requirements. Project documentation includes:
   - Information provided by the sponsor during the authorization hand-off meeting
   - Stakeholder comments received during the stakeholder identification process
   - Business case and feasibility study
   - Correspondence
   - Procurement documents
   - Regulatory documents
   - Historical documents from prior projects
2. Identify stakeholders who can provide information on detailed project and product or service requirements.
3. Determine the best data-gathering techniques to collect project or product requirements based on the organization's culture and project. These include:
   - Interviews
   - Brainstorming
   - Observation

- Questionnaires and surveys
- Facilitated workshops
- Prototypes

4. Document and validate each stakeholder's requirements by soliciting feedback.
5. Consolidate and prioritize the requirements.
6. Review the requirements with the sponsor. Solicit the sponsor's input and modify the requirements accordingly.
7. Provide or ensure the final requirements report is available to all stakeholders.

CHAPTER 7

DEFINE THE PROJECT SCOPE

Covered in this chapter:

- Formalizing the project with a scope statement
- Clarifying the project description and requirements
- Refining the project objective(s) using SMART logic
- Identifying constraints, assumptions, risks, exclusions, and acceptance criteria
- Summarizing the cost estimates and timeline
- Signing off on the scope statement

It is common to hear people say, "Let's just get started. We know what we want." The project manager and sponsor have met and discussed the project. The project manager is clear on management's vision. The project stakeholders have been identified, their levels of interest and expectations have been elucidated, and their requirements have been defined. So, why not just start? The answer is no one has taken time to define the final deliverable, what constitutes success, or the boundaries of the project. Failing to do these things causes achieving success to be almost impossible.

When more aspects of a project are defined in a clear, concisely written, and an agreed-upon scope statement, the chance for project success is better. Time spent and costs incurred early in the project to define the work effort will be far less than fixing a problem after the work has begun or the project has been completed. The quality of the scope statement is one of the most important factors impacting project success.

WHAT IS A SCOPE STATEMENT?

Many experts believe the scope statement is the most important project management document because, if not "right," the project is "wrong" from the beginning. A scope statement highlights what the project will and will not accomplish. It assists with defining the work and the level of effort. A scope statement is a formal document written in common, everyday language with enough detail to avoid ambiguity. Industry-specific terminology or jargon is clearly defined. A scope statement can be thought of as the "contract" between the sponsor (management), stakeholders, and the project manager (team).

The project manager is responsible for composing the scope statement and building consensus so that everyone agrees on what is an acceptable final product or service and the criteria to measure success. The document is based on what is known today and what stakeholders and subject matter experts think will happen in the future. Depending on the project, a review of a prior project's documentation might be necessary, appropriate, and helpful.

Not only is a scope statement a communication tool, but it is also a great reference document. As time passes, details are forgotten. A written scope statement avoids future conflict by memorializing the intent of a project and by assisting with eliminating or minimizing misunderstandings, false starts, rework, and the unauthorized addition of features and functionality.

For smaller projects, the length of a scope statement may only require two or three pages while larger projects could have a document of twenty or more pages. Consider including:

- Project description
- Objective(s)
- Requirements
- Exclusions
- Constraints, assumptions, and risks
- Acceptance criteria
- Cost estimates
- Deliverables and milestones
- Sign-offs

A scope statement is *not* an optional project document. Although a scope statement is a mandatory formal document, the exact information included varies by organization and project. Projects are by nature unique; therefore, the project manager or sponsor might deem that certain information unique to the project must be included in the scope statement. For example, some organizations include sections such as special resource requirements, the criticality of the project to the organization, and change management processes and procedures while other organizations prefer not to include cost estimates.

The project manager, sponsor, and any appropriate stakeholders sign off on the scope statement, confirming a common understanding. Think of the document as an agreement, a contract, between all of the players. If there are changes to the scope, just like a contract, the scope statement is to be amended and new signatures obtained.

Although all project management methodologies mention creating a formal written document that defines and provides basic information about the project before planning or project execution begins, there is no one "right" format for a scope statement. Instead of being called a scope statement, the document might be referred to as a *project definition* or *project initiation* document. Instead of being one document, the document could consist of two documents, such as a *project charter* or *project authorization* (see Chapter 4) to authorize the project and then a scope statement refining and expanding on the project charter.

Additionally, an organization may create other documents instead of or in addition to a scope statement. Two common documents are a *contract* and a *contractual statement of work*:

- A formal *contract* is a legally binding agreement between two or more parties. A formal contract provides project-related specifics such as a description of the product or service to be delivered, timeframe, cost estimates, and acceptance criteria and legal requirements such as insurance requirements, nondisclosure, and warranties. For example, a formal contract is used when an organization hires a building contractor to expand the facility.

- A *contractual statement of work* (also referred to as a Statement of Work or SOW) is part of the contract or an amendment to the contract and is used to authorize work. A statement of work has an agreed-upon description of the product or service to be delivered, timeframe, cost estimates, and acceptance criteria. For example, an organization has a contract with a third-party vendor for outsourced computer network maintenance. Any additional work, such as a major network upgrade, requires creating and signing a statement of work referencing the contract.

The foregoing material clearly indicates that there are different opinions concerning the name for the formal document as well as the information and the level of detail to be included in a scope document. The one point all practitioners agree upon, however, is that a formal written and signed document that defines the project leads to a greater chance for project success. To assist with illuminating the importance of a scope statement, consider the following story.

John, a project manager, and two team members were excited about the website they had designed and built. Not only did they think it looked great, but they also completed the project on time and within budget. You can image their surprise when they learned that the sponsor was disappointed with the results. The sponsor thought the navigation was clumsy and the graphics were not crisp—the website just did not present the "right" image. From the sponsor's perspective, the project was a failure. The team had failed to deliver an acceptable final product.

John was confused. He thought the requirements had been met. The website they designed and built was similar to the websites the sponsor "liked" and it had been completed on time and within budget.

So what went wrong? The sponsor thought the project failed because his product requirements, although not properly articulated and not formally documented, were not met. The project manager thought the project was a success because the team met the project requirements (on time and within budget) and met what the team thought were the product requirements (a website similar to the websites the sponsor liked).

Project success requires delivering project and product requirements within the time and budget requirements. Without a written document defining the work and key project and product requirements, it is easy for misunderstandings to occur. The website project was a smaller project, so the sponsor did not think a scope statement was necessary, nor did he have time to explain his expectations, requirements, or what was an acceptable final product. Consequently, John guessed at the requirements and acceptability rather than pressing the sponsor for answers. He assumed "liked" meant the sponsor wanted a website similar to the other websites—which apparently was not the case. The project manager and sponsor could have eliminated frustration and ended up with an acceptable website if they had taken the time to discuss requirements and had created a formal written scope statement.

Although the project manager in the story was internal to the organization, the sponsor could have hired a third-party vendor to create the website. In that case, the third-party vendor would have required a signed contract or statement of work before starting to work on the project. When defining the scope of a project, there should be no difference between a project composed of internal staff and a project in which a third-party vendor is hired.

WRITE THE SCOPE STATEMENT

Although writing a scope statement should not be an onerous, complicated process that takes forever, getting lost in the detail can be easy, particularly if writing a scope statement is a new task for the project manager. Keep it simple. Keep in the mind that the intent is to memorialize the project in writing. The document is a communication and management tool highlighting what the project will and will not accomplish. It is used to define the work and the level of effort— it is the "contract." The format that works for one organization or one project might not work for another organization or another project or a document such as a formal contract might be used instead of a scope statement. This section continues with a walk-through for writing a scope statement.

Three Key Scope Statement Sections

Although all sections are important, a scope statement has three key sections: project description, objective(s), and requirements. The description and objective(s) are the starting point for defining the requirements and were discussed in Chapter 4. Requirements were discussed in Chapter 6. All of the other sections found in a scope statement build upon the description, objective(s), and requirements.

Project description. The project description is prose that briefly explains the purpose and the work to be performed. It is a refinement of the original description discussed during the hand-off meeting and is used during the requirements-gathering process. On a smaller project, the description might only be one or two sentences or two or three paragraphs. For example:

Description: This project includes selecting an educational training web application for nurses and physicians' assistants to enable them to remain current on the latest medical advances and techniques. Also included are reviewing the requirements (provided by a different project); identifying potential software applications; assessing vendors, product demonstrations, and evaluations; and making an application decision.

Project objective. Management should have defined the project objective(s) before the project was authorized, and the project manager and sponsor should have discussed the objective(s) during the hand-off. Objectives are essential to a project because they assist with defining the project's final product or service and are based on the project description. An objective that ties to the educational training web application description above could be:

Objective: By July 1, select an educational healthcare web application for nurses and physicians' assistants to enable them to obtain instruction on the latest medical advances and techniques and to provide weekly tracking of their testing results.

Review the original objective(s), refining it if necessary and ensuring that it is realistic, attainable, and measureable. If your objective(s) is not measurable, is not Specific, Measurable, Attainable, Realistic, and Timely or SMART—keep refining it until it is SMART. (For more on creating SMART objectives, refer to Chapter 4). Alternatively, many project managers have been handed a project objective(s) that is written following SMART logic only to walk away with their heads hung low, muttering words such as "ridiculous, totally unrealistic" or "what are they thinking?" Creating an objective that does not provide a challenge to the team or having an objective that is so impossibly difficult to achieve that it is not accepted as a possible result by the team is easy. The "best" project objective is well stated, is realistic and attainable, can be committed to, and can be embraced by all on the project team.

If there is no objective, the project manager needs to take the lead, solicit the sponsor's assistance, and write the objective(s). Some sponsors, when asked, take the initiative and write the objective(s) for the project. Others, even if they want to assist, will be too busy.

Suggestion: Take initiative when creating an objective(s). If the sponsor is too busy to assist with defining the project objective(s), consider two options:

- Ask the sponsor if he or she can recommend a key stakeholder to assist with defining the objective(s).
- Write a draft of the objective(s) with the assistance of the core team and then ask the sponsor to review the draft. Work with the sponsor's schedule to ensure the sponsor's input is received. This approach can be a great team building exercise because it helps ensure that the project manager, sponsor, and the core team have the same understanding of the project's objectives.

Requirements. The level of detail and how many requirements are included in the scope statement is a judgment call. The project and product requirements in the scope statement should be the high-level requirements, the key requirements. They should tie back to the objective(s). These are the requirements that can make or break a project. Not meeting these requirements results in stakeholders thinking the project was a failure, but if met, the project was a success. For example, three requirements for the selection of the educational training application might be:

- The web application needs to have the ability to track the names and dates of courses taken by each nurse and physician assistant (product requirement).

- The web application needs to support our current training videos and PowerPoint presentations (product requirement).
- The web application needs to be implemented and ready for use by the November rollout of our new on-going training requirement initiative (project requirement).

There will be additional requirements expressed by the stakeholders, some of which are quite detailed that are not listed in the scope statement, but these additional requirements are needed to plan the project work.

Other Scope Statement Sections

Other sections to consider including in a scope statement are exclusions; constraints, assumptions, and risks; acceptance criteria; cost estimates; deliverables and milestones.

Exclusions. Exclusions are the features, functions, or work not included in or prohibited from being a part of the project:

- The educational training web application is not for doctors.
- The dinner event will not include entertainment and dancing.

Constraints, assumptions, and risks. Constraints are factors that limit the way the project can be planned and managed. Start with the triple constraints. Ask the sponsor and key stakeholders for any known scope, time, or cost issues that could influence the project approach:

- The educational training web application must be implemented by November 1, which is when the new training program is being rolled out.
- The total cost for the dinner event cannot exceed $50,000.
- For every day the deliverable is late, the company will be fined $10,000.

Assumptions are statements regarding the project that are assumed to be true or false:

- The educational training web application will be accessible 24/7.
- Dinner will be held on the outside patio at The Cape Restaurant.
- The core team will be assigned to the project for the project's duration.

Risks are uncertain events or conditions. If these events occur, they could have a positive or a negative impact on the objective(s):

- Some of the budgeted dollars for the educational training web application may need to be used to upgrade computer equipment.
- Rain will cause the dinner to be moved inside to the hotel ballroom.
- Our key web developer could resign requiring replacement.

As the planning starts, ask the sponsor and key stakeholders if other uncertainties or risks need to be considered. Also ask the core team if they know of any potential risks.

Acceptance criteria. Acceptance criteria are provided as a defined and measureable list of conditions (not necessarily objective—the criteria can be subjective) that must be met before a project can be considered completed and for the project deliverables to be accepted by the sponsor:

- The educational software must follow our easy-to-use and easy-to-access standards (defined separately); provide instruction on the latest medical advances and techniques; and provide weekly tracking of testing results.
- A software implementation plan must be created before this project is considered complete.
- All guests are to be served the main course within a ten-minute window.

Cost estimates. Money is a project constraint. Management might have estimated a total project cost when the project was authorized. This amount of money could be on target, but it could also be unrealistic because it was determined with limited knowledge of the expectations and requirements of the project. If as project manager you are comfortable with the dollar amount targeted by management, use it in the scope statement. If not, consider using an order-of-magnitude estimate, also known as an "educated guess." Use management's targeted project cost estimate, project documentation, historical information, and the actual cost from a similar project as a starting point. Evaluate the current project against the collected data. Ask questions such as, "Is this project a more complex project? Do we need to adjust for increased material costs?" For example, if raw material costs have increased by five percent since this time last year, increase last year's actual project cost by five percent and use the new number as the new estimate. This type of estimate is normally too high or too low, but it is a starting point for planning purposes. Be prepared to explain to the sponsor and key stakeholders how the budget will be determined during project planning and solicit their input. If there is a budget risk, note the risk under project risks. If a more sophisticated approach to estimating is required, numerous books are available that provide a more comprehensive discussion of the different cost estimating techniques.

Key deliverables and milestones. Key or major deliverables and milestones that are product- or service- as well as project-related are listed with their associated completion dates. To clarify, the project management discipline uses the term *deliverable* to mean any tangible product, service, or document that must be produced to complete the project or part of the project and is subject to approval of the sponsor or customer. Examples of product or service deliverables are a website, an annual dinner, or the product documentation. Project management deliverables are the scope document and project plan. To eliminate confusion, some organizations referred to deliverables as project-related deliverables, interim deliverables, or key deliverables. Milestones mark the start or finish of a significant task or group of tasks or the completion of a key deliverable. A milestone has no duration, cost, or resource requirement associated with it—just a date(s)—but these dates help set project goals and monitor the project's progress. Think about the milestone markers along the side of a road that serve as reference points to assure travelers that they are on the right path. Milestones concerning project checkpoints might include points where the project team checks to see if they are still on the right path. Questions are asked such as, "Are we still on schedule? Do we need to adjust the delivery date based on our findings?" Project start and project end are always project milestones. For example:

Project starts	November 15
Project management plan completed	January 5
Vendor request for proposal issued	January 14
Vendor proposals due	February 15
Vendor contract signed	March 12
Educational software selected	April 15
Educational software contract signed	April 30
Project implementation plan	June 30
Project ends	July 31

OBTAIN SIGN-OFFS

Even in a flat organization, people forget details. People get busy and time passes. By signing the scope statement, everyone understands the project's parameters, even if they do not agree on all the points. The scope statement should be signed-off on by the project manager and sponsor. If there are key stakeholders, consider having them sign the statement as well. With a signed statement, the project manager and core team start planning the project. Any changes to the deliverable or the scope now need to go through a change control process.

Suggestion: Hold a meeting. One of the top reasons projects fail is because they are poorly defined. A poor definition can result in the project team successfully delivering a product or service, but the sponsor or customer being disappointed with the results. The more the project manager and core team can do to ensure that everyone understands the project scope before the planning and work is performed, the better. When the scope statement is ready to be signed, consider having a meeting with the project manager, sponsor, key stakeholders, and the core team. Provide everyone a copy of the document. Explain the various sections. Then open the meeting up to discussion. Clarification of wording can occur, any discrepancies or concerns can be resolved, and any last-minute changes can be made before the project manager, sponsor, and any stakeholders sign off on the scope statement.

Table 7.1 (at end of chapter) illustrates a completed scope statement that was created for the educational software selection project discussed in this chapter. The format is based on a scope statement template that could have been an organization's standardized scope statement template or a generic scope statement template found on the internet. When using a template, review the format and modify it as necessary to fit the needs of each project.

IN REVIEW

- A scope statement is the most important project document. It is a mandatory formal document for all projects in all organizations, even flat organizations. The scope statement is "the contract" between the sponsor (management), stakeholders, and the project manager (team). It memorializes the intent of the project by defining the final deliverable, the boundaries of the project, and the acceptance criteria.
- A scope statement for a flat organization with smaller projects may only be two or three pages in length, but it should include the project description, objective(s), and key requirements as well as high-level information on exclusions; constraints, assumptions, and risks; acceptance criteria; cost estimates; and deliverables and milestones.
- The format of a scope statement varies by organization and project. It may have supplementary documents, such as a project charter or project authorization form, or take the form of a formal contract or a statement of work.
- The scope statement requires a sign-off by the project manager, sponsor, and, if applicable, any key stakeholders.
- The scope statement is referred to and amended throughout the project. It is used to confirm that the final product or service meets the agreed-upon scope and acceptance criteria.

STEP-BY-STEP INSTRUCTIONS

When creating a scope statement, the project manager and core team:

1. Review project-related documentation such as:
   - Project reason, justification, and expectation documentation
   - Business cases, feasibility studies, and any other related studies
   - Memorandum and email correspondence
   - Regulatory and procurement documents
   - Historical documents from prior projects
2. Review and update the project description and project objectives discussed during the initial meeting between the project manager and sponsor.
3. Review the project requirements and determine the key requirements.
4. Create a scope statement. If there is a standardized format, review and modify it for the project. If there is no standardized format, consider including:
   - Project description
   - Objective(s)
   - Requirements
   - Exclusions
   - Constraints, assumptions, and risks
   - Acceptance criteria
   - Cost estimates
   - Deliverables and milestones
   - Sign-Offs
5. Review the scope statement with the sponsor. Solicit the sponsor's input and modify the scope statement accordingly.
6. Distribute the scope statement to stakeholders for review. Obtain feedback from the stakeholders and refine the scope statement, as appropriate.
7. Obtain consensus and formal sign-off signatures from project manager, sponsor, and key stakeholders.
8. Review the finalized and signed-off scope statement with the core team. Clarify any core team questions or concerns.

This book has free material available for download from the
Web Added Value™ resource center at *www.jrosspub.com*

Table 7.1. Scope Statement

Project Name:	Educational Training Web Software Selection
Prepared by:	Project Manager
Date:	November 15

Revision History:	
Revised Date	Revised Change

Project Description:
This project includes selecting an educational training web application for nurses and physicians' assistants enabling them to remain current on the latest medical advances and techniques. This project includes reviewing the requirements (provided by a different project); identifying potential software applications; assessing vendors; product demonstrations and evaluations; and an application decision.

Objectives:
Objective 1: By July 1, select an educational healthcare web application for nurses and physicians' assistants to enable them to obtain instruction on the latest medical advances and techniques and to provide weekly tracking of their testing results.

Objective 2: ...

Requirements:

1. The web application needs to have the ability to track names and dates of courses taken by each nurse and physician's assistant (product requirement).

2. The web application needs to support our current training videos and PowerPoint presentations (product requirement).

3. The web application needs to be implemented and ready for use by the November rollout of our new on-going training requirement initiative (project requirement).

4. ...

Exclusions:

1. The educational training web application is not for doctors.

Acceptance Criteria:

1. The educational software must follow our easy-to-use and easy-to-access standards (defined separately); provide instruction on the latest medical advances and techniques; and provide weekly tracking and reporting of test results.

2. A software implementation plan must be created before this project is considered complete.

Constraints, Assumptions, and Risks:
Constraints:

1. The educational training web application must be implemented by November 1, which is when the new training program is being rolled out.

2. ...

Assumptions:

1. The educational training web application will be accessible 24/7.

2. ...

Risks:

1. Some of the budgeted dollars for the educational training web application may need to be used to upgrade computer equipment.

2. ...

Key Deliverables and Milestones:

Key Deliverables and Milestones	Dates
Project starts	November 15
Project management plan completed	January 5
Vendor request for proposal issued	January 14
Vendor proposals due	February 15
Vendor contract signed	March 12
Educational software selected	April 15
Contract signed	April 30
Project implementation plan	June 30
Project ends	July 31

Cost:
Estimated Cost: $50,000

Other Comments:
Cost estimate includes cost for an outside vendor to assist and advise us with determining the right solution. Internal staff costs are not included in the estimated cost.

Signatures:

Project Sponsor: Sarah	Date: November 30
Project Manager: Elizabeth	Date: November 30
Project Stakeholder: Daniel (Technical Person)	Date: November 30

SECTION 3

BUILDING THE ROADMAP

A trite expression says: "Those who fail to plan, plan to fail." No project manager can afford not to properly plan and schedule a project, but planning is time consuming. Another cliché says: "The devil's in the details." Rarely can a project manager plan in isolation—assistance is needed to determine all of the work and to estimate the time, resources, and cost required for every task. The core team is a key asset for providing this assistance because team members have firsthand knowledge of each task's level of effort. The core team members are accountable for completing the various tasks, so it behooves them to provide realistic time and resource estimates. Input and feedback from a sponsor and the stakeholders are instrumental as well. Sponsors and stakeholders can provide business-related information that can influence the project's success. Following a systematic approach and careful analysis of the details will enable the project manager, sponsor, core team, and stakeholders to properly plan and balance the triple constraints of scope, time, and cost.

The outcome of the chapters in this section will be a functional project work plan, schedule, and budget collectively known as the *project plan* which can be used to monitor, manage, control, and report the progress of a project. This section covers:

Chapter 8. Determine the Work: Focuses on starting the creation of a project plan by dividing the work into manageable pieces using a technique known as the work breakdown structure, a hierarchical breakdown of a project's deliverables, work packages, and tasks

Chapter 9. Sequence the Work: Builds on the work that has been determined and, with the aid of a network diagram and logical relationship diagrams, identifies the dependencies, interdependencies, and relationships of the work so that work is organized in the right order

Chapter 10. Estimate the Time and Resources: Explains how to estimate the duration, level of effort, and resources needed to perform the work using various estimating techniques; the planning time for unknown and unexpected events and contingency reserves; and common estimating mistakes

Chapter 11. Create the Schedule: Focuses on determining which tasks are on the critical path, the sequence of work that takes the longest to complete, so that the project's completion date can be determined; assigns start and finish dates to all of the work creating a schedule; and then compresses the schedule, resulting in a project work plan and schedule

Chapter 12. Assign Resources: Uses the resource estimates to determine the staff skill sets needed and non-staff resources requirements; assigns staff and other resources to the tasks in the work plan; and modifies the schedule accordingly

Chapter 13. Determine the Budget: Leverages all of the planning work; creates a project budget and budget baseline; and a final cost estimate to provide to management enabling them to decide if the project is to proceed or a different course of action needs to be taken

CHAPTER 8

DETERMINE THE WORK

Covered in this chapter:

- Characteristics of a work breakdown structure
- Defining and organizing the work
- Incorporating project management work
- Determining work package ownership

With an approved scope statement, the project plan can start to be created. The first step in the process is breaking down the requirements into workable and manageable pieces. Simply put, the final product or service is broken down into project deliverables, which are then further broken down into the necessary work that needs to be completed to have a successful project. This breakdown is the backbone of the planning effort.

THE WORK BREAKDOWN STRUCTURE

A *work breakdown structure* (WBS) is a hierarchical breakdown that organizes and defines all of the work to be completed during the project's execution phase. A WBS expands on the high-level description and requirements in the scope statement by adding details and is the first step in creating a project plan. The goal of a WBS is to assist with:

- Organizing the project and creating a work plan (a plan that lists all the work to be completed)
- Identifying the deliverables and milestones
- Determining the time and cost estimates

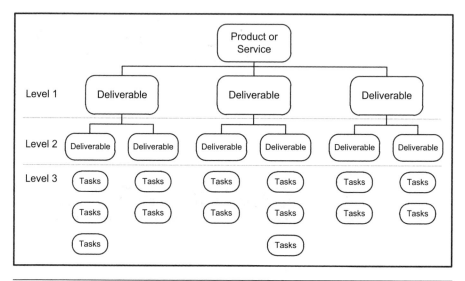

Figure 8.1. Visual work breakdown structure.

- Determining resource needs and assigning responsibilities
- Identifying the work that needs to be completed to produce the final product or deliverable

Whether displayed as a hierarchical graphical diagram (Figure 8.1), also known as a tree structure, or in a textual format (Table 8.1), a WBS is a great tool because it helps the project manager and core team clarify and expand upon the scope statement.

CREATE A WORK BREAKDOWN STRUCTURE

Creating a WBS is not difficult, but it does require the project manager and core team to be thorough when deciding on the detailed work that needs to be completed and determining the best way to categorize the work. There is no right or wrong WBS format. The "right" WBS format is what is "right" for the organization and for the particular project. Work will likely be missed because as the WBS is used to determine the time, cost, staff, and other resources, any additional work required and deliverables can be added or removed. A WBS can be created following either a top-down or a bottom-up approach. The top-down approach discussed in this chapter works well in flat organizations.

If an organization has a project work plan from a prior similar project, consider using the project work plan as a template, a starting point, and modify

Table 8.1. Textual Work Breakdown Structure

Product or Service	
Level 1	Deliverable
Level 2	Deliverable
Level 3	Task
	Task
	Task
Level 2	Deliverable
Level 3	Task
	Task
Level 1	Deliverable
Level 2	Deliverable
Level 3	Task
	Task
	...

it accordingly. Templates save time, make life easier, and provide consistency within the organization for similar projects. Think of templates as project work plans without the time, cost, and staff (or other resource parameters) filled in. For example, use the annual dinner project work plan, a template, from last year as a starting point for the current year's annual dinner.

Identify Elements of the Work Breakdown Structure

Start creating the WBS by identifying the main deliverables required to complete the final product or service. The main deliverables are then *decomposed* (broken down) into various other deliverables. Each deliverable or *branch* is further decomposed into smaller deliverables or smaller "chunks" of work (Figure 8.2). The smallest deliverables, those at the lowest realistic level, are called *work packages*. A work package is composed of a number of manageable and executable pieces, each with an expected duration, called *tasks* or *activities*. In this book, these manageable and executable pieces are referred to as tasks.

Tasks are not a "how-to" or a large, unmanageable "to-do" list. Tasks are "what needs to be done," discrete action items. Tasks roll up to a work package; are in a verb-noun format, such as "write script" or "print brochures" or "conduct training;" and are action related, whereas a deliverable is a summary of the underlying work packages and tasks and is expressed in a noun format, such as "screen content" or "brochure and manual" or "sales training." A deliverable has a name.

When has a WBS been decomposed "enough?" The amount of decomposition requires reliance on the judgment and experience of the project manager. As

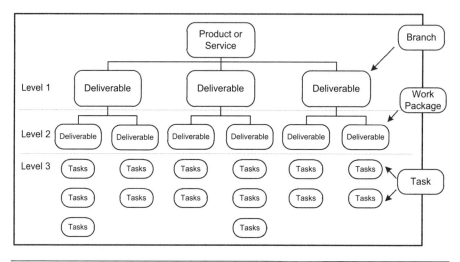

Figure 8.2. Parts of a work breakdown structure.

the work is decomposed, the project manager will determine if the WBS has the work packages and tasks defined at a small enough level of detail so that it is possible to estimate time, cost, staff, and other resources. The "right" level of detail is when the WBS contains enough detail to be meaningful, but not so much that it is overwhelmingly complicated.

Suggestion: Use a work package rule. When decomposing a WBS, an extremely helpful technique known as the *work package rule* can be used. When determining work packages, the project manager develops a guideline or rule for work packages, such as "work packages should be of at least *X* hours and no more than *XX* hours." This requirement forces the project manager and core team to carefully analyze each deliverable, task, and work package based on the rule. The 4/40 rule, in which work packages are of at least 4 hours of effort and no more than 40 hours, is a good guideline for very small projects. The 8/80 rule, in which work packages are of at least 8 hours of effort and no more than 80 hours, works well for many smaller projects. For example, on a project to revamp marketing literature, one of the work packages is a marketing brochure with two tasks: write content and create images. The 8/80 work package rule would be applied by asking, "Is it possible to write the content and create the images in 80 hours?" If the answer is "yes," no more decomposing of the marketing brochure work package is necessary. If the answer is "no," then the marketing brochure work package is not the lowest level and needs to be decomposed further. Although the suggestion at this point is to apply a 4/40 or an 8/80 rule to determine if the WBS is at the right level, the actual time estimates have not yet been determined. At this point, the project manager and core team are making educated guesses concerning the time required. As planning progresses, adjust the work packages in the WBS as required.

Organize the Work Breakdown Structure

The top box of each branch, Level 1, is not only a deliverable level, but also a project organization level or management level. This is the level that the project manager uses to organize and manage the project. For example, does the project manager want to organize and manage by phase (requirements gathering, design) or by deliverable (venue, food and beverage)? Alternatively, does the project manager want to manage by organizational or functional responsibility (Accounting, Sales) or geographical location (East, Midwest, Asia, or Europe)? Even though there is no right or wrong way to organize a WBS, do not mix organizational types.

The two most common ways of organizing work are by phase and deliverable. A WBS could be organized by phase for a software selection project (Figure 8.3) or by deliverable for an annual dinner event (Figure 8.4). Depending on the size of the project, the software selection project might be divided into smaller projects. The subprojects might be organized by deliverable instead of by phase. The preferred approach depends on a number of factors, such as the project, the organization's project management methodology, and the project manager's preferences. Technical projects such as a network upgrade or selecting new software tend to be organized by phase, whereas business process-related projects such as an annual dinner event or changes to a department's operational processes tend to be organized by deliverables.

Determine the Levels

How many levels should a WBS have? The number of levels is dependent on the project. A WBS with three levels is common for smaller projects, but having five or more levels is also possible. Additionally, each branch of the diagram can have a different number of levels because the number of levels for one branch may not be adequate for another branch. Branches do not need to be symmetrical. If, however, the number of levels is disproportionate, such as one branch has two levels and another has fifteen, consider revisiting the work decomposition. To help keep track of levels in the WBS, assign an ID number to the boxes to assist with managing each of them (Figures 8.3 and 8.4).

Suggestion: Use the brainstorming technique. Identifying the required project work is not a one-person job. It is a team effort with input provided by the

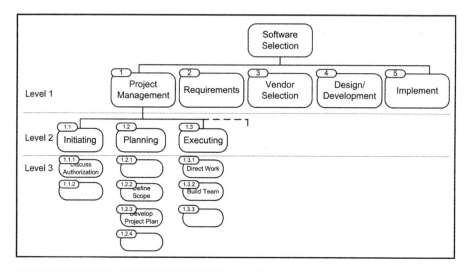

Figure 8.3. Work breakdown structure by phase.

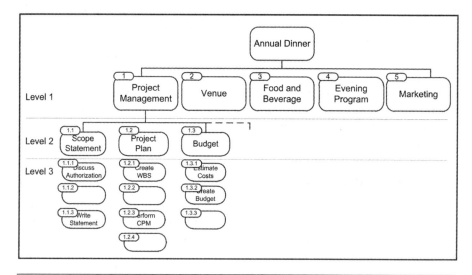

Figure 8.4. Work breakdown structure by deliverable.

project manager, core team, sponsor, stakeholders, and third-party experts who know what needs to be done. A great technique to determine the work required is to brainstorm. Brainstorming not only assists with determining the work, but it is also a great team building exercise because it enables people to get to know one another. When brainstorming, use Post-it® Notes and a blank wall or whiteboard. Start with the deliverables and work down to the work packages and then to the tasks. Keep decomposing until all tasks are identified. Evaluate each task to determine if it is necessary or if the work could be completed in a more cost-effective manner. Check the group's work by starting at the bottom and working up each branch, reevaluating the tasks to ensure that no tasks have been missed and the work package can be created. If the project manager has decided to create documentation for each work package or task, now is a great time to complete the documentation.

Include Project Management Work

Project management work should be budgeted for as well as scheduled because it is work and consumes resources. Project management has deliverables, work packages, and tasks, as well as other related costs. Consider the following story of how a project manager addressed a question about project management with his sponsor.

Catherine, a senior project manager, picked up the telephone to hear, James, a project manager, say, "I thought I'd call instead of sending an email. Do you have a few minutes? My sponsor wants to know why project management deliverables and tasks are included in the WBS. I don't know what to tell him."

James went on to explain that during the annual planning process, a new regulatory requirement had been overlooked. Due to the nature of the regulatory requirement, there now was an emergency. Management had authorized obtaining a fixed-price proposal from a vendor just in case the internal staff could not be shifted away from current projects.

James had a WBS that appeared to be complete, but he was struggling with the project management branch of the WBS. The reason was the sponsor had asked James why project management was included in his WBS while the vendor's fixed-price proposal never mentioned project management. James' initial solution was to remove project management from his WBS.

After Catherine and James spoke, James did not change his WBS. Instead, he met with the sponsor and explained that there is work, time, and cost associated with managing a project and the project management branch was just that—the planned project work, time, and cost required by the project. (The amount of time to manage a project depends on the project, but using 5 to 15% of the total hours is a good starting guideline to follow when estimating the project management level of effort.)

Why was project management not included in the vendor's proposal? It was, but it was hidden. When the sponsor asked the vendor about the project management costs, the vendor explained that justifying project management expenses to many clients is difficult. Therefore, because the vendor was asked to provide a fixed-price, the vendor decided to eliminate questions and confusion by treating project management as an overhead expense and not list project management tasks in the WBS provided.

Suggestion: Create a work breakdown structure in Excel. Once people are comfortable with the work that has been defined, consider migrating the WBS to an Excel spreadsheet. Why? Determining the work is the first step in planning the project. The work needs to be sequenced; the duration, level of effort, and resources needs to be determined; and a budget needs to be created. With Excel, rows and columns can be added or moved around. It is easy to add numbers and create various charts, graphs, and visual aids. Many people are able to perform basic tasks in Excel so no or limited training is necessary. If at a later point in time, a decision is made to use a project management software application, many applications provide the ability to import an Excel spreadsheet.

Create Work Package Documentation

Depending on the project, creating documentation for the work package may be necessary. The reason to document the work package is to provide enough information to assist with estimating the time, cost, staff, and other resources needed for completing the task. Another reason is that people are added and removed from projects all the time, so the documentation can provide a reference point. For some projects, however, particularly one-person projects, the benefits of creating work package documentation may be less than the value of the effort needed to create it; documentation is therefore unnecessary.

There is no right way or one way to create work package documentation. Documentation can be simple, with a brief description of the work package and the related assumptions, constraints, and exclusions. Depending on the project, documentation may need to be more extensive if the project manager thinks that additional information such as quality requirements or specialized skill sets should be noted. For some projects, creating a work package document in an Excel spreadsheet or a Word document is normally adequate (Table 8.2). As a project manager, use your judgment, "keep it simple," and remember that the intent is to provide the information needed for planning and reference.

ASSIGN WORK PACKAGE OWNERSHIP

Although the project manager is responsible for the completion of the project, the core team members as well as other team members are responsible for completing the tasks that are assigned to them. One way to assign the work is to assign ownership or responsibility at the lowest-level deliverable, the work package,

Table 8.2. Work Breakdown Structure: Annual Dinner Work Package Documentation

Project: First Annual Dinner (Work Package Documentation) **Prepared by:** Dave **Date:** May				

		Work	Description	Assumptions, Constraints, and Exclusions
...	...	...		
3		Food and Beverage		
	3.1	Reception (Work Package)	Cash bar before and during dinner	Soda and ice tea available for no charge; wine and beer for purchase
	3.2	Dinner (Work Package)	Sit-down dinner with appetizer, entrée, and dessert	Only one entrée selection provided; allocated $35.00 per person per meal
...	...	...		
5		Marketing		
	5.1	Invitations (Work Package)	Formal Invitations to be sent to all guests	Invitations to be black and white
...	...	...		

to the various core team members that are familiar with the work that needs to be completed. By assigning ownership early in the planning process, the core team members are able to take an active role in defining the level of effort or the amount of time to complete the task, the duration or the lapse time needed to complete each task, cost, and assignment of staff.

THE FIRST PLANNING CHECKPOINT

With a WBS in place and realizing that the planning effort is still far from complete, the project manager and sponsor will meet to discuss the preliminary project work plan. The goal is to determine, based on the anticipated work, if the planning effort should proceed or not or if it should be modified by changing the scope. This is an ideal time to evaluate and analyze the WBS because not much time and money have been spent on the project to date. If the project needs to be modified or halted, now might be the right time. Some sponsors prefer to wait until estimating the time and resource requirements is complete to evaluate, analyze, and decide to proceed or not (another checkpoint) and bypass this checkpoint. Exactly when proceed-or-not analysis begins varies by organization and project, but it should occur throughout the planning process.

Start refining the original time and cost estimates by asking questions such as:

- Based on the WBS, what is a guess as to how long it will take to complete the project? How does this compare to the anticipated completion date in the scope statement?
- Is the cost estimate in the scope statement still valid?
- Do we have staff with the required skill sets available to complete the work? If not, can we find people to assist at a price we can afford?

If the project manager and sponsor think the WBS is in line with the scope statement, the planning effort will continue. Also possible is that the work outlined in the WBS is far more than ever anticipated and the organization does not have the money or the project cannot be completed even close to an anticipated completion date. The number of staff required to support the effort also may not be available, at least not at this time.

In these circumstances there are a few options. One is to modify the scope before additional planning occurs. Another is for the sponsor to discuss the preliminary project plan with management to obtain ideas such as other ways to find additional funds. A third is to halt the project, either completing it at a later time or postponing it indefinitely.

All this theory seems terribly imposing and difficult, but it is not. The easiest way to understand how simple it is to create a WBS is to use a real life scenario, an annual dinner event, and walk through the process following a top-down approach:

1. Dave, the project manager, decides to hold a brainstorming session with the core team and include the sponsor. A meeting is set up. Copies of the scope statement and requirement notes are given to all the participants. This project is the organization's first annual dinner, so no historical documentation or prior dinner WBS templates are available to reference.
2. Dave and the sponsor agree on organizing the WBS by deliverable.
3. With the assistance of a whiteboard and Post-it Notes, the group starts with brainstorming the possible deliverables. They decide on five key deliverables: venue, food and beverage, the evening program, marketing, and project management. Before deciding on the five key deliverables, however, they questioned whether the key deliverable should be marketing with invitations as a marketing work package or whether the invitations should be a key deliverable

and marketing should be another key deliverable. The decision is up to the group; there is no right or wrong way.

4. The group starts by organizing the Post-it Notes, placing them in a hierarchical format. Deliverables are added and removed. Deliverables that are identified, but are out-of-scope deliverables such as raffle tickets and prizes are segregated. The sorting continues until the group is comfortable that all of the deliverables have been identified.

5. The deliverables at the lowest level, the work packages, are assigned to individual core team members.

6. The group starts brainstorming the tasks associated with the lowest-level deliverable, the work package, listing them below the deliverable in no specific order. Appropriate work package documentation is created. Sequencing the tasks or placing them in the right order occurs later in the planning process. (Alternately, the group could have decided that each individual core team member is to be responsible for decomposing their assigned work package into tasks and creating appropriate work package documentation.)

7. The group validates the tasks and deliverables by using a bottom-up approach. They start at the bottom of each branch, ensuring that the tasks create the appropriate deliverable, the work package, and then continue up the branch until they are sure all of the deliverables create the final product or service.

8. A final comparison is performed between the scope statement, the requirements documentation, and the WBS to ensure that nothing that is required has been missed or anything extraneous was added during the process.

9. After the group is comfortable with the deliverables, work packages, and tasks, Dave enters the information into an Excel spreadsheet and adds ID numbers. Although Dave has entered the information into a spreadsheet, he knows this is the first draft and that there will be changes because the tasks may or may not be in the right sequence and some tasks might be missing. He decides to add the work package documentation so that all planning performed to date is in one place. Table 8.3 is part of the Excel document Dave created. It will be the starting point for the rest of the planning activities.

10. Dave reviews the completed WBS with the sponsor and the appropriate stakeholders for review and comment. He makes a point of asking them if they think anything has been missed. At the same time, he discusses the next steps in the planning process with the sponsor and stakeholders.

Table 8.3. Work Breakdown Structure: Annual Dinner Tasks

Project: First Annual Dinner (Tasks)
Prepared by: Dave
Date: May

		Work	Description	Assumptions, Constraints, and Exclusions
...	...	...		
3		Food and Beverage		
	3.1	Reception (Work Package)	Cash bar before and during dinner	Soda and ice tea available for no charge; wine and beer for purchase
	3.1.1	Determine Hors d'oeuvres (Task)		
	3.1.2	Determine Beverages (Task)		
	3.2	Dinner (Work Package)	Sit-down dinner with appetizer, entrée, and dessert	Only one entrée selection provided; allocated $35.00 per person per meal
	3.2.1	Determine Meal/Beverages (Task)		
...	...	...		
5		Marketing		
	5.1	Invitations (Work Package)	Formal Invitations to be sent; RSVP required	Invitations to be black and white
	5.1.1	Create Mailing List (Task)		
	5.1.2	Address and Mail Invitations (Task)		
	5.1.3	Design and Print Invitations (Task)		
	5.1.4	Select Printer (Task)		
...	...	...		

IN REVIEW

- A work breakdown structure (WBS) is a hierarchical graphical or textual breakdown of a project's deliverables and tasks. It is the backbone of the project planning process. The intent of a WBS is to determine all of the work that is required to complete the project and to assist with organizing the project; to identify the deliverables and milestones; to determine the time and cost estimates; and to determine resource needs and assign responsibilities.
- For many people working within flat organizations, the best way to create a WBS is by following a top-down approach.
- Each WBS is unique to a particular project. All projects have deliverables, work packages, and tasks. Standardized WBS templates can be used as a starting point when creating a WBS, but modify them to fit the particular project. Slightly different functionality and feature requirements, different stakeholders, and different project managers influence the final agreed-upon WBS format.
- With a WBS, the project manager and sponsor start discussing whether the project is realistic (or not) based on the organization's money, time, staff, and other resources. This discussion is the first decision point for determining whether the project should proceed, be modified, or be halted.
- If necessary, create work package documentation. The intent of work package documentation is to provide enough information for the project manager to continue building a project plan and to provide a reference point for team members as they perform the work.
- Assign ownership and responsibility of work packages to core team members, enabling them to have an active role in planning the work for which they are accountable.

STEP-BY-STEP INSTRUCTIONS

When creating a work breakdown structure (WBS), follow a top-down approach:

1. Gather and review project-related materials, including:
   - Scope statement and related notes
   - Requirements documentation
   - Historical documentation and templates

2. Create a WBS, either graphically or in a text format, including:
    - Determining how the work is to be organized, such as by phase or deliverable, and managed
    - Identifying the project-related deliverables starting with the key deliverables and milestones listed in the scope statement
    - Determining the Level 1 deliverables, the deliverable that starts each branch
    - Decomposing each branch into smaller deliverables until the lowest deliverable level, the work package, is identified
    - Decomposing each work package into tasks
3. Assign ownership of work packages to core team members. Document the work packages.
4. Validate the WBS, using a bottom-up approach. Start at the bottom and work up each branch of the diagram, reevaluating the tasks to ensure that no tasks were missed and the work package can be created. If necessary, modify the WBS.
5. Compare the WBS to the scope statement and requirements. Pay particular attention to the project exclusions in the scope statement. For example, has a key deliverable been included in the WBS that was excluded in the scope statement? If so, determine if the key deliverable is to be excluded from the WBS or included in the scope statement. Adjust the appropriate document, as necessary.
6. Review the WBS, with the sponsor and key stakeholders. Explain: "This is the work we think needs to be completed to produce the product or service. Do you see anything we have missed? Should we proceed?" Although a sign-off is not necessary, communicate and work with the sponsor and key stakeholders to ensure that the information is complete and the requirements are being met.
7. Discuss the future planning steps with the sponsor and key stakeholders. It is important for sponsors and key stakeholders to understand that although the work has been determined, there are still a number of planning steps to be completed before there is a project plan such as sequencing the work; determining the level of effort and duration for each task; determining the start and finish dates for tasks; and establishing a budget.
8. Review the comments received from the sponsor and key stakeholders with the core team. Clarify any core team questions or concerns.

CHAPTER 9

SEQUENCE THE WORK

Covered in this chapter:

- Definition of a network diagram
- Determining the dependency and interdependency relationships
- Creating a network diagram using the Precedence Diagramming Method
- Using a logic relationship table and network diagram to sequence the work

When a project starts, people in the organization naturally become anxious. Although the sponsor and stakeholders want the project to be completed as soon as possible, when they learn that the work has been defined, they have a tendency to question the project manager about the completion date in the scope statement. The sponsor and stakeholders want to know if the date is realistic. Unfortunately, all the project manager knows at this point in the planning process is what work needs to occur, not how long that work will take to complete. More work has to be done to determine if achieving the completion date in the scope statement is feasible. The next step in the process is sequencing the work to determine if any work has been overlooked, which positions the project manager to determine the time, cost, and resource requirements.

THE NETWORK DIAGRAM

Think of projects you have worked on. Did one task need to be completed before the next task started? Were some tasks performed concurrently? By creating a *network diagram*, which is a flowchart, a team is able to visualize the sequence or order of the tasks necessary to have a successful project. A network diagram is a great tool for finding missing tasks because it is a walk-through of the work that needs to occur and takes into account the relationships between tasks. No matter how diligent the effort was when the work packages and tasks were defined, or how many eyes reviewed the final work breakdown structure, work can be missed.

The *Precedence Diagramming Method* (PDM) is the most commonly used network-diagramming method because it is easy to create, understand, and explain. A PDM diagram shows the tasks as boxes and uses lines with arrows to connect them and indicate the relationship between the tasks. Except for the start and finish boxes, each box has an arrow in and out. The goal of a PDM diagram is to show the project tasks in the proper order or sequence. When the PDM diagram is complete, the team is in position to start estimating the time and resource requirements for the tasks.

Dependency Concepts and Terms

Before tasks can be sequenced and a network diagram can be created, understanding task relationships and the impact of these relationships on a project's timeline, and later its execution, is important, including understanding:

- Successor and predecessor tasks
- Dependency relationships and types
- Leads and lags

Successor and Predecessor Tasks

Sequencing tasks requires the project manager to analyze each task and ask:

- What task occurs before this task?
- What task occurs after this task?

The task performed directly before another task is the *predecessor*. The task performed directly after another task is the *successor*. In Figure 9.1, the invitations are printed (the predecessor) before they are addressed (the successor).

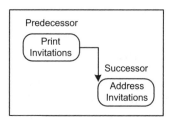

Figure 9.1. A predecessor and successor relationship.

Dependency Relationships and Types

A *dependency* is the relationship of a preceding task to a succeeding task. Tasks can have a single preceding or succeeding task or multiple preceding and succeeding tasks. There are four dependency relationships to consider when creating a network diagram:

- Finish-to-start (FS)
- Start-to-start (SS)
- Finish-to-finish (FF)
- Start-to-finish (SF)

The most common relationship is *finish-to-start* (FS). Task A (the predecessor) must finish before Task B (the successor) can begin. In Figure 9.2, the invitations (the predecessor) must be designed before they can be printed (the successor). For many projects, a FS relationship is the primary, if not the only, relationship between tasks that a project manager needs to consider when sequencing tasks.

A *start-to-start* (SS) relationship between tasks occurs when a project manager determines that the estimated completion date cannot be met and, in an effort to shorten the project timeline, the project manager attempts to overlap tasks or change their sequence. For example, have you ever attended a dinner event and heard, "To save time, I would like to provide an update as dinner is being served." This is an example of a SS relationship. SS relationships are used when Task B (the successor) in the relationship cannot start until after Task A (the predecessor) begins. SS relationships do not require that both tasks start at the same time—just that Task A begins before Task B. In Figure 9.3, the mailing list is being created (the predecessor), but the envelopes for the invitations cannot start to be addressed (the successor) until creation of the mailing list has least started (the predecessor). There is no need to wait until a complete mailing list is created to start addressing the invitations.

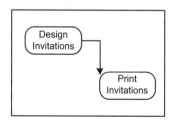

Figure 9.2. A finish-to-start relationship.

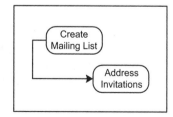

Figure 9.3. A start-to-start relationship.

A *finish-to-finish* (FF) relationship occurs when one task cannot finish before another task finishes. An FF relationship does not require that both tasks be completed simultaneously, only that Task A (the predecessor) finishes before Task B (the successor) can finish. In Figure 9.4, all of the invitations need to be addressed (the predecessor) before all of them can be mailed (the successor).

The fourth dependency relationship is *start-to-finish* (SF). The SF relationship is rarely used. In an SF relationship, Task B (the successor) cannot finish until Task A (the predecessor) starts, but Task B (the successor) can finish at any time after Task A (the predecessor) starts. In Figure 9.5, the company is invoiced as soon as the printer is selected and a contract is signed (the predecessor), but the printer is not paid until a later point in time (the successor).

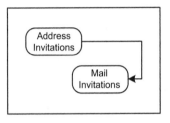

Figure 9.4. A finish-to-finish relationship.

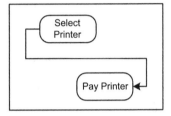

Figure 9.5. A start-to-finish relationship.

As important as it is to understand dependency relationships, dependency types also need to be understood. Dependency types fall into one of three categories:

- A *mandatory* dependency exists between tasks because of the way the work must be performed to achieve the expected outcome: the invitations must be received from the printer before they can be addressed and mailed.
- A *discretionary* dependency is based on a preference or the way the project team wants to perform the work: if a mailing list is necessary, the list can be created before the invitations are designed and printed or after the invitations are received from the printer.
- An *external* dependency involves an event or a third party outside the project on which a project task is dependent: the dinner invitations are designed, ordered, and printed by a third-party vendor.

As tasks are sequenced, the project manager evaluates each task and asks questions, such as: "Is there a mandatory predecessor? Is there an external predecessor? Knowing which tasks are discretionary will become important when scheduling staff, leveling a team member's work, or shortening a timeline.

Leads and Lags

Think of lags and leads as the extra time between tasks. A *lag* is the delay between the predecessor task and the successor task or the wait time before the successor can start. In Figure 9.6, the lag time between selecting a printer and being invoiced and then paying the printer could be two months. A *lead* occurs when a successor task starts before the predecessor finishes. In Figure 9.7, an allowance of one month of lead time may be needed before addressing the invitations is possible. Confusing leads and lags is easy, but the concept that is important to understand is that there can be extra time between tasks that needs to be considered when creating a network diagram.

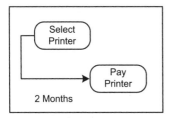

Figure 9.6. A two-month lag time relationship.

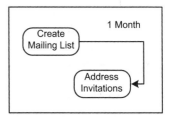

Figure 9.7. A one-month lead time relationship.

If a network diagram was created using the four dependencies and lags and leads as described, the diagram might look like Figure 9.8. In reality all of the dependency types are not used for every project, particularly smaller projects.

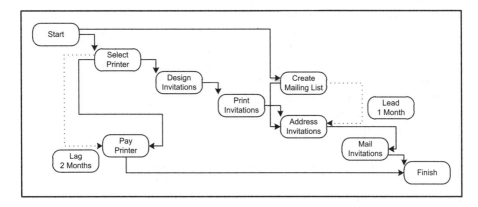

Figure 9.8. Network diagram 1: create and mail invitations, using the four dependencies and lags and leads.

Table 9.1. A Logical Relationship Table

1	2	3	4
Identifier	Task Description	Preceding Task Identifier	Comments (Optional)
	Start	–	
1	Create Mailing List	Start	
2	Address Invitations	1,7	
3	Mail Invitations	2	
5	Select Printer	Start	
6	Design Invitations	5	
7	Print Invitations	6	
8	Pay Printer	7	
	Finish	3, 8	

CREATE A NETWORK DIAGRAM

Two basic steps are required when creating a network diagram:

- Determine the dependencies using a logical relationship table.
- Draw the network diagram using the Precedence Diagramming Method (PDM).

Create a Logical Relationship Table

An easy way to determine dependencies and if tasks are in the right sequence is to create a logical relationship table. Table 9.1 illustrates a logical relationship table for the tasks related to invitations for the annual dinner. In the first column, enter a unique identifier such as 1, 2, 3 (or A, B, C). In the second column, list each task to be sequenced. In the third column, enter the unique identifier of the immediate predecessor tasks for each task. To determine predecessor tasks, first identify the task that ends the project. Then evaluate each task by asking: "What does this task need before it can start?" By asking this question, determining the tasks that are predecessors for the task being evaluated is possible. The fourth column for comments is optional. For some project managers having a comments column is useful for recording notes about the dependency type (mandatory, discretionary, and external), if the relationship is not FS, any lead or lag information, or other points they do not want to forget.

Is using a logical relationship table always necessary? No, but a logical relationship table helps to ensure that nothing is missed. For example, think of what can happen if you send a person to the food store for ten items, but do not provide an itemized list. How often did they come back with all ten items? Did they forget one or two items? Did they purchase an item that was not on the list because they thought it was?

It is best to document and determine the dependencies between the tasks. How the dependencies are documented depends on the project manager and the organization's project management methodology. For example, an experienced project manager may decide to skip creating a logical relationship table if a project is small—ten or fewer tasks. The key word is *experienced*. The reason is experience may enable the project manager to evaluate the tasks and visualize the dependencies and the predecessor and successor tasks without taking the time to record the relationships in a table.

Draw a Network Diagram

Using the logical relationship table in Table 9.1, create a network diagram. Begin the diagram by starting on the left and creating a **Start** box. Create task boxes for all tasks that do not have an immediate predecessor. These tasks can start as soon as the project is started and can occur concurrently. Next, create task boxes for the tasks that are successor activities to the boxes already created. Beginning with the **Start** box, draw arrows from the predecessor activities to the successor activities. Continue working from left to right until all tasks are included on the diagram and arrows indicate their precedence relationships. When this process is complete, include a **Finish** box. Verify that no tasks have been overlooked or missed. Figure 9.9 represents the task dependencies and their sequences from Table 9.1 and uses an FS dependency relationship, the relationship most often used in projects, particularly smaller projects. Notice the differences between Figure 9.9, which uses only the FS dependency relationship, and Figure 9.8, which uses all the various dependency relationships and leads and lags.

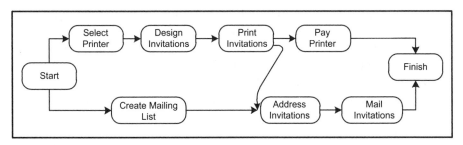

Figure 9.9. Network diagram 2: create and mail invitations, using the finish-to-start dependency relationship.

Suggestion: Use the brainstorming technique. Some project managers prefer not to use a logical relationship table. Instead the project manager and core team use Post-it® Notes and a wall, brainstorming the flow of work until a network diagram has been created. This process is similar to the brainstorming that occurred when defining the work.

In theory, a network diagram needs to be created for every project, but in reality it does not. Typically, creating a network diagram is skipped to save planning time. Creating a network diagram is a project manager's judgment call:

- A project manager might not create a network diagram if a project template that has been used year after year for similar events is available; the project manager is comfortable with the WBS; the tasks are sequenced; and the critical path is known. (The critical path is the path through the network diagram that takes the longest total time to complete and therefore determines the shortest time in which the project can be completed. Determining the critical path is discussed in Chapter 11.)

- A project manager might decide to create a network diagram for only a particular deliverable branch or a work package. For example, for the annual dinner project, the project manager might decide to create network diagram for the invitation work package, but to sequence the rest of the work using a logical relationship table.

- A project manager might use a textual plan that has been created and sequence the work within the textual plan. For example, the work packages and tasks listed in Table 8.3 (the work breakdown structure created during the real life scenario in Chapter 8) could have been clarified, refined, and sequenced, creating an updated list of work packages and tasks similar to Table 9.2.

IN REVIEW

- A network diagram is a flowchart that enables a project manager and core team to visually see the work required to successfully complete the project. The most commonly used network diagramming method is the Precedence Diagramming Method (PDM).

- Sequencing the work highlights missing tasks and makes it possible to see task relationships and the dependencies and interdependencies between two or more tasks. Not all of the dependency types are used in every project. For many smaller projects, a finish-to-start relationship, the most common relationship, is the primary relationship a project manager needs to consider when sequencing tasks.

- The goal of sequencing is to get the work that needs to be performed in the right order. Although using a logical relationship table and network diagram are two techniques to assist with sequencing the work, due to the type and size of a project, the relationships and dependencies, the historical information available, and the organization, some project managers might opt to sequence the work directly in a productivity tool or software application.

Table 9.2. Sequenced Work Breakdown Structure: Annual Dinner

Project: First Annual Dinner (Sequenced Tasks)
Prepared by: Dave
Date: June

		Work	Description	Assumptions, Constraints, and Exclusions
...	...	...		
3		Food and Beverage		
	3.1	Reception	Cash bar before and during dinner	Soda and ice tea available for no charge; wine and beer for purchase
		3.1.1 Determine Hors d'oeuvres		
		3.1.2 Determine Beverages		
	3.2	Dinner	Sit-down dinner with appetizer, entrée, and dessert	Only one entrée selection provided; allocated $35.00 per person per meal
		Determine Meal		
...	...	...		
5		Marketing		
	5.1	Invitations	Formal invitations to be sent; RSVP required	Invitations to be black and white
		5.1.1 Create Mailing List		
		5.1.2 Select Printer		
		5.1.3 Design Invitations		
		5.1.4 Print Invitations		
		5.1.5 Address Invitations		
		5.1.6 Mail Invitiations		
		5.1.7 Pay Printer		
...	...	...		

- During the planning phase, understanding relationships and dependencies is necessary to determine the critical path, the path that takes the longest to complete with no slack. The critical path and the project start date determine the project completion date.
- During the project's execution, the project manager needs to understand relationships and dependencies so that the impact of a delayed task on cost, staffing, and, most importantly, the project completion date can be recognized and corrective action evaluated and taken.

STEP-BY-STEP INSTRUCTIONS

When creating a network diagram:
1. Identify logical relationships. Use a logical relationship table to determine the relationships between tasks and predecessor tasks.
2. Create the network diagram using the Precedence Diagramming Method (PDM). Start with the logical relationship table and begin the diagram by starting on the left and moving to the right:
   - Create a **Start** (milestone) box.
   - Create task boxes for all tasks that do not have an immediate predecessor. These tasks can start as soon as the project is started and can occur concurrently.
   - Create task boxes for the tasks that are successor activities to the boxes already created.
   - Beginning with the **Start** box, draw arrows from the predecessor activities to the successor activities.
3. Continue drawing the network diagram. Continue work from left to right until:
   - Tasks included in the work breakdown structure (WBS) are included on the diagram and arrows indicate their precedence relationships.
   - Tasks that were missed and overlooked when the WBS was created are added to the diagram.
   - Leads and lags are included.
   - The **Finish** (milestone) box is created.
4. Verify the accuracy of the network diagram. Check to ensure that:
   - All tasks required to complete the project are included in the diagram.
   - Arrows going from the predecessor activities to the successor activities correctly indicate all precedence relationships.
   - Known leads or lags are indicated on the diagram.
5. Compare the network diagram to the WBS. Make sure all the WBS tasks are included on the network diagram. If a task was added to the network diagram and is not included in the WBS, update the WBS. If a task is not included in the network diagram and should be removed from the WBS, remove the task from the WBS.

CHAPTER 10

ESTIMATE TIME AND RESOURCES

Covered in this chapter:

- Defining time, resource, and cost estimates
- Using estimating tools and techniques
- Estimating the duration and level of effort
- Determining and consolidating time and resource estimates
- Estimating mistakes

Being able to accurately estimate the time and resources needed to complete the required work is essential to creating a realistic project plan because these estimates drive the deadlines for the project. If time and resources are underestimated, not only are deadlines missed, but the team may also be placed under undue stress. If time and resources are grossly overestimated, the sponsor might consider cancelling a project because the project has been estimated incorrectly and will take much longer and cost more than anticipated. Loss of credibility can occur from under- or overestimating project time and resources.

THE ESTIMATION PROCESS

An *estimate* is a rough calculation, a best guess about something. When planning a project that *something* is the time, cost, and resources. A project manager, the core team, and anyone else involved in the process of determining how long the work will take, how much it will cost to complete the work, and what and how many resources are needed to complete the work must understand how to

Table 10.1. Time Estimates

Term	Definition	Example
Duration	The lapse time needed to complete each task or the number of working days to complete each task using the available resources	Start on Thursday and finish on Monday. Saturday and Sunday are not workdays. Duration is 3 days.
Level of Effort	The amount of time to complete the task without any interruptions	Work on: Thursday for 3 hours Friday for 3.5 hours Saturday for 0 hours Sunday for 0 hours Monday for 3 hours Level of effort is 10.5 hours.
Calendar Days	The number of days shown on a calendar to complete a task	Start on Thursday and finish on Monday. Saturday and Sunday are not workdays. Number of calendar days is 5 days.

estimate each of them. In addition to the work required to complete a project, normal events such as internal organizational meetings, illnesses, emergencies, missed deliveries by vendors, supplier mishaps, equipment breakdowns, and quality-control problems need to be considered when creating estimates. Partly because people are unfamiliar with the estimating process, over- or underestimating the amount of time, cost, and resources needed to implement a project is easy.

Estimating is not an exact science. Projects are uncertain and have a degree of risk associated with them. To make matters more challenging, projects change over time due to new requirements, unexpected events, or unknown factors, resulting in changes to the estimates. At this point in the planning process, the goal is to be approximately right about the amount of time, cost, and resources required rather than precisely wrong.

Time Estimates

Time estimation is the determination of the *duration, level of effort,* and the *calendar days* required to complete each task (Table 10.1). Time estimates can be expressed in hours, days, weeks, or months. Duration is normally measured in days; level of effort is normally measured in hours. The time measurement used can vary by project, but the same work period unit needs to be used for an entire project: the level of effort for one task should not be measured in days if the level of effort for a different task is measured in hours. Be consistent.

If you are still confused about the differences between level of effort and duration, think of it this way. You are going to take a trip that requires a passport. It takes you two hours to obtain a picture, complete the paperwork, and drop the picture and paperwork off at the Passport Office (or Post Office) for processing. The normal processing time for new passports is six to eight weeks after the paperwork is submitted. The duration, or the lapse time, is eight weeks. The level of effort is two hours.

Resource Estimates

Resource estimation is tied to the practical matter of how planned tasks are to be completed because it determines how many resources are needed to complete the planned tasks, including staff, consultants, equipment, materials and supplies, facilities, and any other unique resource required for a particular task. Every task has a resource estimate. Think of a resource estimate as two estimates—one estimate for people, the staff and consultants, and another estimate for the other resources, the equipment, materials and supplies, and facilities. Accurately estimating resources requires understanding the resources that are available or are going to be available and the available opinions and alternatives.

Cost Estimates

Cost estimation is the determination of the cost for every task. The work effort for each task and the rates (or cost) for each resource are used to create the cost estimate. The cost estimates are used to create the budget, but the cost estimates are not the budget. Estimating the cost is mentioned in this chapter because many of the same estimating tools and techniques are used to estimate cost as to estimate time and resources. (Cost estimating and creating a budget based on the estimates are discussed in detail in Chapter 13.)

ESTIMATING TOOLS AND TECHNIQUES

Using a combination of different estimating tools and techniques to estimate a project's time and resources is a common practice. If you are uncomfortable with estimating a project, consider working with an expert, leveraging their knowledge and obtaining their opinions about:

- The duration or how long a task will take
- The level of effort or how many hours the task will take
- The resources needed

Table 10.2. Estimating Tools and Techniques

Tool or Technique	Description	Accuracy Level	Example
Expert Judgment	Leverage an expert's knowledge and opinions on the work effort, resources, and cost needed for specific tasks.	Accurate	A discussion occurs with a project manager who has completed a similar project.
Analogous Estimating (This technique is also known as a top-down or historical approach.)	Actual high-level cost and time are available from a similar project or projects.	Less accurate than other tools and techniques because planning is at a top level	Last website took 2 months to create. Estimate duration of 2 months to create a new website.
Bottom-Up Estimating	The lowest level or bottom tasks are analyzed. Cost and time estimates are determined for each task and then the amounts are summed.	Most accurate and reliable tool and technique to use, but is the most time consuming and costly to create	For each computer work station it takes a half hour to take the workstation out of the box, 1 hour to run software updates, 15 minutes to add to the network, etc. Individual tasks add up to 4 hours. Estimate 4 hours per work-station for the level of effort.
Parametric Estimating	A formula based on prior experience is used to predict duration, level of effort, or cost. Industry-specific mathematical models are available.	Normally more accurate than analogous estimating, but validity depends on quality of the parametric data	Based on prior experience it takes 4 hours to configure and set up a computer workstation. There are five workstations. The duration to set up all workstations is 4 × 5 or 20 hours. Estimate duration of 20 hours.
Three-Point Estimating (PERT is the most common three-point estimate.)	Three numbers are used to create a time estimate: a realistic or most likely estimate, an optimistic estimate, and a pessimistic estimate. The final estimate is based on a formula and is an average. The PERT estimating technique formula is: (Optimistic + (4 × Most Likely) + Pessimistic)/6 = Expected Duration (used only for time estimates)	Varies, but three-point estimating accounts for uncertainty and takes into account risk	Using PERT, an optimistic estimate is the website can be completed in 1 month; a pessimistic estimate is 4 months; and a realistic estimate is 2 months. Using the PERT calculation: (Optimistic + (4 × Most Likely) + Pessimistic)/6 = Expected Duration or Cost) or (1 + (4 × 4) + 4)/6 = 3.5 months Estimate duration of 3.5 months.

Table 10.2. Estimating Tools and Techniques (continued)

Tool or Technique	Description	Accuracy Level	Example
Vendor Contracts	Estimates are provided by a vendor to provide a product or service. The three major types of contracts are fixed price, cost plus, and time and materials.	Depends on type of project (Fixed-price contracts are more accurate than time and materials contracts.)	Vendor A estimates it will take 2.5 months to gather requirements, design, code, and test the website. Estimate duration of 2.5 months.
Contingency Reserve	The contingency reserve amount is the time and funds added to a plan to cover unplanned and unexpected events. Time or amount of money is expressed as a percentage of the budget or a number added to the overall project plan.	Not at all accurate	It should take 20 hours to configure and set up five workstations. Add a contingency reserve of 10%. Add a 2-hour contingency reserve to the project plan.

An expert can be the sponsor, a stakeholder, an experienced project manager, a key team member on a similar project, an industry specialist, or even an outside third-party consultant. Talk to the expert about the best approach to use to estimate the project. Obtaining information and advice from an independent expert can increase the accuracy and the confidence level of any estimate.

In addition to using an expert's opinion to assist with estimating time and resources, other estimating tools and techniques that work well are analogous estimating, bottom-up estimating, parametric estimating, three-point estimating, vendor contracts, and contingency reserves. Estimating tools and techniques are used individually or in combination with one another. A common combination of tools and techniques is expert judgment, bottom-up estimating, and analogous estimating. To make it easier to understand each estimating tool and technique and when using each is appropriate, refer to Table 10.2.

Contingency reserves tend to be ignored or forgotten for smaller projects, but contingency reserves provide a project manager with the time and money to respond to the unexpected opportunities and difficulties experienced on all projects. Talk to the sponsor and management about adding extra time, which normally equates to extra money.

The amount of time or money, either as a percentage or number of hours, that should be added will depend on the project and factors such as degree of risk, type of work, and the culture of the organization. A contingency of 5% might be fine for a low-risk, routine project that does not rely on third parties or a low-risk, repeatable project such as an annual dinner for which the actual result has been within 2% of the budget for the last five years. For a high-risk project with many project unknowns, such as implementing beta software for which there is no historical information, 20% might be a more appropriate amount for a contingency reserve.

To determine the right contingency reserve for the project, talk to the expert and review the project's assumptions and risks, industry guidelines, and similar prior projects. Then decide if the contingency is to be applied at the project level, at the deliverable or work package level, or at the task level. For smaller projects, applying a contingency reserve percentage at the project level is usually adequate. The following story is an example of how different estimating tools and techniques can be combined.

A project manager and core team need to determine the time, costs, and resources for the fifteenth annual company summer picnic. The picnic is to be held at a rented facility and the company is to provide the food, games and prizes, and entertainment. Because this is not the first summer picnic the company has held, the project manager and core team decide to rely on historical records to determine the work required and to estimate the project time, costs, and resources. The process includes:

- Using historical time and resource estimates from prior plans for setting up the facility (analogous estimating)
- Using historical resource estimates to determine the supplies necessary for the games (analogous estimating)
- Collecting current costs for food, supplies, and prizes (bottom-up)
- Reviewing contracts for cost of the facility and the band (vendor contracts)
- Having discussions with last year's project team (expert judgment)
- Increasing the time planned by 5% and the dollars budgeted by 10% for unplanned events (contingency reserves)

Regardless of the tool or technique or the combination of tools or techniques used, documenting assumptions and any known constraints for later use is important. For a variety of reasons, estimates will be revisited as a project progresses. Three months into the project, a team member might not remember the reasons for a task estimate or a new team member might need to understand how the estimates were determined for a task.

TIME AND RESOURCE PLANNING

Project managers and sponsors have different opinions and preferences when estimating a project, but all project managers need to carefully plan the estimation process. Before any estimates are created, ask questions such as, "What is estimated first—time or resources? Can time and resources be estimated together? Should the estimate be at the task level or the work package level? What measurement unit do we use for duration and level of effort? What estimating tools and techniques should be used? Who should be involved in the estimating process? How should the information be collected?"

There is no right or wrong approach to estimating time and resources, but a project manager needs to carefully think about the best approach to determine, collect, and consolidate the estimates for a particular project. For example, in a flat organization with team members only able to work on the project part-time, the project manager might find it easier to estimate the duration, level of effort, and resources all at the same time as a "unit." One way to estimate the duration, level of effort, and resources as a unit is to ask the potential team member (the resource) to compare and analyze his or her day-to-day operational and project responsibilities (duration and level of effort). Ask the potential team member to determine if there is enough time to complete all the work required or if additional resources are needed. With the feedback provided by the potential team member, the project manager can ask additional questions and better estimate the duration and level of effort for a task or to determine if a different person needs to be found to perform the work.

The project manager might also ask a core team member to assist with the estimating process. Asking a core team member to assist with estimating provides another level of validation, particularly if the core team member has firsthand experience with a particular work package. Using a core team member can result in the project manager providing a more realistic duration, level of effort, and resource estimates.

As the time and resource estimating process is planned, do not forget to review organizational policies and procedures such as who is on the approved vendor list because the organizational policies and procedures could impact the planning and then estimating decisions. Consult historical information and lessons learned from similar projects for any additional insights.

Determine the Duration and the Level of Effort

One of the first planning decisions is determining if duration and the level of effort should be measured in hours, days, or weeks—referred to as the *measurement unit*. Duration and level of effort can use different measurement units, but the same measurement unit needs to be used for all duration planning (normally days). The same measurement unit also needs to be used for all level of effort planning (normally hours).

A measurement unit of hours for level of effort is easy for everyone to understand. If there are 8 hours of work required to complete a task, the level of effort is 8 hours. When defining duration, however, making a mistake is easy. Carefully evaluate and plan the duration measurement unit because it is used to:

- Determine the number of people needed to complete a task
- Determine the critical path
- Assign work start and finish dates to tasks

If duration is defined incorrectly, the time and resource requirements for an entire plan could be either over- or underestimated.

Many project managers use a 7- or 8-hour day as the measurement unit for duration, particularly because a 7- or 8-hour day eases the assignment of calendar days to tasks. A 7- or 8-hour day, however, might not be the right duration measurement unit for a project, particularly if team members are not working on the project full time. A mistake some project managers make is not taking the time to properly define duration or what is meant by a "day" in terms of hours. The result: during project execution, they run into difficulties when managing the tasks and meeting committed dates.

People commonly say that a task has a duration of 5 days or will take a week to complete, but they do not say that the task has a level of effort of 40 hours and that the task needs to be completed in 5 days. Could this task be completed in 5 days if the work day is 7 hours? Not with one person because 5 days or a week with 7 hour work days totals only 35 hours. The task could, however, be completed in 5 days, one work week, with two people. If a work day really were 8 productive hours, one person, in theory, could complete the task.

Why in theory? Most people think of a day as being 7 or 8 working hours, but is thinking that people are productively at work 7 or 8 hours a day realistic? Probably not. People attend internal meetings that take time away from their daily tasks or work, get a drink of water, make a quick personal telephone call, or just plain need to walk away from their desk.

On projects when team members are not working full time or there are volunteers, a day probably does not equal 7 or 8 hours. Maybe a day is only 3 or 4 hours. In extreme cases, a day might only be 1 hour. This situation requires a project manager to think about how many hours a person is able to productively work in a day on a project. Discuss the appropriate number of hours to use for duration with the sponsor and define duration as a specific number of hours per day.

The key to estimating time (Duration, D, and Level of Effort, LOE) and staff (resources) is establishing the "right" hours for duration because duration links the Level of Effort Required (LOER) and the Level of Effort Available (LOEA) for every project task. Armed with these three values, a project manager can evaluate a task to determine the number of staff needed to complete a task of a given duration or increase the time (either staff hours or duration) given the number of staff available. The relationship is mathematic, but only involves simple arithmetic to solve.

Up to this point, for each task, the project manager has determined:

- Estimated LOE (LOEE), the estimated level of effort in hours for the task
- Duration (D), the duration in terms of days for the task

From these values, the Level of Effort Required (LOER) per day of Duration (D) can be determined by:

$$LOER = LOEE/D \qquad (10.1)$$

The LOER represents the required average number of hours to complete the task in the number of days specified by the task duration.

The project manager has also determined (for each team member) the Level of Effort Available (LOEA). LOEA is equal to the team member available hours per day. Armed with the estimated Level of Effort Required (LOER) and Level of Effort Available (LOEA), the project manager can calculate the number of required staff (team members) to complete the task given the duration as follows:

$$Required\ Staff = LOER/LOEA \qquad (10.2)$$

People cannot be divided, so a fractional required staff should be rounded up to the next higher whole number. Equation 10.2 can be rewritten to determine what the LOEA must be to complete the task given a staff level and the LOER:

$$LOEA = LOER/Staff \qquad (10.3)$$

Equation 10.2 can also be rewritten (with values substituted from Equation 10.1) to determine what the Duration (D) must be to complete the task given the LOEE, number of staff (Staff), and LOEA:

$$D = LOEE/(Staff \times LOEA) \qquad (10.4)$$

These four equations enable a project manager to evaluate a task to determine the time and resources needed to complete that task. In preparing a project plan, the project manager's job is to find, for each task, a practical combination of duration, required level of effort, available level of effort, and number of staff. That practical combination is memorialized by the project plan.

In theory, when estimating time and resources needs, names should not be assigned yet, but in reality in a flat organization, many times it makes sense to assign a name to a task while estimating time, particularly if the task requires a person with a certain skill set. By assigning a specific person to the task, the time estimate for the task is based on that person's ability to complete the work. If this approach is taken, each task is estimated as a "unit," concurrently estimating the duration, level of effort, and resource requirements for a particular task.

Does estimating sound complicated and complex? It really is not. The easiest way to understand the concept of estimating is with an example: the creation of a mailing list for the annual dinner using three scenarios. In all three scenarios, duration is defined in terms of a day, with a day equaling 3 hours, and the level of effort is defined in terms of hours. How did the project manager and sponsor determine that a day is 3 hours if a normal workday (excluding a lunch or dinner break) is 8 hours? They agreed that a person probably takes at least two 15 minutes breaks a day, leaving 7.5 hours. Then they decided that some administrative time should be taken into consideration, such as the time associated with stopping work on daily tasks and starting the project work, writing internal communications such as emails, and attending occasional meetings. They also acknowledged that each team member could only work on the project half of the available time of any workday because there are operational requirements that needed to be met.

Scenario 1. All staff (team member) resources are available (LOEA) to work 3 hours a day, task duration (D) is 7 days, and the task estimated level of effort (LOEE) is 20 hours. How many team members are required to complete the task? Applying Equation 10.1 determines LOER:

$$LOER = LOEE/D$$
$$LOER = 20/7 = 2.86$$

Applying Equation 10.2 determines required number of team members:

$$Required\ Staff = LOER/LOEA$$
$$Required\ Staff = 2.86/3 = 0.95$$

Round up and assign one team member to the task for 3 hours per day for 7 days.

Scenario 2. All staff (team member) resources are available (LOEA) 1.5 hours a day, task duration (D) is 7 days, and the task level of effort (LOEE) is 20 hours. How many team members are required to complete the task? Applying Equation 10.1 determines LOER:

$$LOER = LOEE/D$$
$$LOER = 20/7 = 2.86$$

Applying Equation 10.2 determines required number of team members:

$$Required\ Staff = LOER/LOEA$$
$$Required\ Staff = 2.86/1.5 = 1.91$$

Round up and assign 2 team members to the task for 1.5 hours per day for 7 days.

Scenario 3. Determine if a preferred staff person (team member) who is available 2 hours a day (LOEA) can be used as the sole resource to complete a task if the task duration (D) is 7 days and the estimated level of effort (LOEE) is 15 hours. Applying Equation 10.1 determines LOER:

$$LOER = LOEE/D$$
$$LOER = 15/7 = 2.14$$

Applying Equation 10.2 determines required number of team members:

$$Required\ Staff = LOER/LOEA$$
$$Required\ Staff = 2.14/2.00 = 1.07$$

Note that the answer to Required Staff is greater than 1. This result means that the preferred person cannot be used as the sole resource because that person does not have enough time available to complete the task given the task's duration. If the preferred person is to be used, either increase the duration of the task to 8 days (15 hours/8 days = 1.88 hours); evaluate the level of effort to determine if the task can be completed in 14 hours instead of 15 hours (14 hours/7 days = 2 hours); or seek to increase the preferred person's availability by an additional 9 minutes (0.15 hours) per day.

Keep in mind, estimating is not an exact science. Estimating is an integrated and iterative process requiring multiple passes though the data until the project manager is comfortable with the duration, level of effort, and resource estimates for each task.

One last point: If a software package is being used to plan and manage a project, take the time to understand how the package manipulates duration, level of effort, resources, calendars, and start and finish dates. Some software packages use 7 or 8 hours as the default period for a day's duration. If not careful, a project manager will not only be surprised, but frustrated with the results if he or she does not adjust the default duration period.

Determine the Estimation Level

The type and size of the project and the culture of the organization influence whether the project should be estimated at the work package or task level. For some projects, estimating at the work package level (or even the deliverable level) is adequate, particularly if the same person has responsibility for completing all of the tasks, but for many projects, estimating must be done at the task level. This chapter discusses estimating at the task level, following a bottom-up approach.

Determine the Tools and the Techniques

Review the various estimating tools and techniques and determine which tools and techniques are applicable for the particular project. For example, a decision might be made that because estimating will be performed at the work package level and there is limited historical data, using the *Project Evaluation Review Technique* or PERT (refer to Table 10.2 for the formula) is the right option to estimate the project's duration. For an annual project, however, the decision might be to plan at the task level and use a combination of tools and techniques such as analogous, bottom-up, and vendor contracts to estimate the project's duration, level of effort, and resources.

Suggestion: Use PERT. Periodically a project manager will have a situation in which management does not have the time to properly plan a project. Additionally, there is limited (or no) historical information available to leverage. The project manager might even be told to determine the work that needs to occur, but to not spend much time estimating how long it will take. He or she might hear, "We need a back-of-the-envelope number for how long it's going to take to complete the project." When a situation like this occurs, discuss the use of PERT with the sponsor. The PERT formula uses an optimistic (best), most likely (realistic), and pessimistic (worst) duration to determine the expected duration. The PERT formula is:

$$(\text{Optimistic} + (4 \times \text{Most Likely}) + \text{Pessimistic})/6 = \text{Expected}$$

Using the annual dinner as the project, PERT can be used to determine how long it will take to plan and to get ready for the dinner. The project manager was asked to provide a back-of-the-envelope estimate for an annual dinner project. Although the project manager can create these estimates alone, a better option is to brainstorm with the sponsor and core team. During brainstorming, decide the level to be used for estimating, such as final deliverable level or work package. Then write down the assumptions, constraints, and risks for each duration category: optimistic, pessimistic, and most likely. Determine the duration for each category and add a contingency reserve:

1. Optimistic duration: 25 days. Some assumptions, constraints, and risks:
   - The venue used last year is available.
   - The format for food and beverage is the same.
   - Our regular printer is available and able to print the invitations immediately.
2. Pessimistic duration: 90 days. Some assumptions, constraints, and risks:
   - No venues within a 25-mile radius are available for the chosen day. A different date must be selected.
   - The venue selected does not have a caterer. A new caterer must be found or one recommended by the venue must be used.
   - Our regular printer is unavailable. A printer that we have never used must be used.
3. Most likely duration: 45 days. Some assumptions, constraints, and risks:
   - The venue used last year is unavailable, but other local venues are available.
   - The venue will have a caterer. There is no need to use a third party.
   - Our regular printer will need 5 days to print the invitations.

Applying PERT to this example, the project manager can anticipate the project effort to take 49.17 days ($(25 + (4 \times 45) + 90)/6 = 49.17$ days). If a 10% contingency reserve is added (4.91 additional days), the duration would total 54.08 days.

Determine the People to Involve

Determine who should assist with the time and resource estimating process. These people may or may not be part of the project team. If a core team member is assigned responsibility for the completion of a work package, consider having the core team member estimate his or her work package(s). Not only will involving core team members assist with building an effective project team, but it also facilitates having a shared understanding of the time requirements and resource needs.

DETERMINING, CAPTURING, AND CONSOLIDATING ESTIMATES

In flat organizations, two tools that work well when determining, capturing, and consolidating estimating data at the work package or task level are an estimating worksheet, a formal approach, and a spreadsheet, an informal approach.

Flat organizations with limited controls and processes might find a spreadsheet more than adequate when estimating time and resources, particularly if there is historical information to leverage, but an estimating worksheet might be the right approach to use when estimating time and resources for:

- A new project with no history to rely upon
- A core team member who needs to leverage third-party databases and benchmark studies
- A team that needs to obtain expert advice for guidance
- A team that is 100% virtual without a physical location for the team to meet

Using an estimating worksheet can result in the project team using a more formalized process with additional controls.

Create an Estimating Worksheet

Use an estimating worksheet to record duration, level of effort, and staff and other resource needs. Create one worksheet for each work package or task. Table 10.3 provides a sample estimating worksheet, but the actual format used needs to be appropriate for the project (and the organization). In addition to time and staff and other resource estimates, the project manager might want to record information such as cost and potential risks. Why ask for cost or risk information if the project manager is focused on estimating time and resource needs? The information will be needed later in the planning process and, depending on the project, it might be prudent and cost effective to ask for as much information as possible at the same time.

How the worksheets are completed and by whom vary by project manager. One way is for the core team member assigned the work package ownership to complete the worksheet. The core team member has a copy of the WBS, the work package documentation, and the network diagram. If special expertise is necessary to complete a worksheet, the core team member solicits assistance. Another way is for the project manager to complete each worksheet and then verify information with the core team and experts. Regardless of how the estimates are obtained, remember that the project manager is responsible for the final estimates. If core team members complete the worksheets, the project manager still has the responsibility to validate and agree to the estimates.

If estimating worksheets are used, communication is a key factor for success. Consider distributing the worksheets during a meeting in which everyone is encouraged to ask questions. The project manager provides clear and concise instructions that include the time measurement to be used (hours, days), estimating techniques appropriate for the project, how to estimate staff (number of staff

Table 10.3. Estimating Worksheet: Selected Information

Time:					
Duration:					
Level of Effort:					

Staff:					
Skills:		Person:		Amount of Time:	
Skills:		Person:		Amount of Time:	

Other Resources:			
Consultants/Vendors		Cost:	
Facilities		Cost:	
Equipment		Cost:	
Software		Cost:	
Materials and Supplies		Cost:	
Other		Cost:	

Constraints, Assumptions, and Risks:

and related skill sets required), and how to estimate other resources. Some flat organizations add a specific person's name to a work package during the estimating process, but this is not necessary at this time. At this point in the planning process, the primary objective is estimating the number of staff required and related skill sets.

The estimating information is then collected, documented, and consolidated. The easiest way is to create a spreadsheet. A spreadsheet enables data to be analyzed and totaled quickly. If an Excel spreadsheet that lists the sequenced work was created (see Table 9.2), consider expanding the worksheet or creating a new spreadsheet by copying the applicable columns. Table 10.4 is an example of a spreadsheet used to collect estimating data following a bottom-up approach. Remember that the spreadsheet is a working document. A number of changes will be made before the final estimates are established.

Create an Estimating Spreadsheet

An expedited informal approach is to only use an Excel spreadsheet as shown in Table 10.4, bypassing the use of an estimating worksheet. In this case, the project

Table 10.4. Estimating Time and Resources: Annual Dinner

Project: First Annual Dinner
Prepared by: Dave
Date: May

	Work	DESC	D (Days)	LOE (Hours)	Staff	Other	Non-Staff Cost	Assumptions, Constraints, and Exclusions
...	...	...						
5	Marketing	Formal Invitations to be sent; RSVP required						Invitations to be black and white
5.1	Invitations	Create annual dinner mailing list						No master list available to be used as a starting point; will need to collect mailing and email addresses
5.1.1	Create Mailing List		25	40	3	N/A	$0	Plan to use our current printer
5.1.2	Select Printer	Create a custom-designed invitation	1	2	1	N/A		Estimate based on discussions with current printer
5.1.3	Design Invitations		10	16	1	Third-Party Designer	$500	Need to assign a person to review printed invitations for quality
5.1.4	Print Invitations		10	4	1	Print Vendor	$500	
5.1.5	Address Invitations		7	40	3	Labels	$0	
5.1.6	Mail Invitations		1	2	1	Stamps	$200	
5.1.7	Pay Printer		1	1	1	N/A	$0	
...	...							

manager takes responsibility for completing the time and resource estimates for all work packages and tasks and reviews the results with the core team. Another option is for the project manager to meet with each core team member in an informal manner and to jointly complete the sections of the Excel spreadsheet for the work packages and tasks.

Other Options

There can be any number of variations to the two methods. For example:

- Use a combination of both. The estimating worksheet might be the right approach for a few of the work packages, but not for all of the work packages and tasks. Use an estimating worksheet for those work packages and an Excel spreadsheet for the rest.
- Send the Excel spreadsheet to each core team member, asking him or her to add the appropriate information for their work package(s). The project manager still has responsibility for compiling and reviewing the information.

There is no right way to complete the time and resource estimates for the work packages and tasks. Keep in mind the intent of estimating: to determine the time and resources needed to complete each task and work package. Employ an approach that works, is a "fit" with the organization's culture, and meets the needs of the project.

Suggestion: Manage estimating expectations. No matter how often a project manager states to a sponsor, team members, or other stakeholders that an estimate is a best guess, some people will seize on the number and forget to allow flexibility or room for error. Take the time to explain to the sponsor and other stakeholders how and why the estimates were determined. Additionally, explain how adjustments to the estimates will be communicated. Things happen. Estimates can change. The project manager is responsible for making sure the sponsor and stakeholders are not surprised. One way to avoid people seizing on an estimated number and forgetting to allow room for error is to provide more than one estimate. For example, provide a realistic range or three estimates: an optimistic estimate, a pessimistic estimate, and a most likely estimate. Multiple estimates prevent people from seizing on one number, particularly people who have an understanding of the estimating process. Multiple estimates are used by some third-party vendors who base invoices on actual time, thus providing their clients with a better range of the final cost. One negative of multiple estimates is that the project manager still needs to use one estimate to manage and report project progress.

ESTIMATING ERRORS

At times the project manager may be uncomfortable with a request received from the sponsor or key stakeholders or with a message he or she needs to relay to them. Informing management or a sponsor that the initial completion date is not possible can be intimidating. Telling them that estimating errors (known as mistakes) have been made is an uncomfortable situation. Project managers should be realistic when estimating, but they also need to be able to articulate why an estimate is inaccurate or unrealistic.

Underestimating occurs when the project manager remembers what was successful about a prior project, but forgets about what went wrong, such as not including project management tasks in the plan or not adequately estimating the amount of nonproductive team member time (administrative, travel, nonproject-related training, vacations, and holidays).

Conversely, overestimating can occur when the project manager is new to project estimating and no expert is available to help. In this case, the project manager is better off estimating the level of effort that he or she thinks the project should require and then add a reasonable contingency. Just be careful to not add too much to an estimate—unrealistic numbers will be noticed.

Estimating errors can also occur when a "one person plan" is created. Under- or overestimating or missing a strategic resource is easy for a project manager. Take the time to discuss the estimates with core team members who are responsible for completing the tasks and with experts as well. Get their input. There can be alternatives that the "one person" never thought to consider.

IN REVIEW

- Estimating time, resources, and cost is a calculated guess that is reasonable, not over- or underestimated, and takes into account expected as well as unexpected events and delays. The goal is to focus on being approximately right rather than precisely wrong.
- Time estimates include the duration, the lapse time to complete a task, and the level of effort, the amount of time to complete the task without interruptions. Resource estimates determine how many resources (people, equipment, and facilities) are required. Cost estimates are the costs for every task.
- Define the measurement unit for duration and level of effort. If the measurement unit for duration is a day, indicate how many hours constitute a day.

- Estimating tools and techniques can be used individually or in combination. Tools and techniques that work well are expert opinion, analogous estimating, bottom-up estimating, parametric estimating, three-point estimating, vendor contracts, and contingency reserves.
- Add extra time and money, a contingency reserve, to the project for unexpected and unplanned events.
- Flat organizations with informal communication and processes have flexibility when deciding how to determine, collect, and consolidate project estimates. There is no right or wrong way. The process can be as informal or formal as need be based on the type and size of project, and the organization's culture.
- Even though the project manager is responsible for the time and resource estimates, overlooking resources requirements or time constraints is easy. Involve the core team and, if applicable, other potential team members in the estimating effort. Not only does involving team members assist with building an effective project team, but it also establishes a shared understanding of the time requirements and resource needs of the project.
- Be realistic when estimating. Do not assume the milestone end date in the scope statement is nonnegotiable. Do not over- or underestimate the work in an effort to satisfy sponsor and stakeholder requests.

STEP-BY-STEP INSTRUCTIONS

When determining resource and time estimates:

1. Gather and review project-related documentation:
   - Collect project documents created to-date: the scope statement; the work breakdown structure and documentation; the network diagram; and correspondence.
   - Review organizational policies and procedures: approval and sign-off requirements for purchasing supplies; acceptable and approved vendors; and procedures for hiring consultants.
   - Consult historical information: the detailed information and lessons learned from similar projects.
   - Review published information: third-party databases and benchmark studies.
2. Determine the approach for estimating time and resources:
   - If necessary, consult with other project managers and the sponsor to determine the best approach for the project.

- Define duration and level of effort measurement units.
- Decide if time and resource estimates are to be completed as a unit or if each is to be estimated individually and then reconciled.
- Determine if estimates are to be created at the task or work package level.
- Determine the estimating tools and techniques to be used.
- Determine who is responsible for creating the estimates.
- Determine how the estimates are to be collected and recorded: on a spreadsheet or on an estimating worksheet or using a combination of both.

3. If an estimating worksheet is used (if not using estimating spreadsheets, skip this step and move to Step 4):
   - Develop clear and concise instructions and include:
     - How to complete the estimating worksheets
     - How to estimate the resources (Step 4)
     - How to estimate the duration and level of effort (Step 5)
     - The time measurement (i.e., hours, days) to be used for duration and level of effort
     - The appropriate estimating tools and techniques for the project
     - The organizational policies and procedures and historical information that could impact the resource or time estimating effort
   - Set up a meeting. Distribute the estimating worksheets and explain the process. Provide each person with their estimating worksheets, the work breakdown structure, applicable work package documentation, and any other pertinent project documentation.
   - Collect the completed estimating worksheets and analyze them.

4. Estimate the resources:
   - Determine the resources necessary to complete each task, which includes the need for internal people and their skill sets; external people (third-party vendors, consultants) and their skill sets; and equipment, materials, and facilities. At his point, names of people do not need to be assigned. (Assigning and noting the person who has been assigned to a task is common when an organization has a limited number of staff or a particular key person is needed.)

- Determine the quantity of resources necessary to complete each task.
- Indicate any constraints, assumptions, risks, or alternatives, such as no one in the organization has the necessary skill set so third-party resources are required.

5. Estimate duration and level of effort:
   - Determine the common time measurement to be used for duration and level of effort.
   - Verify the accuracy of the estimates.
   - Consider the need for a contingency reserve and document the reasons.
   - Indicate any constraints, assumptions, and risks.

6. Consolidate information in a resource and time spreadsheet:
   - Compare the spreadsheet to the scope statement, the work breakdown structure, and work package documentation to ensure all the resources to perform the project work have been estimated.
   - Add a reserve to the time estimate at the work package level or indicate that a reserve should be considered.
   - Take into account the organization's policies, procedures, and any potential impacts on resources.
   - Analyze the resources available to the project. Discuss staff needs and skill sets with Human Resources.
   - Review constraints, assumptions, alternatives, and risks.
   - Review the time and resource estimates with the core team. Clarify any core team questions or concerns. Modify the spreadsheet accordingly.

7. Review time and resource estimates with the sponsor and, if appropriate, the key stakeholders. As when the work breakdown structure was reviewed, ask if anything has been missed or misunderstood. Additionally, discuss whether the project should be halted or continued.

8. Update the work breakdown structure with any additions or deletions.

9. Review comments received from the sponsor and key stakeholders with the core team. Clarify any core team questions or concerns.

CHAPTER 11

CREATE THE SCHEDULE

Covered in this chapter:

- Determining the critical path using the Critical Path Method
- Assigning start and finish dates to the work
- Determining the project completion date
- Compressing the schedule by descoping, fast tracking, and crashing
- Reporting key deliverable and milestone dates
- Creating scope and schedule baselines

With the work defined and time estimates in place, start and finish dates can be applied to the project work plan, resulting in a project schedule. As the schedule is created, there is a constant refinement and solidification of the work and time required. Task durations are reviewed, task dependencies are reworked, and any redundant tasks are eliminated. The critical path, the sequence of tasks that takes the longest to complete with no slack or extra time, is determined. In an effort to complete the project by the date in the scope statement, the schedule is compressed and alternatives are assessed. Creating an acceptable and realistic project schedule is an iterative process with changes to the schedule occurring throughout the project life cycle.

DEFINE THE SCHEDULE

To create a schedule, analyze all of the planned work performed to date and determine planned start and finish dates for all project tasks and deliverables. In theory, a schedule is not complete until all resources are assigned, but once the critical path is known, start and finish dates can be assigned to the tasks and a preliminary project completion date can be determined. The project manager also has enough information to have a meaningful conversation with the sponsor pertaining to the completion date in the scope statement.

THE IMPORTANCE OF THE CRITICAL PATH

The critical path is the sequence of tasks that requires the longest duration to complete with no slack or extra time. It sets the minimum length of time required to complete the project. Another way to look at the critical path is that it is the earliest date by which the project can be completed. The project manager and core team focus on determining the earliest a task can start and the precise time it takes to complete the task before the next task can begin. Task dependencies and interdependencies are reviewed, and the work is scrutinized, yet again, ensuring that only relevant tasks are included in the project plan.

The tasks on the critical path are not any more important than any of the other tasks, but they do have less scheduling flexibility and require careful monitoring to ensure that meeting the planned project completion date is possible. If a task is not completed on time and a subsequent task is not completed ahead of schedule compensating for the delay, the entire project will be delayed.

Understanding the critical path is a basic planning concept that all team members need to understand, but project managers must go a step further and understand how calculating the critical path assists with determining dates, optimizes efficiency, impacts staff utilization, identifies risk, and influences total project costs. Why? Think of it this way, have you ever stood in front of a cashier at a store and thought, "That total isn't right. It's too high." If you did not know how to add up the cost of the individual items, you might not know that you were spending more than planned or know what questions to ask.

Although there are different techniques for determining the critical path, the most common technique is known as the *Critical Path Method* (CPM). CPM uses the network diagram for the project, each task's relationship to one another, and each task's duration to determine the critical path.

CPM procedures are relatively simple and the calculations easy to perform, resulting in people not needing to have extensive mathematical knowledge or computational skills. These characteristics make CPM the most popular method for determining the critical path as well as being the method used by many project management software packages.

For projects with a small number of tasks and paths, the critical path can be calculated manually or calculated by using a productivity tool such as Excel. For some projects, it is possible for the project manager to determine the path with the longest duration when the work is sequenced because the longest path is easy to visualize, but being the longest path does not guarantee that this path it is the critical path. The critical path also needs to be the path that has no extra time. To determine that a path has no extra time, the start and finish dates need to be assigned to each task.

Manually calculating the critical path for a large project, although possible, can become quite cumbersome and time consuming. For large projects, using a project management software package is a better solution because the software automatically determines the critical path after each task's duration and relationship to one another have been entered. Even if a software package automatically calculates the critical path for the project, the project manager and core team should still perform a reasonability test.

DETERMINE THE CRITICAL PATH

The easiest way to explain how to determine the critical path is to walk through an example. Figure 11.1 is a network diagram with four tasks. In this example, duration is defined in terms of days. The duration for each task is noted above the applicable task box because the task's duration is required to determine the critical path.

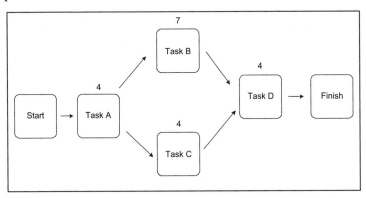

Figure 11.1. Network diagram 1.

Begin at the **Start** box and work left to right. Identify all of the paths in the network diagram. In Figure 11.1, there are two paths:

- Path A follows Start, Task A, Task B, Task D, and Finish
- Path B follows Start, Task A, Task C, Task D, and Finish

Next, add the duration for each of the tasks on each of the paths in the diagram:

- Path A: 4 + 7 + 4 = 15
- Path B: 4 + 4 + 4 = 12

The critical path is the path with the longest duration. In this example, the duration of Path A is 15 days, which is longer than the duration of Path B, 12 days. Path A is therefore the critical path.

Remember that simply choosing the path with the longest duration total does not always, or adequately, identify the critical path because following the method of choosing the path with the longest duration does not explicitly find the path with no extra time. What distinguishes the critical path, making it critical, is that this path has no extra time—time that is referred to as *slack* or *float*. To quantify float requires following a more complicated procedure involving a *forward pass* and a *backward pass*. This procedure requires determining the following for each task:

Early start (ES) = earliest task start time
Late start (LS) = latest task start time
Early finish (EF) = earliest task finish time
Late finish (LF) = latest task finish time
Float (F) = (LS − ES) or (LF − EF)

After determining ES, LS, EF, and LF for each task, calculating the float (F) or the slack for the task, and adjusting for leads and lags, the critical path can be determined.

Walking through an example is the easiest way to understand how to determine the critical path using forward and backward pass logic and each task's float. Figure 11.2 is a network diagram with six tasks and three paths:

- Path A follows Start, Task A, Task B, Task E, Task F, and Finish
- Path B follows Start, Task A, Task C, Task E, Task F, and Finish
- Path C follows Start, Task A, Task D, Task F, and Finish

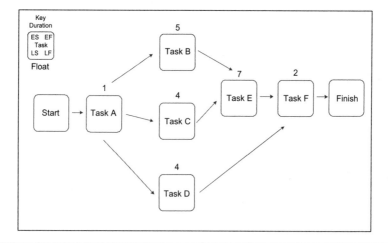

Figure 11.2. Network diagram 2.

As before, the duration for each task is noted above the applicable task box. After each forward and backward pass calculation is performed, display the calculation in the task box on the network diagram. The forward pass calculations are at the top of the task box and the backward pass calculations are at the bottom of the task box as shown in the **Key** in Figure 11.2.

Perform a Forward Pass

Calculate the forward pass which is the ES (early start) and EF (early finish):

- Step 1: Use zero for the first task's ES. For Task A, enter 0 under ES.
- Step 2: The first task's EF is the task's duration. For Task A, enter 1, Task A's duration, under EF.
- Step 3: The ES for each successor task is the latest EF from any of its predecessor tasks. For Task B, enter 1 under ES, Task A's EF.
- Step 4: Calculate the EF for each successor task by adding its duration to the ES. For Task B, enter 6 under EF (Task B's ES of 1 + Task B's duration of 5 = 6).
- Step 5: Repeat Steps 3 and 4 for Task C and Task D.

The resulting network diagram looks like Figure 11.3.

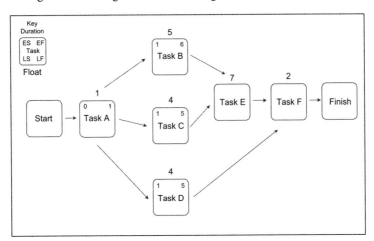

Figure 11.3. Network diagram: forward pass 1.

- Step 6: Calculate Task E. Task E has two predecessors with two different early finishes. Remember, the early start for each successor task is the latest early finish from any of its predecessor tasks. Task B's EF is 6 and Task C's EF is 5. Because Task E cannot start until both Task B and C have been completed, the task with the **latest** EF needs to be used, which requires using Task B's EF of 6 for Task E's ES. Calculate the EF for Task E (6 + 7 = 13).

- Step 7: Task F also has two predecessors with two different early finishes. Task E's EF (13) is later than Task D's EF (5), so use Task E's EF of 13. Calculate the EF for Task F (13 + 2 = 15).

The resulting network diagram looks like Figure 11. 4.

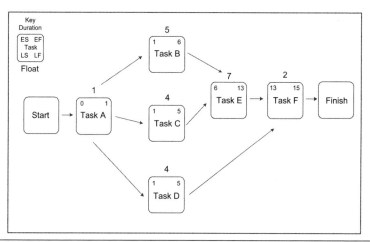

Figure 11.4. Network diagram: forward pass 2.

Perform a Backward Pass

With the forward pass complete, calculate the backward pass, which is the LS (late start) and LF (late finish):

- Step 1: The last task's early finish is the late finish for the task. For Task F, enter 15 under LF.
- Step 2: Subtract the last task's duration from the LF to calculate the LS. For Task F, enter 13 under LS (Task F's LF of 15 – Task F's duration of 2 = 13).
- Step 3: The late finish for each predecessor task uses the earliest late start from any successor tasks. For Task E, enter 13 under LF.
- Step 4: The late start for each predecessor activity is calculated by subtracting its duration from its late finish. For Task E, enter 6 under LS. (Task E's LS of 13 – Task E's duration of 7 = 6.)
- Step 5: Repeat Steps 3 and 4 for Task B, Task C, and Task D.

The resulting network diagram looks like Figure 11.5.

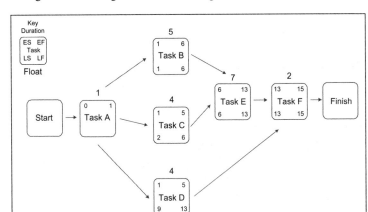

Figure 11.5. Network diagram: backward pass 1.

- Step 6: Next calculate the LF for Task A. Task A has three successor tasks: B, C, and D. To determine Task A's LF, use the earliest LS from any successor tasks. In this example, it is the LS of Task B or 1. Calculate the LS for Task A by subtracting duration from LF (1 – 1 = 0).

The resulting network diagram looks like Figure 11.6.

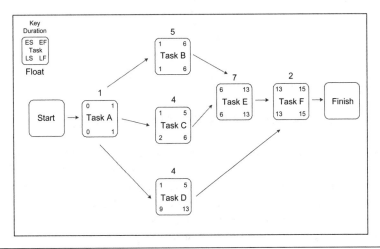

Figure 11.6. Network diagram: backward pass 2.

Calculate Float

To calculate the float for each task, subtract the ES from the LS or subtract the EF from the LF. Both calculations will provide the same answer so it does not matter which calculation is used. If you want to check your work, determine float using both calculations. Display the float for each task at the bottom of the task box. The finished network diagram looks like Figure 11. 7.

Identify the Critical Path

In Figure 11.7, identify the path in which all tasks on the path have zero float: in this case, it is Path A (Start, Task A, Task B, Task E, Task F, and Finish). Path A is therefore the *critical path*, the path that will take the longest to complete and the path that has no slack. Calculate the project's total duration by adding up all of the task durations on Path A. In Figure 11.7, the duration is 15 days (Path A = 1 + 5 + 7 + 2 = 15).

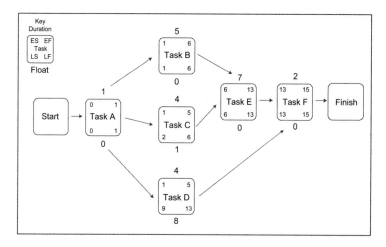

Figure 11.7. Network diagram: float.

DETERMINE THE PROJECT COMPLETION DATE

After identifying the critical path, assign a calendar start date to the first critical path task. Next determine the task end date by using the duration and taking into account nonworking calendar days such as Saturday and Sunday. Repeat this process for all tasks on the critical path. The end date for the final task on the critical path is the new completion date. Do not be disheartened if the critical path indicates that the project cannot be completed by the date in the scope statement. By compressing the schedule, which is discussed later in this chapter, it may be possible for the team to complete the project by the completion date in the scope statement.

If the work breakdown structure was entered into an Excel spreadsheet, enter the start and end dates for tasks on the critical path. Next determine the start and end dates for the remaining project tasks, taking into account each task's time duration and nonworking days. With all of the project work documented, a known completion date, and start and finish dates assigned to the work (Table 11.1), the project manager has a project roadmap, a work plan and schedule, in Excel.

Table 11.1. Schedule: Annual Dinner

Project: First Annual Dinner
Prepared by: Dave
Date: May

			Work	Start Date	Finish Date	Duration
...	...	...				
3			**Food and Beverage**			
	3.1		Receptions			
	3.1.1		Determine Hors d'oeuvres	7/8	7/21	10
	3.1.2		Determine Beverages	7/8	7/21	10
	3.2		Dinner			
	3.2.1		Determine Meal	7/8	7/21	10
...	...	...				
5			**Marketing**			
	5.1		Invitations			
	5.1.1		Create Mailing List	7/9	8/10	25
	5.1.2		Select Printer	6/18	6/18	1
	5.1.3		Design Invitations	7/9	7/20	10
	5.1.4		Print Invitations	7/20	8/3	10
	5.1.5		Address Invitations	8/3	8/13	7
	5.1.6		Mail Invitations	8/22	8/22	1
	5.1.7		Pay Printer	8/3	8/3	1
...	...	...				

If the project looks like it can be completed early, do not rush to announce the early finish. Staff has not yet been assigned and a particular staff person may not be available when required, resulting in a task's start and end dates needing to be modified. Even if this staff person is available, the possibility exists that after other staff members are assigned, the new completion date might be later than the completion date in the scope statement. So, wait until after the staff has been assigned and the schedule has been compressed before announcing the "good news." Talk to management and the sponsor; get their advice. Management or the sponsor may want to consider keeping the extra time as a contingency reserve in case there are any unseen or unplanned events.

Do not assume that the project completion date in the scope statement is nonnegotiable. Attempt to meet the date within the agreed-upon scope, but if the completion date cannot be met without changing the scope, discuss various alternatives with the sponsor and key stakeholders. It cannot be assumed that a talented project manager or team will "figure something out" and somehow meet an unrealistic completion date work. Chances are they will not do so. Although the sponsor and key stakeholders might not be pleased that the date cannot be met, not delivering a quality product or service is worse.

Suggestion: Use backward planning. A project manager might be required to "back into" a completion date. When presented with a mandatory completion date, use backward planning to determine the latest date a project can start and still meet the completion date. There are several different ways to backward plan. The easiest is to create a network diagram and determine the critical path. Then instead of assigning a calendar start date to the first critical task, assign a calendar finish date—the requested completion date to the last critical path task. Work backward, assigning calendar dates based on duration while taking into account nonworking calendar days such as Saturday and Sunday. This process also establishes the amount of time remaining before work must start to meet the end date (the *upfront slack*).

COMPRESS THE SCHEDULE

If the anticipated completion date cannot be met, compress the schedule. There are three techniques to consider when compressing a schedule: *fast tracking, crashing,* and *descoping.* Descoping eliminates some of the project work while fast tracking and crashing shorten the critical path. Descoping normally reduces project cost while crashing normally increases project cost and is not always successful. Fast tracking and crashing both increase project risk.

Fast Tracking

Fast tracking is an effective way of shortening a project schedule if tasks on the critical path can be overlapped or work can be performed in parallel instead of performed sequentially. First, look at the longest tasks on the critical path. Next determine if it is possible to start the next task or overlap tasks. Then look at the tasks that use different resources, analyze each task risk, and determine if these tasks can be performed in parallel.

A perfect example of fast tracking in everyday life is cooking a meal. Tasks can be split, with one person cooking the entree while another person prepares the appetizer. One person could have performed the "work" sequentially, but it would have taken longer to produce the meal.

Crashing

Crashing involves analyzing the critical path to determine if a task's duration can be shortened or reduced by adding additional resources. The critical path is the only place to look for tasks to crash because these tasks are the only ones that can be shortened to reduce the duration of the project. Normally the additional resources are people, but a resource could be a technical or equipment change.

Review the duration of each task first. Is each duration realistic or can it be reduced? Is there a lead or lag that might be shorted? Review the work that needs to be completed for each critical path task. Can additional people be added to reduce the time needed to complete the task? Is there a software application (or a piece of equipment) that could be used to save time?

If it is possible to successfully crash the tasks on the critical path, validate that the path is still the critical path. Crashing can cause another path to now be the critical path.

The "quick, dirty way" to confirm if a path is still the critical path is to add up all the paths and determine if the crashed critical path's duration is equal to or less than any of the other paths. For example, the critical path shown in Figure 11.7 is Path A (Start, Task A, Task B, Task E, Task F, and Finish) with a duration of 15 days. The duration of Path B (Start, Task A, Task C, Task E, Task F, and Finish) is 14 days. If after crashing Path A, the duration is 13 days, then Path B is now the new critical path.

Descoping

Descoping requires removing features or functionality from the final product or service, the deliverable, by reducing the work and in turn the time required. When descoping, use the prioritized requirements list as a starting point. Include the sponsor in the discussions. Be prepared to provide the sponsor with some possible scenarios or solutions:

- "If the project is divided into phases, this is what we can provide in Phase 1."
- "If we remove this feature (or functionality), the product will met 95% of the requirements requested by the stakeholders."

Important: Remember that the sponsor needs to sign-off on the descoped final product or services.

When you compress a project's schedule, consider fast tracking first, crashing second, and descoping last. Work with the sponsor and perform a cost analysis so that the economic as well as the business impacts are known and have been considered. Two suggestions to consider when thinking about descoping, fast tracking, or crashing:

- Even if the date can be met, a project manager might consider compressing the schedule, enabling the project to be completed earlier than the anticipated completion date, providing a time contingency reserve.
- Instead of compressing twice, once after the dates have been applied and then again after the resources are assigned (discussed in Chapter 12), consider waiting until after the resources are assigned to compress a schedule.

REPORT KEY DATES

With the assigning of start and finish dates to the tasks, a project schedule is in place, but there could be differences between the key deliverables and milestone dates in the project work plan and schedule and the scope statement. Review, confirm, and update the key deliverables and milestone dates in the scope statement. Add any new key deliverables and milestones to the scope statement. Similarly, remove key deliverables and milestones from the scope statement that are no longer applicable. Because milestones do not have a start or finish date or a cost associated with them, milestones are easy to forget. Ensure that milestones are identified in the scope statement as well as in the project work plan and schedule—milestones are key dates because they are project checkpoints.

Milestone and Gantt charts are great management and communication tools to highlight key dates. They also work in conjunction with each other. A milestone chart lists milestones with associated end dates (Table 11.2) while a Gantt chart (a bar chart) shows the length of time, the start and completion of tasks or work packages, and summary components in a visual or graphical format (Figure 11.8).

Some project teams tend to omit creating a milestone chart, thinking it is extra work. A common comment: "The milestones are listed in the detailed Excel project plan." Take the time to create a milestone chart. A detailed project work plan and schedule that includes all the tasks, work packages, durations, work efforts, and resource assignments, even if not long, can be cumbersome and hard to read. Many stakeholders who are interested in the project, even the sponsor, do not need the level of detail included in a work plan and schedule. Rather, they need summary information so that they are aware of the key dates—a milestone chart is a good tool to use when providing the status of a project.

Table 11.2. Milestone Chart

Product or Service	
Milestone	**Completion Date**
Start Project	6/18
Finalize Project Plan	7/2
Project Kick-Off	7/8
...	
Contract Signed with Venue	7/26
...	
Contract Signed with Speaker	7/15
...	
Invitations Mailed	8/22
...	
Dinner	10/15
...	
Project Complete	10/20

With the work defined, a network diagram in place, the critical path determined, and milestone dates established, a Gantt chart can be created (Figure 11.8). A Gantt chart is a visual aid enabling everyone to see the big picture and to quickly see the order, duration, and status of all project tasks or work packages. Periodically throughout the project consider creating a Gantt chart for the sponsor and stakeholders at the major deliverable and milestone levels. A Gantt chart is an excellent way to provide a quick and easy visual status of the project to anyone.

CREATE THE SCOPE AND SCHEDULE BASELINES

With the work, key deliverables, and milestones defined and start and finish dates assigned to the work, the project manager has the project scope (work, key deliverables, and milestones) and schedule (start and finish dates) baselines. A baseline is snapshot of the agreed-upon and signed-off on scope and schedule. This snapshot is used to manage, control, and report the project's performance and status.

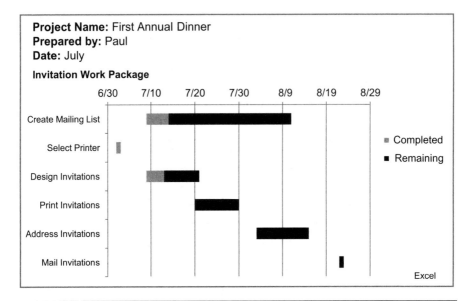

Figure 11.8. Gantt chart.

Scope and schedule baselines tie to two of the triple constraints—scope, the work; and schedule, the time. The budget baseline—which ties to the third triple constraint, cost—is created after a budget for the project has been built. (Creating a budget plan is discussed in Chapter 13.)

IN REVIEW

- The critical path is the sequence of tasks that requires the longest to complete with no slack or extra time and determines the earliest date a project can be completed.
- The Critical Path Method (CPM) is the most popular method for determining the critical path.
- By identifying the tasks on the critical path, the project manager is made aware of the risky tasks that will impact the completion date if they go over schedule.
- After the critical path is known, start and finish dates are assigned, first to critical path tasks so that a completion date can be determined and then to the remaining tasks, resulting in a project schedule.
- Three ways to compress a schedule to meet an earlier completion date are fast tracking, crashing, and descoping.

- Milestone and Gantt charts are great management and communication tools that can be used to communicate status information about tasks, deliverables, and milestones to the sponsor and stakeholders.
- With the approval of the completion date and schedule by the sponsor, project scope and schedule baselines are created, two of the three baselines that tie to the triple constraints.

STEP-BY-STEP INSTRUCTIONS

To determine the critical path and associated dates:

1. Gather the network diagram and information on each task's duration.
2. Decide if a decision table will be used or if the calculations will be displayed on a network diagram.
3. Calculate the forward pass (early start and early finish):
   - Use zero for the first task's early start.
   - The first task's early finish is the task's duration.
   - The early start for each successor task is the latest early finish from any of its predecessor tasks.
   - The early finish for each successor task is calculated by adding its duration to the early start.
   - Move forward through all tasks, repeating the above steps.
4. Calculate the backward pass (late start and late finish):
   - The last task's early finish is the late finish for the task.
   - Subtract the last task's duration from the early finish to calculate the late start.
   - The late finish for each predecessor task uses the earliest late start from any successor tasks.
   - The late start for each predecessor activity is calculated by subtracting its duration from its late finish.
   - Move backward through all tasks, repeating the above steps.
5. Calculate float. For each task, subtract the early start from the late start or subtract the early finish from the late finish.
6. Determine the critical path. Find the path with the longest duration and zero float.
7. Assign dates:
   - Assign a calendar start date to the first critical path task.
   - Add the time duration to determine the task end date.

- Repeat this process for all tasks on the critical path.
- The end date for the final task on the critical path is the new project completion date.
- Assign start and end dates to the remaining tasks.

8. Meet with the sponsor and key stakeholders to review and discuss:
   - The critical path
   - The project schedule
   - The completion date

   Based on this discussion, determine if the completion date is acceptable or if the schedule should be compressed.

9. Compress the schedule by:
   - Fast tracking
   - Crashing
   - Descoping

   Based on the results of the compressing effort, modify the scope and schedule accordingly.

10. Review and update the key deliverables and milestones in the scope statement.

11. Create a milestone chart with key dates.

12. Consider creating a Gantt chart showing the order and duration of the project tasks.

13. Review the schedule with the sponsor and determine if the project should proceed. If the schedule is approved, create the scope and schedule baselines.

14. Review the scope and schedule baselines with the core team. Clarify any core team questions or concerns.

This book has free material available for download from the
Web Added Value™ resource center at *www.jrosspub.com*

CHAPTER 12

DETERMINE THE RESOURCES

Covered in this chapter:

- Assigning staff and non-staff resources
- Determining potential staffing conflicts
- Communicating task assignments
- Leveling overcommitted resources

Before a project plan is complete, the project manager needs to assign resources, which includes the staff, consultants, and vendors as well as other resources such as equipment and software. Assigning non-personnel resources is normally easier than assigning staff. Assigning staff can be time consuming because it involves determining the needed skill sets; identifying the people available who possess these required skill sets; negotiating for the appropriate people; assigning staff; and then leveling the resources to ensure that people are used optimally, not overcommitted or underutilized. As staff members are scheduled, additional modifications to the scope and schedule occur.

ASSIGN RESOURCES

Assigning resources involves inserting the name of a resource, whether a staff person, a vendor, equipment, materials, software, or some other resource, next to the task in the project plan. Non-staff resources may have already been assigned when the resource needs were estimated. In a flat organization with limited staff, a project manager may have assigned staff with key skills to selected tasks during the estimation process. Another project manager, particularly a project manager accustomed to a hierarchical organization with larger projects, may create a human resource plan for assigning staff—a process that is overkill for many flat organizations. Still other project managers prefer to wait to assign resources until after a schedule with a start and a finish date has been determined.

If the project is to start as soon as the project plan (scope, schedule, and budget) is complete, now is the time to assign resources to the tasks. (Creating a budget is discussed in Chapter 13.) If resources were assigned when resource needs were estimated, now is the time to review and confirm. The reason to review and confirm is that planning a project is an iterative process; change happens and must be accommodated. For example, with start and end dates assigned to tasks, there could be a potential scheduling conflict with a staff person—the person is not available when needed by the project even though they were assigned to the task during the estimation process.

Assigning staff is the delegation of work to team members. Assigning staff sounds and is straightforward, but is it always practical and realistic? For example, the project manager has a list of potential people who are available to work on the project. Their skills are matched with project needs. Staff members are then assigned first to the critical path tasks and then to the other project tasks. Next, the project manager creates a *resource histogram* bar chart that shows the amount of time a person or a group will be working over a period of time to ensure the person or the group is not overcommitted or underutilized. Then the project manager creates a project calendar with the dates each staff person is to work on the project. Everyone is preassigned to the project; there are no open tasks and no conflicts. The project manager does not need to be concerned about assigning staff again. Unfortunately, this is a rare scenario. It is not representative of most projects. People resign and get sick or a business emergency occurs. Other things can happen that disrupt the project and project resources.

Use the resource estimations and create a list of skills needed for the project. Highlight the skills and staff resource needs associated with tasks on the critical path because these are the skills needed to complete the project on time. Meet with the sponsor to discuss project staffing needs and options. If staff members are available with skills that match or almost match those needed by the project, it is easy to assign the staff to the project. If the necessary staff members are not available, work with managers and other project managers and negotiate for the appropriate people within the organization. Two other options are to hire temporary people, such as contractors and consultants, or to extend the project timeline until the appropriate staff members are available.

Suggestion: Use creative assignment options. Flat organizations with limited staff require a project manager to be creative and innovative when assigning staff to the project tasks. So, after the potential team members have been identified consider:

- Assigning only the tasks that require a particular staff person with a particular or key skill set: For the remaining tasks, brainstorm with people who are available to work on the project. Ask what tasks they would like to work on and the tasks they are interested in as well as the tasks that would work best with their other organizational responsibilities. People can have skills and knowledge that are beneficial to the project that no one in the organization knows about.

- Asking for a volunteer: If there is a task that no one is interested in completing, ask potential team members for a volunteer. The volunteer might not be a potential team member. Someone else in the organization may be qualified to complete the task and can do so in the most effective and efficient way possible. Do not forget to recognize volunteers. Reward them for their effort and support.

- Training available staff in new skills, particularly if the skills can be used in their day-to-day operational roles: Work with the potential team members to determine if there is a staff person who could benefit by the training, helping the staff person as well as meeting the needs of the project. Another option is to train an interested staff person in a skill needed to perform a task(s).

Armed with a list of potential people, the project manager can start assigning staff. Assign staff to the tasks on the critical path first because not completing these tasks on time impacts the project completion date. Then assign staff to the remaining tasks.

Many projects struggle because a project manager assumes staff will be available when needed. Even if a person has been committed to a project, the availability of the person could change. Day-to-day operations and projects have conflicting needs all the time. If there is potential for conflicting operational needs or a risk that a key person will not be available, discuss these risks with the sponsor and look for alternatives.

CHART STAFFING NEEDS

A number of easy, low-cost tools and techniques are available to assist with determining overcommitted and underutilized staff resources and for communicating staff challenges to a sponsor or stakeholders. Two tools to consider using are a *staff utilization chart* and a *resource histogram*. Not all projects need a staff utilization chart or resource histogram, but both are visual tools that can assist with clarifying or highlighting project resource conflicts and needs.

Staff Utilization Chart

To determine if staff are overcommitted or underutilized, create a staff utilization chart (Table 12.1). Although all of the project work packages and tasks can be listed, many times this technique is only used for work packages or tasks for which a project manager has concerns. First, create a chart with days (or dates) listed horizontally across the top and work packages (or tasks) listed vertically. A person's name is then entered into the associated column and row. Analyze the staff utilization chart. Identify any time or personnel conflicts by following techniques as described for Table 12.1. Brainstorm different staffing ideas with the core team or use the chart as a starting point in staffing discussions with the sponsor.

Table 12.1. Staff Utilization Chart: Annual Dinner

Work Package	Duration (Days)	Level of Effort (Hours)	1	2	3	4	5	6	7
Sponsors	5	24	S	S	S	S	S		
Transportation	3	20				T	T	T	
Software	3	16					S	S	S

S, Sarah; T, Tim.

In Table 12.1, Sarah might be considered to be underutilized if she was assigned to work full time (100%) on the project because she has a total of 56 hours (7 days × 8 hours) to complete 40 hours of work (24 hours for work package "Sponsors" and 16 hours for work package "Software"). In theory, Sarah could complete work package "Sponsors" on Days 1 through 3 and then work package "Software" on Days 5 and 6.

If the scenario changed so that Sarah could only spend 50% of her time working on the project, she would be overcommitted. Ignoring the fact that "Sponsors" and "Software" have one day of duration overlap, the work package "Sponsors" requires 3 days to complete the work, but Sarah only has 2.5 days (50% of 5 days) allocated to work on the work package—20 hours to complete 24 hours of work. Work package "Software" is similar in that it requires 2 days to complete the work, but Sarah only has 1.5 days (50% of 3 days) allocated to work on the work package. Sarah cannot complete the assigned work within the required timeframe.

Resource Histogram

A *histogram* is a bar graph that allows a project manager to compare data characteristics and enables making informed decisions. Many people think of histograms when evaluating the quality of a product because histograms are a visual aid for statistical approximations, such as out of 200 defects, 10 are critical while 175 are low priority. A *resource histogram* can show how many people are needed at various points in a project and can assist with having the right number of people scheduled at the right point in time. Resource histograms are ideal for projects that require a large number of resources during the execution phase, such as construction and technology projects; projects that rely on volunteers; or projects with a significant number of part-time project team members.

In Figure 12.1, the project manager uses the duration, level of effort, and resource estimations for an eight-week project to create a resource histogram. The full-time resource needs are entered into an Excel spreadsheet by category (Management, Staff, and Volunteers). Then using Excel chart functionality, a resource histogram is created. The horizontal axis at the bottom of the graph shows the weeks. The vertical axis shows the number of full-time workers needed each week.

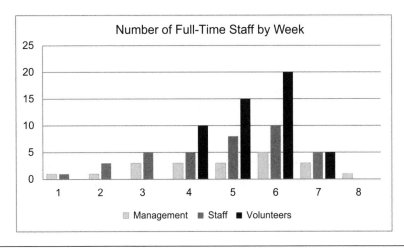

Figure 12.1. Resource histogram: annual dinner project staff required.

After analyzing the histogram, the project manager decides that obtaining 20 full-time volunteers in week six might be unrealistic, so the project manager evaluates other alternatives such as using 40 volunteers on a part-time basis or adding more staff to support the effort. Instead of changing the staff mix at this time, however, the project manager might use the chart to explain the resource needs to stakeholders, such as the board of directors, and to solicit their assistance in finding 20 full-time volunteers.

Responsibility Assignment Matrix

Assigning and reassigning staff to the project can occur for any number of reasons. A simple, but helpful communication tool for ensuring that all tasks have been properly assigned to team members or a group of team members is a *Responsibility Assignment Matrix* (RAM). A basic RAM has vertical columns with a person's name (or role) and horizontal rows with the tasks, work packages, or deliverables (Table 12.2). The simplest way to use a RAM is to enter a √ or an X in a box to assign each task (or work package or deliverable) to the person who is responsible for completing the work.

Table 12.2. Responsibility Assignment Matrix: Annual Dinner

Work Package	Task	Sarah	Tim	Joe	Mary	Marketing Consultant
Invitations	Create Mailing List				√	
Invitations	Address Invitations	√				
Invitations	Design Invitations					√
Invitations	Select Printer			√		

If a more complex responsibility assignment matrix is necessary, consider a type of responsibility matrix known as a *RACI Matrix* (Responsible, Accountable, Consulted, Informed) in which each task or work package is assigned according to:

- *R for responsible:* the person who owns the work and whose efforts result in the completed task or work package
- *A for accountable:* the person who approves the work before the task or work package can be considered complete
- *C for consulted:* the person who plays an advisory role or contributes some sort of knowledge or expertise
- *I for informed:* the person who needs to be kept informed of the progress of the work

The RACI Matrix in Table 12.3 is by work packages. Originally, work package ownership responsibility was assigned to a core team member when the work was determined. The RACI Matrix takes that responsibility to a higher level by assigning approval, consultative, or informative responsibilities to team members.

Table 12.3. RACI Matrix: Annual Dinner

Work Package	Sarah	Tim	Joe	Mary	Marketing Consultant
Location	A	C			I
Entertainment	A		R	C	I
Decorations	I	C		A	
Dinner Reception	A		C	R	I
Dinner	A		C	R	I
Keynote Speaker	A	R		I	C

LEVEL RESOURCES

When staff or other resources are overcommitted, there are two choices. These choices are to extend the project timeline or to level the work. If the timeline cannot be extended, consider leveling the resources by:

- Adding people to the schedule, either from the organization or by using outside temporary workers. Unfortunately, adding more staff might not be the answer. For example, if it takes 2 months to complete a task regardless of how many people are working on the task, adding staff to reduce the time will not be effective.
- Taking a hard look at the float. A person may be scheduled to work 14 hours over 2 days on a task with a duration of 6 days. If this person has dual responsibilities, they might not be able to commit to the 14 hours over 2 days, so spread the work out over the 6 days, instead of 2 days. Spreading the work over the 6 days will eliminate the overcommitment. The alternative of spreading the work out will not work if the task is on the critical path and the end date cannot be extended.
- Changing the resource mix so that instead of using staff, technology will be used. Sometimes a task's duration can be shortened with the use of technology or by using a different type of technology. For example, a software developer needs to test an application. The work, as defined, has the developer creating test scripts and manually testing the application. An alternative resource might be using a third-party tool or a test automation service, which automates the process, shortening the timeframe and enabling the current staff to focus on fixing problems and continuing with the development effort.

If after leveling the resources, the anticipated completion date still cannot be met, consider compressing the schedule by fast tracking or crashing the project.

If fast tracking or crashing is not possible and the only option is to descope the project, discuss this situation with the sponsor. (Compressing the schedule by fast tracking or crashing is discussed in Chapter 11.) If the project scope is modified, remember to modify the scope statement accordingly.

Although descoping, fast tracking, and crashing are techniques that compress a schedule, consider the trade-offs. Adding resources can damage a project's success as much as help the project succeed. If new people who do not have the required skill sets join the team, they will need to be trained, increasing time and cost. New people can also be less productive just because they are new to the team, thus requiring more support time from the current team members as well as the project manager. More time may be required to manage the project or coordinate the work. Spreading the work effort out over more days tends to require additional administrative time because there will be additional starts and stops. If performing the tasks sequentially is better, but to save time tasks are overlapped, also consider the impact to the triple constraints, such as increasing the risk of needing rework or the potential for increasing costs.

IN REVIEW

- Assigning resources is inserting the name of the resource, whether staff, vendor, equipment, materials, software, or some other resource, next to the task in the project plan. Assigning staff is the delegation of work to team members.
- Day-to-day operations and projects routinely have conflicting needs. A project manager within a flat organization that relies on staff with dual responsibilities needs to be creative and innovative when assigning staff.
- Consider using tools and techniques such as a staff utilization chart or resource histogram to assist with determining and communicating overcommitted and underutilized staff resource challenges.
- When staff are overcommitted, extend the project or level the resources by adding people, taking a hard look at float, or changing the resource mix.
- Communicate the assignment of work to staff with the use of a Responsibility Assignment Matrix (RAM) or a RACI Matrix (Responsible, Accountable, Consulted, Informed).

STEP-BY-STEP INSTRUCTIONS

To assign and level resources:

1. Determine the skill sets and staff resource needs:
   - Create a list of skills needed to support the project.
   - Highlight the critical path skill sets and staff needs.
2. Determine the right staff mix. Work with the sponsor and Human Resources to match the needs with potential staff. If staff are not available:
   - Negotiate with managers or other project managers to acquire staff
   - Ask for volunteers
   - Use temporary workers such as contractors and consultants
   - Train people
3. Assign staff to the project by assigning people to tasks along the critical path and then assign people to the remaining tasks.
4. Create a Responsibility Assignment Matrix (RAM) or a RACI Matrix (Responsible, Accountable, Consulted, Informed) to assist with communicating assigned tasks.
5. Analyze the schedule. Determine if people are overcommitted or underutilized. If necessary, create a staff utilization chart or a resource histogram.
6. If people are overcommitted, level the resources by:
   - Extending the project timeline
   - Leveling the work
7. If after assigning resources, the anticipated date cannot be met, compress the schedule by:
   - Fast tracking
   - Crashing
   - Descoping
8. Update the project work plan with the resource and staff names. Update the schedule with any modified start and end dates. Modify the scope and schedule baselines accordingly.
9. Review the project work plan and schedule with the sponsor and stakeholders.
10. Review the comments received from the sponsor and stakeholders with the core team. Clarify any core team questions or concerns.

CHAPTER 13

DETERMINE THE BUDGET

Covered in this chapter:

- Differentiating cost, budget, and forecast numbers
- Identifying direct and indirect costs
- Building a budget using estimating tools and techniques
- Reporting a realistic budget
- Reconciling the proposed budget
- Creating a budget baseline

Now that a scope and a schedule baseline have been created and approved, the original financial resources authorized by management and the cost estimates in the scope statement can be replaced with a realistic, fact-based project budget. With a realistic, fact-based budget, a final project cost estimate is provided to management and an educated decision to proceed with the project is made. If the budget estimate is larger than the funds set aside, management decides to allocate additional funds, reduce the scope, evaluate alternative project approaches, postpone the project, or completely cancel the project.

COST, BUDGET, AND FORECAST NUMBERS

The project's cost, budget, and forecast numbers are three important financial figures that every project manager needs to understand to properly monitor and control the financial health of the project. Project *cost* is the actual expense that the project has incurred or paid for resources, such as equipment, materials, salaries, and vendors. A project *budget* is the amount of money that is allocated or set aside to support the total work effort and the resource needs over the project's life cycle. A project *forecast* is a glimpse into the future providing management with a projection as to what the expenditures are expected to be based on what has occurred to date. A project budget is created during the planning phase of a project while a forecast is created as the project is executed and performance updates are provided.

Unless there is a major change to the project scope that impacts the resource needs, the budget normally does not change—it is the expense dollar amount to which a project manager manages. At the end of the project, the actual costs are compared to the budget. The more accurate the budget estimates are, the better the chances are of having a successful project. Informing a sponsor that additional funds are needed during a project's execution because of an inaccurate budget can be a difficult conversation.

On all projects, two types of costs need to be budgeted: direct and indirect. Direct costs are the costs for resources used only on that particular project: such as materials, supplies, equipment, travel, legal fees, insurance, third-party vendors, and subcontractors. Indirect costs are the shared services for overhead or allocated costs such as rent for office space and furniture, utility expenditures, and management and administrative salaries. Staff costs often are included in a budget. A staff person's salary is a direct cost while employee benefits such as health insurance and vacation expenses are indirect costs. For help understanding direct and indirect costs, speak with the CFO or an accountant.

CREATE A BUDGET

In an ideal world, a project manager can spend whatever amount he or she needs for project success. Many organizations, however, begin projects with limited funds, requiring a project manager to be prudent and thrifty when he or she budgets project expenditures. The challenge: it is the project manager and sponsor's responsibility to ensure the organization has sufficient funds to successfully complete a project. In theory, the project manager is responsible for compiling the cost estimates and creating a realistic budget, based on the available funding and organizational or cultural standards and requirements. The sponsor's responsibility is to ensure the actual funds are available. Some organizations:

- Do not consider that tracking actual project costs against a budget is necessary while others track every cost associated with the project
- Track only the direct costs or selected portions of the project budget, eliminating the tracking of costs felt to be too sensitive or immaterial
- Require a project manager to remain within the authorized budget amount, resulting in the project manager needing to work with the sponsor to descope the project if the estimated budget is over the authorized amount.

Before embarking on the task of building a budget, the project manager meets with the sponsor, the CFO, an accountant, or other appropriate persons to obtain guidance about building and managing a project budget. Questions should be asked, such as:

- What level of detail is required? Should budget estimates be at the task or at the work package level? Is managing the budget at the work package level acceptable?
- Should the budget include direct as well as indirect costs?
- How should salaries and benefits be estimated? Is there a *blended* (or *loaded*) salary rate?
- Is an overall contingency reserve adequate? Or is a contingency reserve required at a work package level?
- What reporting format is required?
- Are there any cost concerns or cost risks the project manager needs to know about?
- Which estimating or combination of estimating tools and techniques are acceptable to determine the costs estimates?

Although the core team might assist with collecting cost-related information, some organizations prefer that the project manager work directly with the sponsor and CFO to develop the budget. Some flat organizations estimate budgets at the task level, but manage a budget at the work package level. Still others estimate budgets at the work package level. Work closely with the sponsor to determine the optimum approach for creating a budget.

After meeting with the sponsor and CFO, gather and compile any relevant cost information, including the estimating worksheets and spreadsheets, industry-specific project templates, and historical project documentation. Determine the estimating tools and techniques (expert opinion, analogous estimating, bottom-up estimating, parametric estimating, and vendor contracts) or the combination of tools and techniques required to determine the project cost estimates or missing cost estimates. For example:

- Use analogous estimating or a top-down approach if limited detail is available, but a similar project or historical cost information can be used for comparison purposes.
- Use bottom-up estimating if detail is available by work package or task, providing a more accurate cost estimate.
- Use parametric estimating if industry guidelines and templates can be used (for example, the number of dollars per square foot for construction material).

Also discuss adding a contingency reserve—the additional expenses for unexpected and unplanned events. For some projects, a percentage of the total budget is adequate and appropriate. Some organizations refer to this reserve as a *project reserve* or *managerial reserve*. (Refer to Chapter 10 if the estimating tools and techniques, including contingency reserves, are unclear.)

One approach to ensure that every work package (and task) has a cost associated with it is to use the estimating spreadsheet that was created earlier in the planning process and review and update it with missing task cost data. Verify that the assumptions, constraints, and risk factors are still valid. Table 13.1 builds on the estimating worksheet created in Chapter 10 (Table 10.4) by confirming that cost estimates were provided for all tasks, a bottom-up approach. The dollar amounts were then summarized at the work package level because in this case, a decision had been made to create the budget at the work package level.

Table 13.1. Budget Estimating Spreadsheet: Annual Dinner

Project: First Annual Dinner
Prepared by: Dave
Date: May

		Work	Non-Staff Cost	Assumptions, Constraints, and Exclusions
1		Project Management (Total)	$1,000	
...	...	...		
2		Venue (Total)	$37,500	
	2.1	Location	$25,000	
	2.2	AV Equipment	$5,000	Only necessary if venue does not provide AV equipment
	2.3	Entertainment/Music	$6,000	
	2.3	Decorations	$1,500	
3		Food and Beverage (Total)	$25,000	
	3.1	Reception	$7,000	
	3.2	Dinner	$18,000	Cost based on $35 per meal for 400 guests plus miscellaneous expense such as taxes, gratuity, etc.
4		Evening Program (Total)	$12,000	
...	...	...		
5		Marketing (Total)	$4,500	
...	...	...		

The easiest costs to estimate (or budget) are the direct costs for specific project resources such as supplies, equipment, travel, and vendors. A vendor's cost is a direct cost and needs to be posted on the spreadsheet and included in the project's budget. (Chapter 16 provides guidance on procuring products or services from vendors.)

The most sensitive cost for many organizations to estimate is salary cost, a direct cost, and related employee benefits costs, an indirect cost. Common, particularly on smaller projects, is to exclude salary and benefit costs in a project budget because an organization has potential confidentiality concerns. Some organizations may view salary and benefit costs as *sunk cost*, a cost that has already been incurred and cannot be recovered, and opt to eliminate salary and related employee benefit costs from the project budget. Still other organizations think eliminating salary and benefit costs provides an incomplete cost picture, so they opt to use a weighted approach.

A weighed approach is used by many vendors and consultants. Staff are classified into categories such as management, business analyst, construction worker, or engineer. Each category is then assigned a salary rate:

- *An average salary rate:* Everyone's salary in a particular category is added together and divided by the number people in the category. A different rate or percentage is used for employee benefits.
- *A blended (or loaded) salary rate:* The median salary rate for the category plus the employee benefits are used to determine a single rate. This single rate also could include allocated dollars for other indirect costs such as office space. A single blended (loaded) rate of $85 per hour for each business analyst is easier to budget (and later manage) than a salary rate of $56 per hour, benefits that are 33% of the hourly rate (or $18.48 of $56), and $10.50 for office space, equipment, and administrative costs.
- *A unique salary rate:* A rate that is unique to the organization based on the organization's budgeting process.

The blended or loaded salary rate by staff category or by organization, particularly if the rate includes indirect costs, is the preferred rate by some project managers because there is only one rate by staff category, which eliminates the need to budget and later manage multiple expense categories and simplifies work for the project manager.

Suggestion: Use a notional budget. If your organization does not monitor and control the project budget, consider asking the sponsor if creating a notational budget—an imaginary or hypothetical budget—is possible. The reason to do this is that a project manager needs to understand the financial aspects of the project, including how to build, monitor, and control the budget and how to use the tools to keep the project on track for success. Monitor and control involves calculating project variances, which requires budget and actual costs. When creating a notional budget, attempt to use realistic estimates.

REPORT THE BUDGET

After reviewing and estimating costs for the deliverables, work packages, and tasks, create a budget report (a budget plan report). The purpose of the budget report is to assist the project manager with the management of actual costs against the budgeted dollar amounts. As the project is monitored and controlled, the project manager will use the budget report to provide updates of expenditures to management and forecast future expenditures. The budget report provides information about the amounts of money expended, when the money was expended, and how much budgeted money remains to be expended.

Decide on the format for the budget report during the project's planning phase. An organization might have a specific preferred budget report format, but one common format ties expenses to the work packages and deliverables in the project work plan and schedule and includes a contingency reserve category. Table 13.2 is an example of a common format. In this example, the actual dollar amounts posted in the month and year-to-date columns are zero because the project is still in the planning process and there have been no expenditures as of yet. Based on the schedule, the project will start start in June. Do not wait until there are expenditures to create a budget report.

RECONCILE THE BUDGET

With the budget plan complete, compare the budget estimate to the original budget authorized by management and the cost estimates in the scope statement. It is possible for the final budget estimate total to be larger than the amount of money set aside for the project. To reduce the budget, reconcile the budget by following a process similar to compressing the schedule. Look for ways to reduce the task costs. Determine if there are alternative resource options or find additional funding sources. Talk to the sponsor. He or she might know of some additional funding sources. The goal is to reduce the overall cost, but to not reduce the quality of the final product or service. Some possible actions include:

- Reviewing the estimates to ensure they are realistic because overestimating potential costs is easy

- Using a staff person instead of a consultant or considering using a lower-cost consultant if they can provide a satisfactory level of quality
- Considering the possibility of using standard stock materials (if the same deliverable quality is possible) instead of the custom or high-end materials budgeted
- Considering leasing instead of purchasing equipment

Another option is to descope the project by removing (or postponing to a later project) some of the deliverable's features and functionality. If the project is descoped or alternatives are implemented, update the scope statement and obtain sponsor sign-off. Then rework the scope and schedule. Regardless of how much the overall cost is reduced, the possibility exists that once the sponsor and others in management review the budget plan, the project will be placed on hold until additional funding is available or they may decide to cancel the project.

Table 13.2. Budget Report: Annual Dinner

Project: First Annual Dinner
Prepared by: Dave
Date: May

			Month 1: June			Year-to-Date		
		Work	**BUDGET**	**ACTL**	**VAR**	**BUDGET**	**ACTL**	**VAR**
1		Project Management (Total)	$250	0	0	$1,000	0	0
...	...	...	...	...	...	...	...	...
2		Venue (Total)	0	0	0	$37,500	0	0
	2.1	Location	$2,000	0	0	$25,000	0	0
	2.2	AV Equipment	0	0	0	$5,000	0	0
	2.3	Entertainment/Music	0	0	0	$6,000	0	0
	2.4	Decorations	0	0	0	$1,500	0	0
3		Food and Beverage (Total)	0	0	0	$25,000	0	0
	3.1	Reception	0	0	0	$7,000	0	0
	3.2	Dinner	$1,000	0	0	$18,000	0	0
4		Evening Program (Total)	$1,000	0	0	$12,000	0	0
...	...	...	...	...	...	...	...	...
5		Marketing (Total)	$100			$4,500		
...	...	...	...	...	...	...	...	...
		Contingency Reserve	$5,000			$5,000		
		TOTAL	...	...	...	...	...	...

CREATE THE BUDGET BASELINE

Once the project budget has been prepared and approved, a *budget baseline* is created. Think of the budget baseline as a snapshot of the potential costs. It is this baseline that will be used by the project manager to track actual cost against the budgeted dollar amounts and to create the forecast. With the budget baseline in place, all three of the triple constraints—work (scope), time (schedule), and cost (budget)—now have baselines established. Each baseline is used to manage and control the project as the work (the execution phase) is performed.

IN REVIEW

- Three financial numbers a project manager needs to understand are cost, budget, and forecast. The project budget is the amount of money set aside based on the work and resource needs of the project. Project cost is the actual expenditures. The forecast is the project's expected future expenditures based on current to-date expenditures.
- Although it is the project manager's responsibility to estimate and compile direct and indirect costs and create a realistic, fact-based budget for the project, the project manager needs to work closely with the project sponsor and CFO.
- The same estimating tools and techniques are used to estimate cost as to estimate the project's time and resources.
- If contingency reserves are not applied at the deliverable, work package, or task level, consideration should be given to applying a contingency reserve that is a percentage of the total budget amount for unknown and unexpected expenditures.
- Compare and reconcile the proposed budget to the original budget authorized by management and the cost estimates in the scope statement. The reconciliation continues until the budget estimate reaches an acceptable dollar amount, which enables the project to proceed or a decision to be made to halt the project.
- With an approved budget, a budget baseline is established. Create a budget report to be used in reporting performance information about the actual cost, budget, and forecast.

STEP-BY-STEP INSTRUCTIONS

When creating a budget:

1. Meet with the sponsor and the CFO (or an accountant) to determine the appropriate budget detail level and format.
2. Gather and review project-related documentation:
   - Collect project documents created to date: estimating worksheets, spreadsheets, and related notes.
   - Review organizational policies and procedures: standard budget report formats, budgeting level, and approach to estimating salaries and related indirect costs.
   - Consult historical information to obtain detailed cost planning information from similar projects and lessons learned.
   - Obtain industry-specific project templates and third-party resource rates.
3. Determine the estimating tools and techniques or the combination of estimating tools and techniques to use. Consult with experts, the sponsor, or other project managers to obtain advice.
4. Estimate the costs for each deliverable, work package, or task:
   - Determine the costs necessary to complete each work package and task.
   - Indicate any constraints, assumptions, alternatives, and risks for each work package and task.
5. Determine the contingency reserve(s) either as a percentage of the total budget or by deliverable, work package, or task.
6. Create a budget report.
7. If the budget estimate is more than the original estimated cost or order of magnitude cost, reconcile the budget by:
   - Reviewing cost estimates to ensure they are not overestimated
   - Evaluating alternative costing options
   - Obtaining additional funds
   - Descoping with the assistance of the sponsor
8. Review the budget with the sponsor and determine:
   - If the project should proceed
   - If the project proceeds with modifications
   - If the project is to be postponed or halted

9. If modifications are necessary to the project plan, modify the work plan and schedule accordingly, creating "new" scope and schedule baselines.
10. If the budget is approved, establish a budget baseline.
11. Review the budget baseline with the core team. Clarify any core team questions or concerns.

SECTION 4

STILL MORE PLANNING

The scope, schedule, and budget are now in place, but the planning process might not be complete. Before starting to execute the project, your organization may need to create a few additional plans: risk, quality, procurement, or communication. All of these plans are considered part of an overall project management plan, but all of them might not be required for a particular project. Other plans that are unique to the project or organization, such as a logistics plan, may also be needed.

The timing for creating these additional plans varies. For example, creating a procurement plan before estimating the resources might be prudent if there is heavy reliance on a third-party vendor for a particular raw material necessary to build a product. For a high-risk project, a project manager might want to start creating a risk plan as soon as the planning process starts so that risk strategies are considered as the project plan is written. A project manager might also decide that a particular plan, such as a quality plan, is a "deliverable" that needs to be created during the project's execution. The project manager would then build the work and time required to create the quality plan into the overall project plan. Regardless of when these additional plans are created, if they impact the scope, schedule, or budget baselines, modify and establish a new baseline(s) prior to starting the project execution phase.

A point to remember as this section is read is that a plan does not need to be a formal written document. A plan is a method or an approach for doing something. In a flat organization, depending on the project as well as the organization, the plan could be a formal, written document or a very informal approach that is only discussed and then followed. This section covers:

Chapter 14. Determine Project Risks: Focuses on the identification, assessment, prioritization, and rating of potential positive and negative risks based on impact and probability, risk response strategies, and the creation of a tracking mechanism to assist with monitoring and managing risk

Chapter 15. Ensure Quality: Explains the relationship between quality criteria and the scope statement, different quality tools and techniques, and the need to monitor and communicate a quality standard

Chapter 16. Procure the Right Resources: Focuses on understanding an organization's procurement process, the make-or-buy decision in a project setting, the importance of vendor relationships, and engaging a vendor

Chapter 17. Communicate the Right Information: Explains basic communication concepts and the need to define the best ways to share information, interact, and exchange ideas

CHAPTER 14

DETERMINE PROJECT RISKS

Covered in this chapter:

- Definition of risk
- Identifying project risks
- Assessing, prioritizing, and rating risk
- Planning risk response strategies
- Monitoring and managing risk using a risk register
- Modifying the project plan based on potential risks

Precisely predicting the future is impossible. All projects are plagued by unknowns, uncertainties, and unexpected events known as *project risks*. If the planning process to date has been thorough and realistic, project risks will be minimal, but what if an unexpected event does occur? What if there is a need to respond to a setback? To address these possibilities, the project manager and core team should take the time to identify, assess, and prioritize potential project risks. Then they should develop a strategy to avoid or minimize negative risks and a plan to optimize the benefits of positive risks. A risk strategy, even an informal strategy, that addresses potential risks, their probability of occurrence, their impact to the project, and the contingency plans for the risky events is a must. A project may have only a few potential risks of concern, but just one unplanned event can influence the project's overall success.

WHAT IS RISK?

Risk is an unexpected event or condition that, if it occurs, will have a negative or positive impact on the project. Thinking about risk and documenting potential risks commenced when the project was authorized. Potential risks were considered as the work was determined, the timing was understood, and costs were estimated, but now the project manager and core team need to take a harder look at the potential risks and evaluate the probability and impact of unexpected events.

There is a caveat to this statement. The timing of evaluating risk can (and does) vary by project. On occasion, risk planning starts before the work is defined. For example, a project manager for a project that has a regulatory or legal requirement that results in hefty fines if the completion date is not met might start developing a risk strategy as soon as the scope statement is signed. As another example, a project manager might be aware of some potential risks and is concerned that these risks could have a major impact on the scope and schedule. In this instance, the project manager assesses the risks and plans the risk strategies before the critical path is determined and a schedule is created.

Risk management assumes it is possible to anticipate all unexpected events and creates contingencies for each risk. In reality, however, it is always possible to experience an unplanned event for which there is no strategy—there are no contingencies. Risks can be overlooked and missed; it happens. The goal of risk planning is to identify the risks that are likely to happen, plan contingency responses in case they do happen, and then monitor the potential risks for changes throughout the remainder of the project.

IDENTIFY RISK

The easiest way to identify risk is to ask: "What can go wrong with this project?" Think about the "what if's." *What if* a key team member is no longer available due to daily operational demands? *What if* the materials are delivered too early or too late? *What if* a task cannot be completed in the allocated timeframe? *What if* it rains the day of the outdoor event? There is more to risk management, however, than just asking what if questions to identify risks. Start by identifying categories (or sources) of risk; then consider negative and positive risks and the internal and external risks.

Consider the risk categories. There are two categories of risk: project management-related risks and categories related to the final deliverable or the various work packages. For each category, ask questions. It is possible that there will be some overlap when questions are asked in each category, but the chances of overlooking a risk will be minimized. Project management-related categories and questions could include:

Staff:
- Does everyone have the required training?
- Does everyone on the team work well together?
- How will the resignation of a key team member be handled?

Work:
- Has the project been tried in the past and failed?
- Is the deliverable to be moved into operations? If so, have any operational quality requirements been overlooked?
- Are there any regulatory or compliance issues?

Schedule:
- Have the estimates been created as a unit—duration, level of effort, and resources? If not, are there any potential time problems?
- Have the right people been involved in the estimates?
- Has the schedule taken into account other organizational priorities?

Cost:
- Does the possibility exist that the project budget might be cut?
- Is there a cash flow shortage that could affect when supplies and materials are purchased?
- Are there any cost-related contract issues that could influence the schedule?

Final deliverable or work package related categories and questions could include:

Environmental:
- If the deliverable is an outdoor event, what will happen if there are severe storms?

Logistical:
- If the deliverable is a product that requires materials so that it can be built, what will happen if there is a transportation strike?

Technical:
- If heavy reliance on a technology is required to build the product, what will happen if a key equipment component fails?

Testing:
- If the final deliverable is a software application or a new website, is the test data realistic?

Next review the scope, schedule, and budget as well as project documents and determine the worst events or mishaps that could happen in each risk category. Consider the events that could cause the project to deviate from the plan either positively or negatively. Pay particular attention to the tasks on the critical path because a delay in a critical path task impacts the completion date.

Consider the negative and positive risks. Typically, risk is thought to be *negative* or a threat. For example, a union strike is a risk that could delay the receipt of raw materials. If the raw materials are needed to complete a task on the critical path, the project completion date could be impacted. Risks, however, can also be *positive* or an opportunity. For example, a rain-free period is a risk that can result in outside building work being completed two days ahead of schedule, but a positive risk does not necessarily mean the project will be completed ahead of schedule. Ask: how can the opportunity be exploited? Then use the answer to craft the risk response strategy.

Consider the internal and external risks. *Internal risks* are events that occur within the bounds of the project that the project manager can manage and control. For example, the project manager could manage and control the internal risk of:

- Substandard work products by implementing a good quality-control process
- A key staff person resigning by ensuring that the key person has a backup

External risks are events that the project manager has no control or influence over. External risks are often unknown or hidden, making it difficult, if not impossible, to identify them beforehand. For example, the project manager has no control over:

- A hurricane, a flood, or some other natural disaster
- The closing of a major highway due to an accident

CREATE A RISK REGISTER

Document each risk in a *risk register*. A risk register provides details on all risks, including the category, description, impact, probability, response (including status), and owner. After each risk is identified by category, the risk is documented in the risk register and then each risk is assessed and prioritized. The risk register is used to monitor and manage risk throughout the project.

Suggestion: Use the Delphi technique. One way to obtain opinions, ideas, and a consensus is to use a method known as the Delphi technique, which is an anonymous information-gathering method. The Delphi technique can be used to gather information to determine (or estimate) the likelihood of the risk occurrence and the outcome of future risk events. A person (often called a facilitator) sends questionnaires to the key stakeholders or experts. Then the responses are consolidated and returned to the respondents with a request for additional feedback. Responses and comments to the questionnaire are then sorted by category and additional comments are requested. This process continues until there is a consensus and comfort level with the risks identified and the response strategies. The Delphi technique is anonymous—no names are attached to the comments, opinions, or responses to the questionnaires—people therefore tend to give honest feedback.

ASSESS AND PRIORITIZE RISK

A simplified approach to assessing and prioritizing each risk is to rate the impact and probability of the risk by using a high, medium, and low rating system. *Impact* refers to the effect the risk will have on the project's constraints—scope, time (schedule), and cost (budget)—and the potential quality of the final deliverable. *Probability* refers to the likelihood that the risk will occur. In a high, medium, and low system, each risk is assigned a rating for impact and another rating for probability. The combination of the ratings results in a priority rating.

Before rating each risk, define the objective criteria or what is meant by high (or serious), medium (or significant), and low (or minor) so that everyone will have the same understanding. The objective criteria need to be based on facts and should not be based on the opinion of an evaluator (a subjective assessment). For impact, high, medium, and low definitions might be:

- *High:* The risk has a catastrophic effect that could result in the project being cancelled, such as having a project objective in the scope statement that is no longer feasible or attainable, forcing a major change in possibly all of the constraints.
- *Medium:* The risk does not cause the project to fail or be cancelled, but a requirement might not be attainable, forcing a change in one or more of the constraints.
- *Low:* The risk results in no or only minor changes to the constraints.

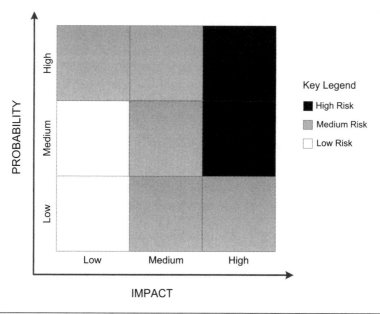

Figure 14.1. The probability-impact matrix.

For probability, high, medium, and low definitions might be:

- *High*: The risk is likely to occur or the chance of occurrence is more than 67%.
- *Medium*: The risk might occur or the chance of occurrence is between 34% and 66%.
- *Low*: The risk is unlikely to occur, but it could; the chance of occurrence is less than 33%.

After the impact and probability of each risk are rated, prioritize each risk. Priority is determined by combining the probability rating with the impact rating. Assign a high-probability, high-impact risk a high priority rating; assign a low-probability, low-impact risk a low priority rating. The Probability-Impact Matrix is a tool that assists with assigning risk (Figure 14.1). Using the matrix, plot each risk. Then update the risk register with the priority rating for each risk.

PLAN FOR RISK

A project manager and core team need to be adaptable, flexible, and creative when resolving unplanned events, but having a potential response enables an action to be executed quickly if an unplanned event does arise. A risk response strategy does not need to be created for every risk, but a response strategy should be created for each high-priority risk. Medium-priority risks may or may not require a response strategy. Some project managers think all medium-priority risks require a strategy. Other project managers only monitor medium-risk priorities and create a strategy if it is thought that the impact or probability of occurrence has increased. Still other project managers use their judgment, selectively deciding if a medium-priority risk requires a strategy. For example, a project manager might think that a strategy should be determined for any medium-priority risk that has high-probability and medium-impact ratings. Low-priority risks may only require periodic monitoring. The low-priority risks normally are placed on a "watchlist" so if something *triggers* a change in a risk's priority, the project manager can respond quickly before damage occurs to the project. A *trigger* is an event, a signal, indicating that a risk event is likely to happen. If the trigger occurs, the project manager should start watching for the risk event and managing the potential risk closely.

When developing risk responses, there are four response techniques for negative risks: *avoid, transfer, mitigate,* and *accept.* There are also four response techniques for positive risks: *exploit, enhance, share,* and accept. Acceptance is a response technique used for both positive and negative risks.

Negative Risks: Avoid, Transfer, Mitigate, and Accept

Avoid. Avoidance is the best response to negative risk, but avoidance requires identifying an alternative approach. Whenever possible, attempt to avoid a risk or eliminate as many possible causes of the risk as you can. Avoiding a risk normally requires changes to one or more of the triple constraints and might require modifications to the scope, schedule, and budget:

- A start-up business has been offered low-rent retail space, but just before signing the lease, the business owners discover that a road expansion project is scheduled. The road will be under construction for the next 18 months making it hard, if not impossible, for potential clients to visit the retail space. Instead of signing the lease, a new location is found avoiding the risk of no or limited clients being able to visit the retail space.
- A company needs to purchase a physical security product to control access to the raw materials needed for a product development effort. A physical security hardware manufacturer reports that their hardware has a 0.00001% chance of malfunctioning, but a recent industry report cites higher-than-expected failure rates for the hardware. The

company makes a decision to use a different physical security product avoiding the risk of having a physical security problem.

Transfer. Transfer of risk occurs when the risk is assigned to another person or a third party. Normally some sort of payment is involved, such as purchasing insurance or a warranty or providing some sort of guarantee:

- A project manager purchases flood insurance because a flood could seriously damage a product prototype being created at a manufacturing facility. The risk of damage to the prototype and the facility is transferred to the insurance company.
- The project manager signs a *fixed-price service contract* (a service provided for a specific price) with a third-party consultant. The risk of a cost overrun is transferred to the consultant.

Mitigate. Mitigation is the lowering of the probability of a risk occurring by lessening the probability of the occurrence or the degree of impact. Mitigation could require adding additional tasks and updating the project plan. Some mitigation strategies are relatively easy and low cost to implement:

- A project has a tight deadline constraint and the preferred vendor used in the past is not known to deliver parts in a timely fashion. Even though the preferred vendor's cost per part is lower than others in the industry, the project manager might decide to mitigate the risk by using a different, more reliable vendor or by signing a contract with a more reliable vendor to deliver a portion of the parts required for the project.
- The chance of rain occurring is 50%. If it rains, the fundraising event will need to be cancelled indefinitely. To mitigate the risk of the event being cancelled, tents are rented and set up.

Accept. Using acceptance as a response technique to a negative risk means accepting the possibility of the risk and, other than monitoring it, not doing anything about the risk.

- A business decides to be the first in their industry vertical to implement a software application. Because the project team performed a thorough evaluation of the software and the vendor is willing to provide some implementation support free of charge, the project manager and the sponsor are willing to accept the risk that the software is unproven.

Positive Risks: Exploit, Enhance, Share, and Accept

Exploit. Exploiting is doing everything possible to take advantage of a potential opportunity, which could include assigning the best staff available to a task or to a series of tasks:

- Business at a small café has been slow because a major retailer has closed a nearby store, but a new retailer has just finished renovating the space and has planned a grand opening. The café owner exploits the grand opening of the new store by creating a marketing campaign with flyers, email announcements, and Facebook postings suggesting that the café is a great place to take a break from shopping and eat lunch or dinner.
- A website needs to be updated with information about a fundraising event, but there is no money to pay anyone for their time to update the website. The organization's director knows of a volunteer who might be able to assist with the update and not charge a fee. The director asks the volunteer if he or she would be willing to donate their time.

Enhance. Enhancement is making an effort to increase the odds of the opportunity occurring by making the opportunity more likely to occur. The enhancement could be used in combination with another response approach:

- The small café that is exploiting the new retailer's grand opening with a marketing campaign, might consider enhancing the campaign by providing free samples and a discount on lunch and dinner purchased the day of the retailer's grand opening.
- People are always generous during an organization's annual canned goods food drive. This year a local grocery store chain has pledged to increase the number of turkeys they donate by 15% if the number of canned and dried goods donations increases by at least 10%. To enhance the chances of receiving additional turkeys, the organization solicits the assistance of a major local business to collect canned goods donations. The business agrees to place canned goods donation boxes in strategic locations in their office building.

Share. Sharing occurs when taking advantage of an opportunity is harder without the assistance of someone or something:

- Holding an in-house training program requires a minimum of ten people, but the organization has only six people. Another organization wants the same training, but only has five people. By combining efforts, the two organizations are able to hold an in-house training session and share the cost.

- Two different, but related, projects need the same application expert to assist with an implementation effort. The person is only available on a full-time basis, but neither project needs the person full time. To increase synergy and assist with keeping both projects on schedule, the two project managers decide to jointly hire and share the same person so that the person works full time, splitting the time between the two efforts.

Accept. Using acceptance as a response technique to a positive risk is similar to using acceptance for a negative risk in that nothing is done. If a positive risk does occur, the project manager lets the opportunity to benefit the project pass without taking action:

- While performing an internet search, a project manager found a free, new-and-improved marketing newsletter application that claimed it would save time and was easy to use, but instead of changing and using a different application, the project manager decided to continue using the organization's current newsletter application which was costly and difficult to use. The project manager accepted the risk of missing the work package completion date and opted not to decrease the project cost.

For each identified risk, update the risk register with the potential risk response and assign an owner. For smaller projects, all risks might be assigned to the project manager, but a risk could also be assigned to a core team member or a key stakeholder. For example, a key stakeholder might be the person who signed the contract with a third-party vendor. Any risks associated with the vendor are therefore the stakeholder's responsibility to monitor and resolve.

Suggestion: Brainstorm risk possibilities. One of the best ways to identify project risks and responses is to hold a brainstorming session with the project manager, core team, sponsor, stakeholders, and experts. To identify potential risk, the group should discuss topics such as:

- What happens if a task *not* on the critical path with a small float is all of a sudden late due to a problem, placing the delayed task on the critical path? What if the late task causes a delay in the project?
- Are a number of different risks due to the same root cause?

- Are time and resource assumptions made during the estimating process still valid?
- Is there anything that could make the project easier so that it could be completed sooner?
- How do we handle something that reduces the overall cost?

Then review the risks and assumptions in the scope statement and determine if they are still valid or if any other risks are associated with the assumptions that need to be considered. For each risk, walk through possible scenarios and imagine what could happen. Focus on how each risk will affect the project's objective(s) and goal. Jointly rate each scenario's impact on scope, time, and cost. Determine the probability of the scenario occurring. Discuss each risk's priority, potential courses of actions, and potential triggers.

A Scenario: A Risk Register for a Website Project

The easiest way to understand risk is to create a risk register for a project. In this scenario, a business is replacing their current website. A project plan has been created and a website designer has been hired. There are six work packages: project management, requirements, design, development, testing, and implementation. Lauren, the project manager, and the core team decide that the best way for them to determine if they have missed anything during planning is to brainstorm. The brainstorming session will consist of a detailed review of the project plan's scope, schedule, and budget each work package.

Although a number of potential risks are discussed during the brainstorming session, Lauren and the core team think that if the project is managed and everyone does their job that the risk of having problems will be minimal. They did, however, identify three risk categories that they think need to be monitored:

- *Staff:* The stakeholders responsible for updating the website with event information were not included in the website prototype review, which could result in an unacceptable design.
- *Work:* The contract with the vendor describes the final deliverable, but the team is not sure how they are to verify that the website meets the expected organizational requirements and standards.
- *Vendor:* The business knows very little about the website developer. Although they have seen some of the developer's work, there are concerns that the completion date could be missed, impacting the rollout of a new product launch.

Table 14.1. Risk Register with Three Categories to Be Monitored

Project Name: New Website							
Date: May							

	CAT	Description	Impact	Probability	Priority	Response	Owner
1	Staff	Stakeholders responsible for updating website with event information were not included in website prototype review.	High	Medium	High	Meet with stakeholders the team thinks should be included in prototype review; update schedule.	Wayne
2	Work	Contract with vendor described final deliverable, but team is unsure how they will verify that website meets requirements outlined in contract.	High	High	High	Create quality checklist to use to accept website; update scope and schedule.	Victoria
3	Vendor	Website consultant has committed to a delivery date, but team is concerned that date might not be met, impacting rollout of new product launch.	Medium	High	Medium	Meet with vendor to discuss project expectations and discuss concerns.	Wayne

The project team decided to come up with a strategy to *avoid* the first risk, *mitigate* the second risk, and *accept* the third risk. The project plan was adjusted accordingly and a risk register was created using Excel (Table 14.1).

Identifying, assessing, and prioritizing risks and then developing risk response strategies are major parts of creating a risk plan, but before stating that the risk plan is complete, review the scope, schedule, and budget to determine if they require modifications. Additionally, evaluate the funding set aside as a contingency reserve and determine if it is adequate in light of the risk plan.

TO REVIEW

- A risk is any unexpected event or condition that impacts a project negatively or positively.
- Even if the number of negative risks that need to be planned for is minimal, the risks cannot be ignored because these risks could hamper the project's success or result in the project being cancelled.
- Risks can be negative (a threat) or positive (an opportunity) as well as internal (can be managed by the project manager) or external (cannot be managed by the project manager—he or she has no control of or influence on these risks).
- Potential risks are assessed and rated based on their impact (or the effect the risk will have on the scope, time, cost, and quality) and the probability (or the likelihood) that the risk will occur. The assessment can be as simple as using a high, medium, or low rating system. Risk priority is determined by combining the probability rating and the impact rating.
- Based on each risk's priority and an organization's approach to responding to risk, a risk strategy is created. There are four response techniques for negative risks: avoid, transfer, mitigate, and accept and four response techniques for positive risks: exploit, enhance, share, and accept.
- Before a risk plan is complete, the project plan is reviewed and modified accordingly.

STEP-BY-STEP INSTRUCTIONS

To determine a project's risks and a risk strategy:

1. Gather and review project-related documentation.
   - Collect documents created to date: the scope statement, the scope, schedule, and budget baselines, and related notes.
   - Consult historical information: risk strategies from similar projects and lessons learned.
   - Review published information: project success stories and benchmark studies.
2. If there is no organizational standard for rating and prioritizing risks, determine:
   - How the impact and the probability of the identified risks will be rated and prioritized
   - The level of detail that will be documented for each risk

3. Determine how the risks are to be identified, including:
    - The participants, such as the project manager, core team, sponsor, and stakeholders
    - The technique(s) to be used, such as reviewing documentation, interviews, brainstorming, questionnaires, or another technique
4. Determine the risk categories. Using a risk register, identify and assess potential risks:
    - Group the risks into the risk categories.
    - Provide a description of each risk and what will occur if the risk event happens.
    - Identify the impact and probability for each risk.
    - Determine the priority for each risk.
    - Determine risk response strategies.
    - Document the response plan.
    - Assign an owner to each risk.
5. Determine if the project plan (scope, schedule, and budget) needs to be modified. If so, update the project plan and modify the baselines accordingly.
6. Communicate and discuss the risk strategy with the sponsor and key stakeholders.

CHAPTER 15

ENSURE QUALITY

Covered in this chapter:

- Definition of quality
- Difference between quality assurance and quality control
- Linkage between quality and risk
- Determining quality criteria
- Monitoring quality with tools and techniques

A common cause for project failure is the final deliverable does not conform to requirements. One way to ensure a satisfactory product or service is to create a quality plan. Creating a quality plan does not need to be an onerous task nor does a quality plan need to be a formal, detailed written document. A quality plan builds on the acceptance criteria in the scope statement by developing measurable criteria; requires formal and informal actions to be implemented so that the final deliverable conforms to requirements; and ensures the project is executed efficiently. The hardest task for a project manager when creating a quality plan might be determining the right balance between the cost of implementing quality assurance and control and the cost of producing the final product or service.

WHAT IS A QUALITY DELIVERABLE?

A high-quality plan for a project ensures that the project follows the organization's project management methodology, but a high-quality plan for the final deliverable ensures that the final product or service is of high quality and meets, if not exceeds, the acceptance criteria outlined in the scope statement. The quality plan for the deliverable builds on the description, objectives, requirements, and acceptance criteria in the scope statement. It is based on what is known and what is expected and outlines a course of action to ensure that the project team delivers a final product or service that satisfies the sponsor and conforms to requirements. Conformance to requirements suggests:

- Firmly understanding the *stated and implied requirements* **and**
- Ensuring that the deliverable is the *best product design* or *service fit* based on the customer's needs

Project requirements explicitly stated in the scope statement are used as a starting point. The *implied* or common sense requirements are those that are left unsaid, but that are just as critical to the success of the final deliverable as the stated requirements. It is the understanding of the *stated and implied* requirements that helps ensure that the sponsor is satisfied with the outcome of the project. The combined stated and implied requirements also highlight what the product or service is supposed to do. The *best fit* pertains to the execution phase of the project and ensures that the final deliverable does what it is suppose to do and does it well.

As an example, the pages of a new ecommerce website are easy to read (an *expressed requirement*), but the order-processing navigation is difficult. There are too many required pages to place an order, so potential customers are abandoning the site before their orders are complete. The sponsor never discussed the order-processing requirements, but assumed (the *implied requirement*), based on conversations and the goal of the website, that the order-processing navigation would be simple and easy to use. The final deliverable, although seemingly complete, did not fully satisfy the sponsor, did not confirm to the requirements, nor was it the *best fit* because it did not include easy-to-use order-processing navigation.

DETERMINE THE QUALITY CRITERIA

The first step when creating a quality plan is to determine the criteria necessary to measure how closely the final product or service meets the requirements. As the detailed quality criteria are defined, the project team ties the quality criteria to the requirements documentation and the acceptance criteria noted in the scope statement. As the project team reviews and analyzes the various documents, the project team determines if there are any implied requirements that have not been documented for which quality criteria needs to be defined. Criteria can be based on:

- *Metrics:* The customer's requirement is 95% of the gifts are to be shipped by November 15.

- *Regulations:* Toys cannot be painted with lead-based paint.
- *Standards or best practices:* Application testing must include positive- and negative-scenario tests.

Criteria can be formatted as:

- *Interrogatives:* "Is the company logo the right size on the brochure?"
- *Statements:* The company logo on the brochure is 2 inches by 2 inches.

Next, determine a baseline or the minimum level that is required to provide an acceptable deliverable. When thinking about the acceptable quality baseline level, consider a story about a retail bakery.

During the annual holiday butter cookie sale, the bakery had a sign posted on a wall. The first statement on the sign referred to the "high-quality butter" used that resulted in "the best butter cookies in the region." During previous holiday seasons, customers would wait in line to purchase the bakery's butter cookies. When the ability for customers to place orders via the internet was provided, sales increased 30%. In an effort to save money and increase profits, the owners decided to purchase lower-quality butter. The new butter changed the buttery taste of the cookies. Customers noticed that the cookies were not the quality they expected. Within two weeks, the bakery noticed a decrease in the volume of cookie sales. In this case, although the cookies with the new butter were still buttery, the cookies did not meet the customers' requirements or expectations, the *acceptable quality baseline.*

UNDERSTAND QUALITY ASSURANCE AND QUALITY CONTROL

Quality has two parts—assurance and control. *Quality assurance* is the prevention of problems or are all standards and procedures being followed so that a quality problem does not occur? *Quality control* is the inspection or the reviewing of the deliverable for problems.

The project manager needs to plan for both quality assurance and quality control because preventing a potential problem costs less than fixing the problem later in the project. The challenge is that implementing standards and procedures to prevent problems as well as inspecting deliverables for problems both have costs. To determine the cost of quality, the project manager considers the time necessary to create the tool or technique (such as a process standard or a checklist) and to train the team members in the tool or technique as well as the time that needs to be allocated to the team members to inspect the work.

The project manager then carefully balances those costs against the probability that a problem will occur. For example, if the chances for a problem with the quality of the product are low and the cost to develop and implement a procedure or process to inspect the product to prevent the problem is high (and there are no regulatory or legal requirements), the project manager might decide against designing and implementing a quality plan. When considering the trade-off, remember to factor in the nonfinancial reputational cost of lower quality arising from forgoing quality assurance and control efforts.

MONITOR THE WORK

Just as in the annual cookie sale at the retail bakery, monitoring quality can be as simple and informal as publically posting the quality standards, which is the implementation of a quality assurance measure. In the bakery example, because the list was on the wall, every day the bakery employees were reminded of the bakery's quality standards and the customers' expectations. On some projects, communicating the quality standards and providing simple reminders about them are all team members need.

For other projects, inspecting the product or service or using a checklist to confirm compliance may be the right solution. Inspections and checklists are two common quality tools and techniques that work well.

Inspections

Inspecting a product or service is one of the easiest ways to monitor the quality of the product or service, but also a technique that tends to be overlooked or not even defined for a project, particularly if the project team is accustomed to informal communication and limited controls. Organizations routinely think about inspections in the context of the day-to-day operational aspects of the business. For example, in the candy business, inspection guidelines are in place to ensure a chocolate candy bud is a certain size and shape. The inspection standards are defined, staff members are trained in the standards, and the standards necessary to ensure that quality is maintained are understood.

Inspect common items on projects such as:

- Supplies and materials received from a vendor
- Services provided by a vendor
- The product or service being produced by the project team

Not inspecting supplies and materials received from a third party can impact the product or service being worked on by the project team. Inspect what is received, when it is received, to ensure it meets the quality requirements. Inspect the product or service being produced by the team, ensuring that it confirms to the scope statement. If there is a regulatory standard or requirement, inspect the product to ensure there is compliance with the law.

When inspecting a product or service being produced by a project team, it is easy for a project manager to say to team members, "If there are too many defects, let me know." What does that comment mean? In an effort to maintain informality, the project manager might not take the time to clarify what is meant by "too many defects." The positive in a flat organizational culture is that team members communicate frequently with one another. Additionally, the team members tend to have dual responsibilities, so there could be a better understanding of what "too many defects" means in the organization. The negative is there could still be misunderstandings. Provide inspection guidelines and metrics, such as: "If one out of ten is defective, let me know." Providing clear inspection guidelines is good practice.

Checklists

A checklist can be as simple or complex as necessary. A checklist can be written at any time in a project's life cycle, but the time required to develop the checklist needs to be included in the project plan. How detailed the checklist is depends on the experience and skill level of the team members as well as on the project's requirements. Checklists can:

- Prevent team members from making common mistakes
- Provide a consistent standard for all on the team to follow
- Be used to inspect a product or service to ensure it meets specific features or functionality

Checklists for quality (may also be referred to as quality checklists) can be used on just about every type of project from manufacturing and technical projects to marketing projects and a dinner event. A checklist is a versatile tool that supports quality assurance and quality control efforts. To illustrate how a checklist can be used to support assurance as well as control, consider two scenarios:

Scenario 1: Quality assurance. A nonprofit with fewer than 25 employees held food drive projects (all part of a food drive program) throughout the year to gather food for the needy. In order to hold as many food drives as possible, the nonprofit relied heavily on volunteers, who differed from project to project. Consequentially, there were inconsistencies in how the projects were conducted. Some volunteers, although well meaning, sent mixed messages about the food donations to donors, resulting in the donors questioning the stability of the non-profit and a decrease in the amount of food donated. To address the concerns of donors and to not jeopardize the food drive program, a project checklist was created to assure that the same level of quality occurred on each food drive project. To provide an additional degree of control and consistency to each project, an information sheet was created that included items such as:

- The regional centers that were in need of food donations
- The foods that were in short supply and would be greatly appreciated
- The date of the next food drive

A nonprofit staff person was assigned the role of quality assurance supervisor or, in simpler terms, the "point person" who was responsible for coordinating the quality efforts. Every employee and volunteer on every food drive project used the same project checklist and information sheet, eliminating confusion by the donors and providing an acceptable baseline on every food drive project.

Scenario 2: Quality control. A business manager, working with the project manager, hires a website developer to create a website for the business. The project manager creates a checklist with features and functionality that tie to the contract with the vendor. The checklist is used to "accept" delivery of the website (the final product or service from the website developer) and to pay the vendor for services rendered. The features and functionality checklist includes items that are interrogatives (Table 15.1). If the answers are not affirmative (yes), the deliverable is not ready or complete because it does not fulfill the requirements, the quality standard. The project manager might want to expand the checklist to include features and functionality that do not tie to the contract with the website developer, but do tie to the project's scope statement because the features and functionality are requirements of the project—requirements that must be completed and accepted by the sponsor before the new website goes live. In this scenario, the checklist is being used as a quality control tool.

THE LINKAGE BETWEEN QUALITY AND RISK

Quality and risk planning are interrelated—a potential quality problem can be a project risk. The project manager may perform a cost trade-off analysis and decide that because a project risk is deemed low, there is no need to perform any quality testing, but because there might be a potential quality problem, the potential risk should be added to a risk watchlist. Alternatively, if a project risk is deemed high, a project manager might add the risk to the risk register and develop a quality plan as a mitigation strategy.

Table 15.1. Quality Checklist

Project Name: Website Upgrade — Checklist		
Date: March		

Number	Item	Yes/No
	Identify	
1	Is the logo prominently displayed?	
2	Is it possible to read and understand the home page within 10 seconds?	
	...	
	Accessibility	
10	Is the font size and spacing easy to read?	
11	Does the website load in a reasonable amount of time?	
	...	
	Navigation	
20	Are the navigation labels clear?	
21	Do all of the links function?	
	...	
	Content	
30	Are the major headings clear and descriptive?	
31	Are the URLs meaningful and user-friendly?	
	...	

For example, in the nonprofit scenario above, the checklist mitigated the risk of different messages being given to donors. The nonprofit's risk register might have had a risk listed that indicated the sponsor's concern that inconsistent messages could be given to the various donors due to the heavy reliance on volunteers. The response to the risk might have been the creation of a quality checklist.

Suggestion: Use continuous improvement evaluations. As a project manager and team members work on a project, they should evaluate the work. If a task is creating inefficiencies or a lower-than-acceptable-quality product or service, modify the task or, if the right course of action is to eliminate it, eliminate the task. Just because tasks are in a project plan does not mean they are "right." Project plans need to be continually evaluated and improved. Quality not only applies to a project, but also to the project management methodology being followed by the organization. Take the same approach with the organization's project management methodology. If a standard, a process, or a guideline in the project management plan is inefficient or unrealistic for the organization, recommend changes to the standard, process, or guideline; discuss the recommendations; and if agreed on and appropriate, make the changes.

ADDITIONAL QUALITY TOOLS AND TECHNIQUES

A significant number of different quality tools and techniques are available. In addition to the tools and techniques already mentioned in this chapter, three additional quality tools and techniques that a team might want to plan to use are histograms, benchmarking, and flowcharting.

Histograms. A histogram is a visual aid that shows how frequently something occurs. Using a resource histogram as a way to show how many people are needed at various points in a project was discussed in Chapter 12. As a quality tool, if a project requires testing for defects, such as a product that is being built or a software application that is being written, the defects (or bugs) can be categorized as critical, high, medium, or low. The histogram can be used to graphically illustrate the distribution of defects. Based on the analysis, the project manager and team can then modify the work effort and change any quality checking or inspection processes.

Benchmarking. Benchmarking is a standard against which something can be measured or assessed. The benchmarking technique can be used to compare how a particular project's process and testing results compare to a prior, but similar, project. Another way benchmarking can be used is as a reference point. By knowing the final product or service standard within the industry, the project manager can judge and monitor the project's quality compared to others in the market. In the nonprofit food donation story, benchmarking could have been used in addition to the checklist. The nonprofit could benchmark donations during the current food drive and compare them to what has been received to date at the same point in time during the last two food drives. If the donations are down 15%, the nonprofit might want to evaluate the reasons why.

Flowcharting. Every quality problem occurs because something is not "right," resulting in a problem needing to be identified and corrected. Flowcharting provides a graphical depiction that charts a project's processes and work effort enabling the project manager to see how the work fits together and the source of a potential problem. A commonly used flowchart technique is a cause-and-effect diagram. A cause-and-effect diagram categorizes causes by type (Figure 15.1). A cause-and-effect diagram is also known as a fishbone diagram or an Ishikawa diagram. The diagram is called a fishbone because the visual diagram resembles the spine of a fish with the bones representing vertical branches. The spine represents the root cause of the problem. Each category type, such as materials, equipment, or personnel, is a vertical branch on the diagram. Root causes of the problem for each category are shown as horizontal lines tied to the category type

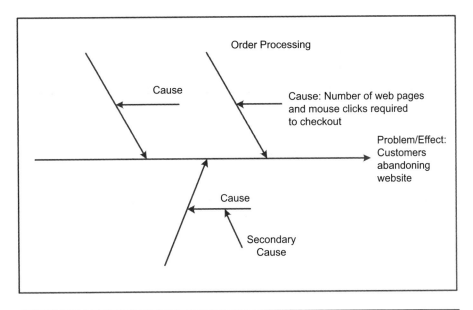

Figure 15.1. Fishbone diagram: cause (root and secondary) and effect of a problem for a website design project.

on the diagram. The diagram is analyzed to determine how to solve the problem. In the nonprofit food donation story, if benchmarking had been used and donations were down more than 15%, a fishbone diagram might have been created to determine the causes and to identify solutions.

IN REVIEW

- Delivering a high-quality product or service means the deliverable fulfills and, if possible exceeds, the requirements the team agreed to when the project started.
- Quality assurance is the proactive act of preventing quality problems while quality control is the reactive act of inspecting the deliverable for the presence of quality problems.
- For the majority of flat organizations, creating a quality plan does not need to be an elaborate process. Simply communicating what is expected of the team may be all that is required.
- Quality and risk planning are interrelated because a potential quality problem can be a project risk. A project risk can be mitigated or avoided with a quality plan.

- Inspection techniques or a simple checklist that can be used to provide consistency may be all that is required to keep the team on track and to assist with producing a quality product or service.
- A number of tools and techniques, such as histograms, benchmarking, and flowcharting, can be used in addition to inspections and checklists to assist with monitoring and controlling quality.

STEP-BY-STEP INSTRUCTIONS

To create a quality plan:

1. Gather and review appropriate project-related documentation:
   - Collect the scope statement and requirements documentation.
   - Consult historical information from prior projects.
2. Identify quality criteria:
   - Review each requirement's acceptance criteria in the scope statement.
   - Identify any required regulations and standards.
   - Review historical data.
   - Determine any metrics or reliability standards.
   - Determine the quality acceptable baseline.
3. Determine how the team will identify potential quality problems and then how quality problems will be corrected:
   - Creation of inspection procedures
   - Creation or modification of checklists
   - Regulatory standards and requirements reviews
   - Benchmarking standards
   - Use of histograms and flowcharting techniques
4. Determine the cost of quality trade-offs:
   - Determine if the quality control and monitoring processes and systems are worth the cost of implementation.
   - Determine how to keep cost under control and still conform to the requirements.
5. Assign the quality assurance role and responsibility.
6. Communicate and discuss the quality plan with the sponsor. Modify accordingly.

CHAPTER 16

PROCURE THE RIGHT RESOURCES

Covered in this chapter:

- Description of the procurement process
- Explanation of the different procurement documents and contract types
- Recognizing the importance of vendor relationships
- Performing a make-or-buy analysis
- Engaging a vendor
- Memorializing the agreement

Flat organizations, particularly those with limited staff, may need to rely on one or two vendors to support a project's resource needs. Relying on vendors requires creating some sort of procurement plan. The plan does not need to be a detailed formal plan, but the project manager is required to clearly define the expectations and requirements of the vendor. With clearly defined expectations and requirements, the project manager can solicit and select qualified vendors, consider potential project risks, and negotiate a signed and effective legal document.

WHAT IS A PROCUREMENT PROCESS?

Some flat organizations have formal, written procurement processes because they have a strong business need, such as a regulatory requirement, while other flat organizations follow an informal process and place heavy reliance on strong vendor relationships. Whether formal or informal, every organization has organizational-related policies and procedures outlining how to communicate with vendors to purchase equipment, supplies, and materials and how to engage subject matter experts and consultants.

Before a project starts, the sponsor may decide to procure a particular product or service, or when the resources are estimated, the project manager may need to have a conversation with the sponsor and CFO about potentially procuring resources. The project manager should consider asking questions such as:

- Who has the authority to commit to a purchase decision?
- Is there a dollar amount limit for which no approval is required?
- Are there operational cash flow requirements that could influence the project's purchasing timeframe?
- Is there a list of preferred vendors?
- What is the process for drafting, negotiating, and signing binding legal documents?

Regardless of when a decision is made to procure either a product or service, the decision is based on factors such as the resource skill sets needed, the type of resource required, and when the resource is needed.

CONDUCT A MAKE-OR-BUY ANALYSIS

A key procurement process is deciding whether to make or buy a specific product or service. Make tends to save money on raw materials, but increases labor costs and the project schedule. Buy could save time, but might jeopardize the final deliverable's quality if the purchased item is not built according to specifications. Consider this make-or-buy story about two different retail businesses: one is a coffee bean roasting company and the other is a bakery.

The coffee bean roasting company sells roasted whole beans by the pound in the company's retail outlet store. Although sales are robust, the owners think they could do better if potential customers have an opportunity to try their various coffee blends. One of the owner's strategic initiatives is to open a coffee shop to provide a place for people to meet and linger while enjoying a cup of coffee with baked goods, such as muffins and cookies. To implement the strategic initiative, the owners have authorized two projects. The first project will expand the store and add a coffee shop to the premises; the second will upgrade the existing employee kitchen so that the coffee shop employees can bake muffins and cookies. Each project, although interrelated and overlapping, will have its own scope statement and project plan.

As the owners evaluated the schedule for the upgrade of the kitchen and the level of effort required to provide an ongoing quality level of baked goods, they became concerned about the potential risks to their main operation—roasting coffee beans. The owners decided to abandon the kitchen upgrade effort and find a baked goods vendor to be a partner. They established a relationship with a local bakery, which included an arrangement with the bakery to provide some exclusive baked goods. The coffee shop would highlight the local bakery's baked goods. In turn, the local bakery would sell packets of coffee and note that their baked goods could also be purchased at the coffee shop. This relationship would enable each retail operation to remain focused on their core product and also provide each business with additional revenue and a new advertising venue. Each business became the preferred vendor of other business, resulting in a "win" for both of the two different retail businesses.

During their make-or-buy analysis process, the owners of the coffee bean roasting company considered the risk to their current operation and several other factors:

- Impact on scope, time, and cost: Cost was not a factor because the owners had adequate funds and had budgeted for the project to upgrade the kitchen. The level of effort and the desire to shorten the project's schedule, however, required a reduction in scope.
- Ongoing operational support needs: The owners realized the operational needs to support a bakery were different from the operational needs of a coffee roasting operation. The more they evaluated the make decision, the more concerned the owners became that the make decision might require them to change the strategic direction of the business, possibly jeopardizing their high-quality coffee bean brand.
- Cost effectiveness: The owners understood roasting coffee, but they did not have experience in operating a bakery. The owners thought it would be more cost effective to engage a vendor because a bakery would require skills and resources that were clearly beyond their current capabilities.

MANAGE VENDOR RELATIONSHIPS

As highlighted in the coffee shop and bakery story, solid vendor relationships can be extremely important in the daily operations of a flat organization. The last thing any organization wants to do is damage a good vendor relationship, but a preferred vendor might not be able to meet a project's demands due to:

- The timing of the request
- The vendor not having the additional quantities requested
- The skill sets required by the project being unavailable

Be flexible and innovative with preferred vendors. Most preferred vendors try to be accommodating, but compromise and flexibility are needed from all parties for some proposals to succeed. For example, a preferred vendor might not able to deliver all of the parts required in one shipment, but would be able to do so in three shipments over a six-week period. This approach might require adjusting the project's critical path, resulting in a change in the completion date. In this example, if the preferred vendor has never been late with deliveries and if there is flexibility with the completion date, the sponsor might agree to adjust the schedule, resulting in the project manager modifying the project plan accordingly. Alternatively, if the schedule cannot be modified, the project manager may agree to receive as many parts as possible from the preferred vendor and obtain additional parts from a different vendor, building a relationship with a new vendor.

ENGAGE A VENDOR

Engaging a preferred vendor is often the best option for a project because the preferred vendor's strengths and weaknesses are known, which keeps unknown project risk low. If a project manager needs to engage a different unknown (new) vendor, unknown risk to the project increases. Before engaging any vendor, preferred or new, the project manager needs to create a list of the expectations and requirements of the vendor and determine the selection criteria. The list should include:

- Expectations and requirements
- Description of the final deliverables
- Key assumptions and constraints
- Roles and responsibilities of both parties
- Timing of the effort
- Acceptance standards for the deliverables
- Regulatory or governmental requirements
- Other organizational-related, project-specific, or selection criteria-related information

The vendor also needs to understand the product or service to be delivered as well as to be able to determine if there is a "good fit" with the organization. *Good fit* works two ways: not only does a vendor need to be a *good fit* for the organization, but the organization also needs to be a *good fit* for the vendor.

Selection criteria are the standards used to evaluate the vendors. Some criteria are objective and can be measured; other criteria are subjective and open to interpretation. Although cost is normally included on a selection criteria list, a project manager should be careful to not make cost the only criteria to consider. Too often a vendor is selected because their proposed cost is the lowest of all the proposals. Later the decision to use the lowest-cost proposal is regretted: in some cases, the cost to repair a problem is more than if a more costly vendor had been originally selected.

When planning for and engaging a vendor, work with the sponsor and CFO and follow the organizational processes and procedures. Some organizations have significant administrative hurdles to clear. For example, the organizational policy may be to take the expectations and requirements list and create a procurement document. The procurement document is then submitted to prospective vendors to solicit proposals for the work.

Procurement documents are designed so that consistent and comparable responses will be received from the vendors. Different types of procurement documents are used to obtain those responses:

- Request for proposal (RFP): Asks vendors for a solution or a strategy as well as pricing information
- Request for quote (RFQ): Asks vendors to quote a price so that a determination can be made as to a fair market price for materials
- Request for information (RFI): Used to find vendors that can solve a problem or provide assistance with an opportunity

For some organizations, RFPs can take too much time and can be expensive for both the organization and the vendor. Furthermore, using an unknown vendor increases the project's risk. Another challenge is a number of good, if not excellent, vendors that work with flat organizations on smaller projects do not respond to RFPs (or RFQs and RFIs). If a vendor does not think they have adequate information to respond to the RFP, does not have an existing relationship with the organization, or thinks the project could potentially contain too much risk, the vendor might pass on the opportunity. The cost to respond may outweigh the potential benefit to the vendor. At this point in the process, the potential client is not a *good fit* for the vendor.

Successful projects require product or service vendors that are a *good fit*— they are a trusted partner. Good vendors want solid, open, honest relationships. They do what is needed to assist the organization and believe an organization's success is their success.

Suggestion: Meet potential vendors. One approach that works well is to follow a more informal process while keeping in mind the primary goal is to perform a comparison of potential vendors and to select one. Ask preferred vendors and people at other organizations for recommendations. Ask about these vendors' strengths, weaknesses, and reasons why they are being recommended. If need be, narrow down the list of potential vendors. Then meet and talk with these vendors. Provide them with the expectations and requirements list and answer their questions. Explain the schedule and any time constraints. If there are cost constraints, discuss them upfront with the potential vendor. Each vendor needs to understand the cost parameters and assess what they can accomplish with the funds available. Evaluate the vendors based on the objective and subjective selection criteria. Determine if there is a fit with a vendor. If you are comfortable with the vendor and if the vendor can provide a product or service based on the cost and time constraints, then ask for a proposal or sign a contract.

MAKE USE OF LEGAL DOCUMENTS

Every agreement with a vendor needs to be memorialized. Think of the agreement as a scope statement between the organization and vendor. Common legally binding agreement forms are a contract or a contractual Statement of Work (also referred to as a SOW). The agreement form selected depends on the organization's policies and procedures as well as project.

Contracts

The point of this discussion on contracts is not to provide legal advice or contract legal points; for that, consult an attorney. This discussion is about the project business points that need to be included in contracts. Business points in project contracts clearly articulate what product or service a vendor is providing to support the project and the sharing of project risk so that a vendor does not overestimate costs nor does the vendor decide it is better to cancel the contract before completion. Cancelling a contract often results in a failed project.

Different types of contracts can be used, but the best contract is one that is a "win-win" for the organization and the vendor. The two common contract types are fixed price or lump sum, and time and materials:

- *Fixed price:* The vendor agrees to provide the supplies or services for a specific price. A fixed-price contract works well with clearly defined specifications and costs that are relatively certain, but a fixed-price contract can be high risk for a vendor. To keep risk to a minimum, the vendor may implement a risk strategy by padding the price for any potential problems and place an emphasis on controlling costs and limiting scope or changes.
- *Time and materials:* The vendor is paid an agreed-upon rate for the actual time spent as well as for the actual cost of all of the materials required to perform the work. A time and materials contract is common type of contract used for engaging subject matter experts or for

staff augmentation. It is a good contract to use if a project manager does not know how long a project need will last. A time and materials contract is a low-risk approach for a vendor, but can be a risky approach for an organization if the project manager does not carefully monitor the work being performed. One risk strategy to implement is to include a *not to exceed* (NTE) clause capping the project time, which reduces the cost risk to the organization, but could increase the scope risk because some tasks might not be completed.

A third type of contract that is not as common is a cost plus or cost reimbursable contract. In this contract, the vendor is reimbursed for the cost of performing the work plus a fixed fee, an incentive fee, or an award fee. Traditionally this type of contract is found in government agency contracts. There are also a number of variations to all three contract types.

Contractual Statements of Work

A contractual statement of work can also be used as an addition or addendum to a contract. A preferred vendor may have a contract with an organization that includes nondisclosure, noncompete, or other legal requirements, but excludes information specific to a project. In this case, a contractual statement of work specific to the project is created as an appendix or an addendum to the contract.

Discuss any legal binding agreement with the sponsor and an attorney. The attorney is responsible for providing the legal points and format while the project manager and sponsor are responsible for addressing the project's business points. Some points to consider having in a contract or a contractual statement of work include:

- Description of the project requirements and final deliverables
- Key assumptions and constraints
- Roles and responsibilities of both parties
- Timing of the effort
- Acceptance standards for the deliverables
- Pricing and payment terms
- Procedures for changes in scope
- Training
- Confidentiality
- Insurance requirements
- Representations and warranties
- Indemnification
- Termination of agreement

Consider the following scenario which highlights similarities between a vendor's legal document (their standard legal contract) and an organization's project scope statement.

A Scenario: Legal Documents for a Website Project

A business decided that to increase their sales, they needed a new ecommerce website. After talking with and providing written requirements to a number of website designers, the sponsor along with the project manager decided on a website design company. The website design company used the discussions with the project manager and sponsor and the written requirement documentation provided by the business to determine the level of effort. A verbal quote was provided by the website company to the project manager.

Because the verbal quote was outside the anticipated range, the project manager and sponsor spoke to and negotiated with the website company. With a few minor changes by the business to the requested requirements, an agreement was reached as to the work to be completed and the associated cost to complete the work. With agreement on the work and cost, the website design company forwarded their standard legal contract to the project manager, providing all legal related requirements, such as confidentiality, warranties, and indemnification, and included a Website Project Statement of Work that outlined the specific work to be completed and other business-related points of the project. (The policy of the design company is to create two documents: a standard legal contract and a statement of work as an addendum to the contract.) Selected sections from a much longer Website Project Statement of Work included:

Project Description and Requirements:
Create an ecommerce website based on the requirements document provided by the business. The business needs:

- To be able to obtain customer-specific data on an ad hoc basis for business analysis
- To be able to send emails to customers based on their purchases and sales
- To have the ability to upload a product list created by third-party vendors and Excel spreadsheets on an as-needed basis
- To have various shipping options to accommodate sending to different locations
- To provide real-time credit card processing

Services and Deliverables:

The four key work steps and deliverables are:

- Requirements Gathering: The first step is to gather information and confirm the requirements. The deliverables are the development of an administrative site map, user site map, and database schema.
- Design and Graphics: In this step, the visual elements of the website are designed and approved, including the page design, product listing design, detail design, cart design, and checkout design.
- Development: …
- Testing and Review: …

Client sign-off of each step is required prior to proceeding to the next step. The assumption is sign-off will occur within 3 days. If sign-off does not occur within 3 days, the timeline will be impacted. Changes to the Services and Deliverables in this Website Project Statement of Work will follow the change control procedures included in the standard contract.

Time and Fees:

This project is will be completed over a 12-week period for a total fixed cost of $20,000. Invoicing will occur upon completion and approval:

- Requirements Gathering: Weeks 1 to 2
- Design and Graphics: Weeks 3 to 6
- Development: …
- Testing and Review: …

Key Personnel:

Tim will be the main website designer and the day-to-day contact person.
…

Roles and Responsibilities:

Website Developer is responsible for:

- Training and documentation of the website
- Initial detailed testing
- …

Client (Customer) is responsible for:
- Providing business expertise and clarification of requirements
- Providing examples of the product files to be imported
- ...

Signatures:

...

The project manager was able to tie the Website Design Statement of Work to the business' Ecommerce Website Scope Statement. Because the sponsor and project manager were both comfortable and satisfied that the website designer's statement of work supported the business' project scope statement, a decision was made to hire the website design company as a vendor.

Table 16.1 shows how a statement of work might look compared to a project's scope statement. A project manager needs to be diligent and thorough when performing a comparison of a statement of work and the project's scope statement, which includes ensuring that the statement of work does not include new work. If the statement of work includes work that is not included in the project plan and for which there is no budget, a project change order normally is warranted. Initiating a project change order is a decision that needs to be made by the sponsor. If a project change order is made, revise the project plan accordingly and notify the core team and stakeholders, particularly if the completion date is impacted.

Table 16.1. Statement of Work and Scope Statement Comparison

Statement of Work	Scope Statement
Project Description and Requirements	Project Description
	Objectives
	Requirements
Services and Deliverables	Key Deliverables and Milestones
	Project Description
	Assumptions
Time and Fees	Key Deliverables and Milestones
	Estimated Cost
Key Personnel	Staff Resources
Roles and Responsibilities	Assumptions
	Exclusions
Signatures	Sign-Off

Finally, as the statement of work is reviewed make sure all pertinent project-related information is included. For example, include:

- Any assumptions in the Services and Deliverables section pertaining to sign-offs (3 days in the example), change orders, and referral to the contract
- References to the standard or master contract
- The acceptance criteria
- An expiration date or a statement such as, "This agreement is valid for thirty (30) days from ... (a specific date)."

Although statements of work will and do vary in form, length, and complexity, once signed, they are binding legal documents.

IN REVIEW

- Follow organizational policies and procedures when procuring products or services for a project.
- Create a list of expectations and requirements that tie to the project's scope statement and determine vendor selection criteria before engaging a vendor.
- Engaging a preferred vendor is the best option when filling a resource need because unknown risk to the project is kept low.
- A vendor needs to be a good fit for an organization and the organization needs to be a good fit for the vendor.
- Fixed price or lump sum and time and materials are two common contract types.
- A formal contract and statement of work from a vendor hired to support a project should tie directly to an organization's scope statement.
- No matter how informal the procurement selection process is, a formal signed agreement is needed between the organization and vendor.

STEP-BY-STEP INSTRUCTIONS

When creating a procurement plan:

1. Gather and review appropriate project-related documentation.
   - Collect documents created to date: the scope statement; requirements documentation; resource requirements; and budget.
   - Consult historical information: prior project vendors' closeout or recap reports; meeting notes that include problems encountered and problem resolved; and lessons learned documents.

2. Identify the project resource needs (equipment, materials, supplies, or subject matter experts) to be fulfilled by a vendor based on factors such as staff skill sets needed, type of resource required, and when the resource is needed.

3. Discuss the organization's procurement process with the sponsor, CFO, and any other appropriate people. The discussions should include reviewing the preferred vendor list, contracts and statements of work process, and the vendor selection process.

4. Perform and document a make-or-buy analysis. Determine if the work can be accomplished by the project team or if a vendor must be engaged.

5. If a vendor is to be engaged, clearly and concisely define for the vendor:
   - Expectations and requirements
   - Description of the final deliverables
   - Key assumptions and constraints
   - Roles and responsibilities of both parties
   - Timing of the effort
   - Acceptance standards for the deliverables
   - Regulatory or governmental requirements
   - Other organization-related, project-specific, or selection criteria-related information

6. Define objective and subjective vendor selection criteria.

7. Follow the organization's vendor selection process.

8. Select a vendor and compare the work proposed in a contract (or contractual statement of work) to the project's scope statement.

9. Memorialize the vendor agreement by signing a contract or contractual statement of work.

10. If necessary, modify the project plan. Update the risk register, if applicable.

11. Communicate the vendor decisions to the core team and stakeholders.

CHAPTER 17

COMMUNICATE THE RIGHT INFORMATION

Covered in this chapter:

- Understanding how communication works
- Recognizing four methods of communication
- Defining who, what, when, how, and why project information is communicated
- Establishing a communication schedule

Detailed large-project communication plans are not necessary for all projects, but the *right* information still needs to get to the *right* people at the *right* time and in the *right* manner. Communication could be a quick, informal conversation in a hallway between the project manager and sponsor in which the project status is discussed, an informal Post-it® Note left on a team member's desk about a project issue, or a formal written statement of work outlining the vendor's commitment to the project. As much as an informal communication process can result in quick resolutions, an informal process can also hinder a project if important information is misconstrued or not communicated in a timely fashion—but a formal, written document takes time to create and time to read. A communication plan determines the *right* balance of informal and formal communications as well as what needs to be communicated and to whom.

WHAT ARE THE BASIC COMMUNICATION CONCEPTS?

Numerous books and studies are available about the best ways for teams to communicate. Before looking for the *best* way, a project team needs to understand two basic communication concepts: the *communication model* and the *communication method*.

The communication model requires:

- A message to be sent from a sender to a receiver
- The receiver to correctly receive the complete message and understand it
- The receiver to interpret the information contained in the message and to appropriately respond

The communication is "successful" if the message received and interpreted by the receiver is the same as the message sent. How the message is interpreted can be influenced by many factors, such as the person's values, attitudes, and perceptions or their native language, culture, or education. If a message is sent, but not interpreted and responded to appropriately, the communication process is not successful. Consider this story in which the project manager sent an email informing the sponsor and three stakeholders of an emergency project meeting.

Tom, the project manager, sent an email informing the sponsor and three stakeholders of an emergency project meeting to be held on Tuesday at 3:00 p.m. The email requested a response only if the sponsor or a stakeholder was unable to attend. Tuesday afternoon arrived, but two of the stakeholders did not show up at the meeting. What happened? When asked, both stakeholders acknowledged they had received the email, but neither interpreted the information correctly, so they did not respond as the project manager expected. Maybe they did not read the email or maybe they forgot to add the meeting to their calendar. Regardless of the reason, the result was an unsuccessful communication process for two of the stakeholders, resulting in rescheduling the meeting and loss of time in an emergency situation.

The communication method is how people communicate and the format of the communication. The four communication methods are formal and informal written and formal and informal verbal:

- Formal written: a scope statement or contract
- Informal written: sending an email or a leaving a note on a person's chair
- Formal verbal: a presentation or speech at an event
- Informal verbal: a face-to-face discussion or a voice mail message

Written communication is the most precise communication method; verbal communication provides the most flexibility. Project documents, such as scope statement or contract, should always be formal written communications. Formal communications are preplanned and standardized while informal communications occur as people think about the information that needs to be shared. All four-communication methods are used on all projects regardless of size. Although informal verbal and informal written are prevalent methods used by flat organizations with modest-sized projects, consider a story highlighting how a project manager's informal approach impacted the project's final cost.

A merger of two small medical offices resulted in the need for a new website. A local website developer was hired, the scope and requirements of the project were defined and documented, and a contract was signed by one of the physicians. The office manager was assigned the project manager role for the new website project.

During a weekly status meeting with the physicians, the project manager questioned why no one considered adding a patient portal to the website because a portal would assist with streamlining the office processes. The physicians agreed that having a portal was a good idea, and after receiving a verbal level of effort and cost estimate from a website developer, agreed verbally to a scope change. As the project progressed, the project manager and physicians asked for additional modifications. When the final website was delivered, although the physicians were pleased with the quality of the website, they were shocked with the final cost—it was double the original contract amount. They did not realize how much every change would cost even though these changes had been verbally discussed and incrementally approved.

What went wrong with the communication process? Being informal and flexible can make it easy to exchange information and can keep a project on schedule, but in this case, being informal caused the project manager and the physicians to overlook the impact of the changes on project cost. The changes to the website requested by the project manager and the physicians were changes to the contract, a formal written project document. These changes should have been formally recognized in a written document.

CREATE A COMMUNICATION PLAN

A *communication plan* defines who, what, when, how, and why for providing project information, interacting, and exchanging ideas. *Who* is the stakeholder, such as sponsor or team member; *what* is the delivery method, such as a team meeting or status report; *when* is the frequency, such as weekly; *how* is the communication method, such as an informal email or formal written report; and *why*

Table 17.1. Communication Schedule

Project Name: Website Upgrade				
Date: March				
Delivery Method (What)	**Purpose (Why)**	**Communication Method (How)**	**Frequency (When)**	**Stakeholder (Who)**
Team Meetings	Discusses work in progress, recently completed work, and upcoming work; ensures risks, issues, and change requests are acted upon accordingly	Informal and verbal	Weekly	Project Manager Team Members
Status Report	Provides a status of the project's work, schedule, and budget	Formal and written report	Weekly	Project Manager Sponsor Team Members Stakeholders
Scope Document	Provides objectives, description, requirements, and acceptance criteria	Formal and written report	After document is signed-off, post in the project file located at: D:\project\ documents\ scope	Project Manager Sponsor Team Members Stakeholders
Deliverable Acceptance Meeting	Ensures requirements and acceptance criteria in scope statement are met	Informal and verbal	Upon deliverables completion	Sponsor Project Manager Team Members

is the purpose, such as to discuss weekly progress. For some projects, particularly smaller projects, instead of a detailed communication plan, consider creating a communication schedule (Table 17.1). A communication schedule might be all that is required by the project.

The communication schedule does not need to be elaborate or fancy nor does it require an enormous amount of time to create: it simply needs to include the information collected about each stakeholder (recall that a stakeholder is anyone impacted by the project) during the stakeholder identification process. If a stakeholder's list was used during the stakeholder identification process, start by reviewing the communication schedule and ask: "Are the stakeholders on the list still valid? Has anyone been missed?" Then review each stakeholder's communication requirements and preferences. If the communication requirements and preferences were not collected, ask each stakeholder questions such as: "How often to you want to receive project status reports?" "What do you need to know about?" Then add the information to the stakeholder list.

Next, the project manager, with the assistance of the core team, determines:

- What information should be "pushed" out to stakeholders (such as status reports)
- When information should be "posted" for the sponsor, stakeholders, and team members to review as needed
- How often face-to-face meetings should be held for interaction with the sponsor and stakeholders to answer questions and address concerns

There can be cultural, organizational, or technical constraints and assumptions that need to be taken into account when determining the *what* (the delivery method), *when* (the frequency), and *how* (the communication method). Give consideration to:

- Are the team members geographically dispersed?
- How technology savvy are the stakeholders?
- What technology and what application systems are available?
- How will stakeholders access the communication?
- Do any stakeholders have time limitations?
- Are there stakeholders, such as volunteers or board members, who will not have access to the organization's network?
- Are traditional methods such as face-to-face meetings the best approach?
- Can newer social media collaboration tools be used?

Stakeholders have different communication preferences, and pleasing everyone is hard. Publish the communication schedule; ensure each stakeholder is comfortable with *what* information they will receive; *how* they will receive it; and *when* they will receive it. The possibility exists that there may be a very good business reason why a particular stakeholder needs information in a different format or at a different time. If that is the case, an exception may be necessary or the approach may need to be changed. If need be, discuss the stakeholder's need with the sponsor.

Team members with dual responsibilities report to two different people: the day-to-day manager and the project manager. Many times the day-to-day

Table 17.2. Communication Requirement Document

Stakeholder	Requirement
Owner	Summary project status information (scope, time, and budget) Summary information on critical project risks and issues
Sponsor	Summary project status information (scope, time, and budget) Summary information on critical project risks and issues Information on proposed project change requests
Project Manager	Summary project status information (scope, time, and budget) Detailed project status information (scope, time, and budget) Detailed information on all risks, issues and change requests
Team Members	Project activity Task status information Risks and issues Time reporting
Team Member's Day-to-Day Manager	Team member's time requirements
...	...

manager is not a stakeholder in a project. Some day-to-day managers want information on a project's status while others only want to know how much longer a team member is needed. These situations require the team member, day-to-day manager, and project manager to develop a communication plan that is unique to the three of them.

Suggestion: Include communication templates in the organization's project management methodology. Create communication schedule and communication requirement templates for the organization's project management methodology. An example of a communication requirement document is shown in Table 17.2. Although the communication schedule and communication requirement templates can used as starting points for any project, they are particularly helpful for recurring projects, such as an annual fundraising event.

IN REVIEW

- The goal of communicating is to ensure the right information gets to the right people at the right time and in right manner.
- Two basic communication concepts project teams should understand are the communication model and the communication method.
- The two most common communication methods for flat organizations are the informal verbal and informal written methods, but

project documents, such as the scope statement or contract, should always be formal written communications.

- A communication plan or schedule defines the *what* (delivery method), *why* (purpose), *when* (frequency), *how* (communication method), and *to whom* (the project manager, sponsor, core team, and other stakeholders) information is to be provided.

STEP-BY-STEP INSTRUCTIONS

To create a communication plan:

1. Gather and review appropriate project-related documentation.
   - Review and update the stakeholder list. Determine if the list is still valid and if any person or category needs to be added.
   - Consult historical information. Review prior project communication plans and the lessons learned.
2. Collect the communication requirements of each stakeholder.
   - Determine *what* and *why* the information is required.
   - Determine the stakeholder's preferred method of receiving the information.
3. Evaluate any constraints or assumptions that could impact the communication plan.
4. Determine the appropriate method for communicating the information to the stakeholders.
5. Create a communication schedule. The communication schedule includes *what* (delivery method), *why* (description and purpose), *how* (communication method), *when* (frequency), and *to whom* (the stakeholder) project information is provided.
6. Discuss the communication plan with the sponsor and core team. Modify the communication plan accordingly.
7. Distribute the communication plan to the stakeholders.

SECTION 5

TIME TO START EXECUTING

Executing a project is all about performing the work defined in the project plan. Successful execution requires a cohesive, collaborative team. In turn, a cohesive, collaborative team requires a project manager to use a blend of management and leadership skills to turn this group of people into an effective team. Effective teams understand one another's strengths and weaknesses, know who is accountable for *what* and *when*, and understand the goals of the project. Team members rely on their project manager to guide them through the project plan so that the project objectives are met, a quality product or service is delivered, and the project is completed on time within budget. This section covers:

Chapter 18. The Project Start: Describes confirming the availability of team members assigned to be on the project team; clarifying roles and responsibilities; creating project guidelines; planning the first team meeting; and announcing the project to the organization

Chapter 19. Build and Manage an Effective Team: Focuses on fostering teamwork and developing effective project teams; describes the differences between management and leadership skills, the importance of interpersonal skills, and a project manager's power; discusses team building tools and techniques and resolving conflict situations

CHAPTER 18

THE PROJECT START

Covered in this chapter:

- Confirming the availability of team members
- Ensuring each team member understands their role and responsibilities
- Starting the project with a team meeting
- Developing project guidelines
- Maintaining and managing project documentation
- Announcing the project to the organization

At this point in the project, planning is complete. Some team members may have been involved with the planning effort while others know nothing more than that they have been assigned to the project team. Begin the execution phase of the project by confirming the availability of each team member and discussing their individual role and responsibilities. If consultants or vendors are to assist with the project, verify their availability and invite them to the first team meeting. The first team meeting enables everyone to meet one another and hear the same message about the project's scope, objectives, requirements and deliverables, the project's operating guidelines, and most importantly what constitutes project success. Finally, announce the start of the project to those in the organization who might be impacted by project work.

CONFIRM THE TEAM

As execution of the project begins, confirm the availability of people who are assigned to the project team. Daily commitments and workloads change. A person promised to the project may not be available at all or their originally committed hours are now reduced. The reasons why a person is no longer available vary, but when staff have day-to-day as well as project responsibilities, the longer the time is between planning and starting the work, the greater the likelihood is that a person will not be available. If a person is not available or the person's commitment level has changed, recruit, negotiate, and select new team members from either inside or outside of the organization or modify the project plan, shifting team members around. If there are tasks for which no team member has been assigned, recruit, negotiate, and assign a person to them.

Confirming availability is more than just asking a person if they are still available. Meet with each person individually to discuss:

- The work they are expected to perform
- The schedule they are expected to meet
- The amount of time (duration and level of effort) they are expected to spend on the project

Ask if the person has any questions. Ask if he or she is clear about their role and responsibilities as a team member. Answer any questions that arise and clarify any points that are unclear. People need to understand their tasks and how their work will contribute to achieving the overall project goals. If a person is anxious about being involved in the project, this is an ideal time for the project manager to discuss the reasons. Two potential reasons the person might be apprehensive are

- The person might be uncomfortable working on a project because he or she has doubts about their ability to perform the work or is unfamiliar with project management concepts. Start reducing their anxiety level by explaining or providing training in fundamental project management concepts.
- The person might think that his or her professional goals and needs will be ignored. Listen to their concerns and then together explore different project-related tasks that might help them with their professional advancement.

Meet with each person's manager to confirm that his or her manager understands and is committed to supporting the project requirements. When team members have dual responsibilities, they need to know that there is collaboration and consensus between their day-to-day operational manager and the project manager. If there is a problem or even the potential for conflict between team members' regular operational and their project responsibilities, discuss the situation with the sponsor and ask for assistance.

HOLD THE FIRST TEAM MEETING

A successful first meeting energizes the group and is the start of building a cohesive, collaborative team. Look at the meeting as a team building exercise. If it is not possible for everyone to attend a face-to-face meeting, investigate other options such as conference call or web conferencing capabilities. The goal of the first team meeting, or what some people might refer to as a *kick-off* meeting, is to ensure that everyone meets one another and leaves the meeting understanding why the project is important to the organization, the implications of a delayed or failed project, and what constitutes project success. Team members should leave the meeting with a clear understanding of:

- Work to be performed
- Objectives and requirements
- Key milestones
- When the project is to start and be completed
- How success will be measured
- How and when status meetings will occur
- Ground rules between the project manager and team members

Although your responsibility as a project manager is to plan the meeting, work with the sponsor to prepare the agenda and to set expectations for the meeting. Use the documents created during the planning process such as the scope statement, responsibility matrix, and project plan and milestone list.

Set a time limit for the meeting, so team members will know when they can return to their day-to-day responsibilities. If the meeting ends early, no one will complain, but if it goes over the allotted time, some team members may leave before the meeting is over. A poorly planned first meeting can give the impression that the project is also poorly planned.

Start the meeting by welcoming everyone. Ask each person to introduce themselves and to include a description of their skills, expertise, and role or perceived role in the project. Talk about other people who will be directly involved, including any external organizations or customers.

If possible, the project manager and sponsor should jointly talk about the project. The sponsor should explain the project's importance and how it ties to the overall strategy of the organization while the project manager should explain the administrative and operational aspects of the project and how the team will function. Unless there is an organizational standard or a request by management, creating a fancy PowerPoint presentation or a formal project team document to explain the project is generally not needed.

Although discussions should have already been held with individual team members, this is the first time the entire team has been gathered to hear the same message. Allow time for questions and answers. At the end of the meeting, explain how the project guidelines will be defined.

CREATE PROJECT GUIDELINES

Project guidelines tie the needs of the team to the needs of the organization by defining how the team will work together and operate. Some guidelines are dictated by the culture and project management methodology of the organization while other guidelines are determined by the team. The optimum approach to creating the guidelines is for the project manager, sponsor, and core team to meet to discuss what is expected of each other and to agree to administrative and operating processes. If the project team is small enough, consider having all team members involved in the creation of the guidelines. If some people are unable to attend a meeting, solicit input from them by email, surveys, or telephone calls because everyone needs to agree to abide by the guidelines. Two types of project guidelines to consider creating are the ground rules and operational and administrative processes.

Ground rules. Ground rules define how team members will work with and treat one another to be effective and productive. Ground rules assist with fostering and building trust and respect. Start by leveraging the acceptable behavior guidelines of the organization and expand on them to create the ground rules for the project team. Potential ground rules could include:

- Understand your role and responsibility. Everyone is responsible for completing his or her assigned tasks on time and in a professional manner.
- Be an active listener. Everyone has a right to speak and to be heard. If a comment is not understood, ask for clarification.
- Provide feedback. If there is a problem or a team member does something incorrectly, provide open, honest, constructive feedback. If a team member does something positive for the project, comment on the great job they did.
- Be patient. Keep the project timeline in mind, but work with each other and help one another to move forward with completing assigned tasks.
- Do not assign blame. If there is a problem, work through the problem and resolve it. Placing blame does **not** move a project forward. Projects are risky by nature and ***mistakes will happen***.

- Ask for and accept help. Do not expect team members or the project manager to know or be able to do everything. Ask for assistance from the "right" people. Sometimes the right person is outside the organization.
- Participate in meetings. Actively participate in meetings by sharing ideas and experiences. All ideas and experiences are worth mention and consideration. Sharing information develops synergy.
- Be proactive. Everyone on the team is responsible for the project's success. If there is potential for conflict, work to resolve the conflict before it becomes a problem.
- Have fun working on the project. Projects are work, but team members should enjoy what they do.

Operational and administrative processes. Create guidelines for operational and administrative processes, such as status meetings and work sessions, communications, decision-making (covered in Chapter 19), issues (covered in Chapter 20), change requests (covered in Chapter 20), conflict resolution (covered in Chapter 19), and status reporting (covered in Chapter 22). A discussion on status meetings might include outcomes such as:

- Status meetings will be held every Friday morning at 8:00 and will be kept to 1 hour or less.
- Cell phones and other mobile technology devices will be turned off (or to vibrate) during status meetings.
- No multitasking will be permitted. No work on day-to-day operational tasks will be done during a project status meeting.
- Status meetings will start with everyone providing an update based on the project's status report format.

Outcomes of a discussion on communication could include:

- Email will be used to communicate project information.
- The weekly status report will be the formal communication document.

The guidelines do not need to be captured and written down in a formal document. They can be informal, such as an informational notice sent by email or a conversation during a meeting. The important point is for team members to understand the ground rules and the operational and administrative processes. The guidelines are to help, not hinder the project. They are to assist the project team in understanding what is expected of them, to eliminate frustration, and to help keep the project on track. Team members need to be empowered to perform their jobs. Be careful—do not create guidelines that are burdensome or add unnecessary overhead; that inhibit the expression of ideas and views; or that prevent calculated risk taking. Although everyone working on a project has tasks to complete and deadlines to meet, a project still needs to be fun.

DETERMINE THE PROJECT DOCUMENTATION APPROACH

Every project has documentation that needs to be collected and stored. If the organization has a standardized approach for collecting and storing documents, follow it. If not, the project team needs to decide what documents to keep and then how and where to store them. Keep it simple. Only keep documents that add value to current project efforts and can be used as a historical reference for future projects. At a minimum, consider keeping:

- Formal project documents (the scope statement)
- Project plans
- Status reports and related notes and minutes
- Issues and change requests

Do not go overboard. Not every memo and document needs to be kept.

Low-cost as well as expensive project management applications and automated collaboration tools are available to assist with collecting and maintaining project documents, but for smaller projects, the team might find these tools too difficult or too time consuming to learn, maintain, and implement. For a smaller project, a low-cost solution such as keeping the documents in a shared folder on a shared network drive might be adequate. Consider this story about a five-person project team.

Each team member works two days a week in the office and three days at home. Although they occasionally meet face-to-face, rarely are all of them in the office at the same time, resulting in many conference calls. Reliance on technology is heavy, so when deciding on an approach for sharing and storing project documents, the team decided that a web-collaboration tool was the right solution. One team member researched the tools and recommended a few solutions. The team members decided on using one of the on-line tools and committed to one another to learn how to use the tool properly.

Suggestion: Keep a project diary. During a project, numerous informal conversations occur. Various undocumented situations can arise that could impact the project or a project manager's decisions. As a project manager, consider keeping a project diary or journal that is a record of your personal experiences, observations, thoughts, and lessons learned. This journal is not an official project document and is not stored in project document files; rather it is to be used by you to manage and lead the project team and to record personal lessons learned for future projects.

ANNOUNCE THE PROJECT TO THE ORGANIZATION

In a flat organization where other staff in the organization work side-by-side with a project team member, consider announcing the project. Why? Remember the "Whisper Down the Lane" communication exercise? How often is the message heard by the last person not even close to the initial message? To ensure the success of the project, ensure that all pertinent people hear the same message by broadcasting the project start.

Although a face-to-face meeting is one option, the announcement could be an email or a formal memo highlighting what the project is expected to deliver; the objectives; when the project is to start and be completed; and information about how and who to contact with questions. If applicable, state how project updates will be periodically communicated.

IN REVIEW

- Confirm the availability of staff members to work on the project. Meet with each person individually to discuss their assigned tasks and the schedule required to complete the work. If a person has dual responsibilities, meet with his or her manager to confirm the manager's commitment and support for the project.
- Energize the project with a team meeting. The project manager and sponsor jointly explain the project's scope statement, how the project ties to the organization's strategy and goals, and the importance of the project. This meeting is the first time the entire team is gathered together as a group. Use it as a team building event.
- Effective, productive teams need guidelines, whether formal or informal, defining acceptable interpersonal project behavior and the operational and administrative aspects of the project, such as status meetings, issue management, and change requests.
- Every project has documentation that needs to be captured and stored, but keep it simple. Only retain documents that add value to the current project and will serve as a historical reference for future projects.

- Announce the project to the organization, particularly if there are people in the organization who might be impacted by the project or will be in the future.

STEP-BY-STEP INSTRUCTIONS

When starting a project, the project manager should:

1. Confirm that the people originally assigned to the project are available; if any are not available, acquire new team members:
   - Meet with each member individually; discuss their individual roles and responsibilities and address any concerns.
   - Confirm that the manager of any person with dual responsibilities understands and is committed to supporting the project requirements.
   - Ask the sponsor for assistance with any staffing conflicts.
2. Hold the first team meeting:
   - Work with the sponsor to prepare an agenda.
   - Ask team members to introduce themselves.
   - Provide the project team with project-related documentation, such as the scope statement, the responsibility assignment matrix, the project plan, and a major deliverable and milestones list.
   - Ask the sponsor to explain key aspects of the project, such as the project scope, objectives and requirements, and success criteria.
   - Explain operational aspects of the project and how the team will function.
   - Answer questions.
3. Establish project guidelines:
   - Define the team ground rules.
   - Define operational and administrative guidelines for processes, such as status meetings and work sessions, communications, decision-making, issues, change requests, conflict resolution, and status reporting.
4. Establish an approach for maintaining project documentation.
5. Announce the project to the organization.

CHAPTER 19

BUILD AND MANAGE AN EFFECTIVE TEAM

Covered in this chapter:

- Differentiating between management and leadership skills
- Recognizing the impact of referent, expert, and legitimate power
- Understanding the importance of interpersonal skills
- Understanding the five stages of team development
- Using tools and techniques to motivate and build a project team
- Anticipating and resolving of conflict

Effective teams support common goals. Team members on an effective team respect and trust each other and exhibit a willingness to collaborate, communicate, and work together. Effective, cohesive teams do not "just happen." They are developed, and maintaining them is an on-going process. To develop and manage a team, attention moves from creating plans to providing motivation to team members when things go wrong and coaching them when they are unsure of the tasks to be completed. A project manager uses his or her management and leadership skills and relies heavily on interpersonal skills to develop and manage a team. The sponsor and stakeholders support and assist the project manager by ensuring that the team is composed of members with the necessary skills. Throughout the project's execution, the project manager works to address the challenges unique to the project team within the flat organization while balancing the needs of the team with the needs of an individual.

MANAGERS, LEADERS, AND POWER

Management skills and leadership skills are not the same, but each is used throughout a project. Managers focus on processes to create project plans and then monitor and implement the plans. Managers continually review potential risks, resolve issues, ensure resources are used efficiently and effectively, and provide communication updates to ensure that all the details are addressed. Leaders focus on the project's vision and mission. Leaders continually work to ensure the right resources are available and encourage and motivate the team members to achieve project goals and take risks. Effective leaders lead by example. Leaders set realistic expectations and work to earn the respect and trust of the team. Interpersonal skills are used every day to communicate and interact with individuals and teams. Managers and leaders must have strong interpersonal skills.

Whether managing or leading, effective project managers realize that they need to take care of the team members, but they also work to motivate their team members so that team members want to do what needs to be done, when it needs to be done. An effective project manager understands how to manage, but knows not to micromanage. The ability to not micromanage depends on the project manager's interpersonal skills and something referred to as *leadership power*, composed of legitimate, referent, and expert power. In a hierarchical organization with formal processes, a project manager generally is in a higher organizational position than the team members. He or she has clear authority (*legitimate power*) to give orders and delegate, following a chain of command philosophy, to ensure operational effectiveness. In a flat organization with less formal processes, a project manager could have the same organizational position as the team members, and although the project manager has legitimate power delegated by management, the organization's culture is different. In this circumstance, the project manager is required to rely on *referent* and *expert power* to influence the team members.

Referent power. Referent power is the ability to influence others based on personal respect and loyalty. Referent power could be based on the perceived trust of an authority figure or based on respect for a person's prior successes. For example, the CEO trusts and respects the project manager's opinion. Therefore, even though the team members may have never worked with the project manager, they respect the project manager because of their trust and respect for the CEO. Another example could be a project manager's last three projects were completed successfully and the team members enjoyed working with the project manager. Based on prior experience and reputation, the current team members trust and respect that project manager. A project manager with strong interpersonal skills can gain referent power. Simple acts of kindness, being supportive and backing team members up when required, being sincere, genuinely caring for people, and keeping promises are all ways to gain referent power.

Expert power. Expert power is the ability to influence others based on a person's experience, skills, or special knowledge. Based on the project manager's expertise, the team members rely on the project manager for advice and guidance. As the project manager provides expertise, the knowledge of the team members increases. For example, a project manager who is experienced with setting up workstations and servers may gain the trust and respect of the team members working on a network upgrade project for the simple reason that the project manager has experience and knows more than the team members.

Referent and expert power tend to be more effective than legitimate power because, in general, team members are motivated by project managers who they respect and trust, not project managers who they have been told they must follow. The "right" leadership power for a particular project depends on a number of factors, such as the overall culture of the organization, the interpersonal skills of the project manager and the team members, the skills of the team members, and the project itself.

STAGES OF TEAM DEVELOPMENT

Much of the success of a project is based on how well team members are able to build relationships and have confidence in each other's capabilities. Part of a project manager's success is based on his or her ability to leverage referent and expert power to help the team members build relationships. Relationships are built as team members move through the various stages of team development. The stages are situational because team members come and go. Individual team members can be in different team development stages based on when they joined the team or how they have personally progressed through a stage, which adds an additional level of complexity for a project manager. Although different terms can be used for each stage, one of the most cited models of team development is that offered by Bruce Tuckman. According to the Tuckman model, the five stages of team development are forming, storming, norming, performing, and adjourning:

- The *forming stage* begins the shaping and molding of the team. The team members are introduced to one another and initial judgments about each person are formed. Conversations are polite. People do not want to reveal too much about themselves. The project manager directs the introduction of team members and shares the project plan, discusses roles and responsibilities, kicks off the project, and provides team building activities to help the team members individually transition into a productive team.

- The *storming stage* is named for the commotion and conflict that arise as team members express different opinions on how the work is to be accomplished and how the team is to make decisions and work together. Differences in personalities are highlighted. The project manager guides and coaches the team members through this process while assuring the team members that they are valued. Team members are encouraged to discuss their project concerns. Team conflicts are acknowledged and managed, but not avoided.

- The *norming stage* sets the standard for acceptable team behavior. Conflict still exists, but the team members now focus on how they will behave toward each other rather than on their personality differences. Over time the team members build commitment toward the project, become supportive of each other, and start to trust and respect one another. The project manager continues to focus on supporting the team members, providing feedback, facilitating more team building, assisting team members to negotiate with one another, and encouraging open and honest communication and collaboration.

- The *performing stage* is the work phase. The team members are working as a unit, collaborating, exchanging information among team members, discussing and solving problems, and trusting each other to place team needs above individual needs. Over time the project team becomes self-managing, requiring little direction from the project manager, which enables the project manager to delegate work and focus on tracking the project's progress, keeping people informed, and recognizing the team's accomplishments.

- The *adjourning stage* is the breakup of the team, with each team member moving to another assignment or to operations and celebrating success. The project manager is responsible for closing the project, which includes showing appreciation for the team's hard work.

Successful project managers continually evaluate the effectiveness of their teams and address each individual person's needs. They use their interpersonal skills as well as their management and leadership skills to move the team through the stages of team development.

INTERPERSONAL SKILLS

Interpersonal skills is a catchall term that includes the ability to write, listen, ask questions, motivate and mentor, problem solve, and make decisions and even to manage stress. Interpersonal skills are valuable assets to have when developing and managing a team. Influencing, negotiating, and decision-making are the three key interpersonal skills that project managers and team members should hone when working in a flat organization:

- *Influencing* is related to power. The more trust, respect, and loyalty that a project manager has, the easier it is for him or her to convince people to do things that they may not want to do. For example, a project manager's personal standard of always being on time for status meetings can influence the behavior of the team members, resulting in everyone always being on time. Constantly not being on time can influence the team as well, but negatively. The message sent to the team members by a project manager being late could be that they are not as important as other people in the organization or that the project is not important, so being concerned with project plan completion dates is not important either.

- *Negotiating* is working together to come to a joint agreement. Everyone listens, discusses the issue, and then everyone compromises so that there is a resolution that addresses everyone's needs. For example, a team member is no longer able to spend as much time working on the project as originally planned. The project manager and two core team members meet and decide that instead of replacing the person, the work will be divided between the two core team members. The two core members discuss, negotiate, and agree on who will take responsibility for which tasks.

- *Decision-making* involves stating the problem, identifying and evaluating the alternatives, deciding on the right solution, and then implementing the decision. For example, will the decision-maker vary based on the issue and factors—the time constraints or the technicality of the issue? Will all team members be included in all decisions or only in selected decisions? Will the decision process be by consensus in which the team decides on the solution or by consultation in which the project manager listens to the team, but decides on the solution? Alternatively, will the project manager make command decisions, never discussing issues with the team, only informing the team after a decision has been made?

A project manager with strong interpersonal skills is usually more success-ful managing a project. Respect from team members and management is quickly gained, making presenting ideas, influencing people and decisions, and obtaining acceptance easier. A person with strong interpersonal skills may even appear bet-ter organized or be perceived as calm, collected and confident—even if he or she is not.

TEAM MOTIVATION

Project managers keep their teams motivated and energized by using a combina-tion of tools and techniques: team building, training, co-location, and recognition and rewards. Many times, however, the tools and techniques that are necessary to build a team are overlooked and not included in the project plan because during the project planning process, the project manager, sponsor, and core team are so focused on the project's work and the deliverables that motivational project tasks are overlooked. The problem with overlooking motivational tools and techniques is if the team members are unable to work together and if they do not have the skills required to complete the work, the planning effort will have been for noth-ing and most likely the project will be unsuccessful.

Discuss the various motivating tools and techniques with the sponsor, taking into account the organization's culture and standards as well as the backgrounds of the team members. Agree on the amount of time and money to allocate for team building, co-location, training, and recognition and rewards.

Team Building

Team building activities are specific actions incorporated in the project life cycle that help team members learn how to depend on and trust each other and help them bond. Team building activities can be formal or informal; very costly or at no cost at all; and be brief five-minute events or extensive multiday events.

As decisions are made about the appropriate team building activities to use, determine why an activity is being organized and what it is trying to achieve: is the objective of the activity to introduce everyone; to encourage collaboration and creativity; to build trust and commitment to the project; and to help team mem-bers with conflict resolution or is the activity to celebrate success by thanking the team members for a job well done?

Offsite workshops can be costly or unfeasible for many projects, but many low-cost team building activities can be implemented:

- Ask a team member to partner with a less experienced team member to provide training, mentoring, and coaching as needed.

- Hold short five-to-ten minute ice-breaking exercises before team meetings.
- Hold a nonmandatory brown bag lunch with a speaker on a topic of interest (not necessarily a topic about the project).
- Find a social activity unrelated to the project in which everyone can participate.

The list of team building activities is endless. Some of the best ideas will come from the team members.

Suggestion: Ask for assistance from the team. Ask a team member to take responsibility for a team building event, such as organizing a pizza outing; an ice breaking exercise; or a nonmandatory lunch or breakfast. If a number of team members are interested in assisting with a team building activity, have a random drawing to select a person.

Co-location

The traditional definition of co-location is a situation in which all team members are in the same physical location. Co-location makes communication easier, enhances team camaraderie, and increases idea sharing. Although co-location is commonly implemented with large project teams, smaller project teams can benefit from co-location just as much as large teams. If co-locating a team is impossible or impractical, consider a creating a communication center or hub. Team members need to be able to meet to talk about and focus on the project. Setting aside a common location for team members to meet and exchange information provides that need. The location could be a cubicle, a small conference room, or a section of a large conference room. Think of the location as a safe place for team members to get away from their day-to-day responsibilities to discuss project issues or listen to others talk about ideas; for the project manager to post information about the project, such as the responsibility matrix, the milestone chart, or communication updates; and for team members to store hard copies of shared documents and project-related books. If creating a physical common location is impossible, consider a digital communication center.

Team building and co-location can complement one another. Consider this story about the importance of team building and how not co-locating team members was impacting an entire project.

During a lunch meeting with colleagues, Paul, a project manager, mentioned that his team of eight people was not working as a cohesive unit and the project's success was in jeopardy. Paul was hoping his colleagues would be willing to brainstorm for a few minutes to talk about potential solutions. As the conversation progressed, three points were discussed:

- Third-party consultants were performing approximately a third of the project work. Their workspace was in the same building, but it was on a different floor than the project team.
- Project plan briefings and project update emails were being sent to the organization's team members or what Paul referred to as "my staff," but the third-party consultants were not receiving project updates because they had "their jobs" to perform.
- Because the team was smaller, team building activities had not been included in the project plan—either in terms of time or money.

The brainstorming discussion highlighted for Paul some project missteps he and the sponsor had made during project planning. The discussion also helped Paul understand that it was his responsibility as a project manager to build a cohesive effective team by helping the team members—both internal and external—learn how to work together. Paul immediately implemented four changes:

- A project briefing document was created for all of the team members. Going forward, periodic communication meetings would be scheduled for all of the project's team members. The third-party consultants would receive the same email communications as his staff.
- The terms *my staff* and *their jobs* disappeared. There was one team. The success or failure of the project depended on all of them.
- With no money allocated for team building, the project manager discussed with the sponsor the need to use some of the contingency reserve funds. The first team building activity, a pizza party, was held so that team members could network in a relaxed environment.
- The project management plan was modified to include other low-cost team building activities.

Why were the third-party consultants not relocated to the same floor as the rest of the project team so that everyone would be working in the same location? In this case, the consultants were not relocated because no space was available anywhere in the building for the team to be co-located without impacting the day-to-day operations.

Training

If a team member does not have the skills needed to perform his or her assigned project tasks, training is needed. The skills needed might be unique to the project or might be required to support the team member's day-to-day responsibilities. Training can cover generic skills or highly technical skills; range from informal on-the-job training to books and e-learning training courses to formal classroom training; and be provided to a specific individual or an entire team. Consider a situation involving a new employee who is working at a small website development company.

After being assigned to her first project for a client, Ellen, a new employee, realized that she did not have all of the necessary programming skills to create the new website. The project manager arranged to have another employee work with Ellen to provide on-the-job technical training and arranged for Ellen to take a formal training course enabling her to complete the website project and meet the client's expectations.

Recognition and Rewards

Using rewards and recognition is a way to thank team members. For example, if a team completes a milestone on time and on budget, consider acknowledging the entire team. Rewards and recognition may be given to an entire team or to individuals, but be aware that recognizing individuals is an unacceptable practice in some organizations and cultures.

Commonly used monetary rewards and recognitions include a bonus based on a project's success; a team lunch or dinner; a gift certificate to a local store or restaurant; a certificate of appreciation; or a token gift personalized with the team member's name. Commonly used nonmonetary rewards and recognition include thank you notes and cards from the project manager or sponsor; written communications from the project manager or sponsor to key stakeholders recognizing the work effort; or a personal thank you from the head of the organization. Consider a situation in which a nonprofit staff person is assigned the task of coordinating the volunteers for an art auction.

During a meeting, a volunteer asked a nonprofit staff person about the possibility of volunteers assisting with handing out flyers and hanging up posters, a task that was not their responsibility. The staff person discussed the request with the project manager and after receiving approval took on the initiative of creating a schedule and working with the volunteers as they handed out flyers and hung posters in local stores. The project manager recognized the staff person during a meeting with a small token gift.

TEAM CONFLICTS

It is a fact: all project teams have conflict. Conflict costs project time and money. Team members become frustrated. In a flat organization, there tends to be more collaboration and compromising, thus keeping conflict on projects to a minimum, but conflict still arises, particularly if the team members have dual responsibilities. The reasons for this conflict include limited staff, scarce resources, conflicting schedules, different organizational priorities, personality clashes and egos, technical and performance issues, communication problems, lack of clarity of a person's role, and cost disagreements.

As a project manager, try to anticipate potential situations that could lead to conflict. Ask questions such as: are the business priorities of the project and the day-to-day operations the same? If not, does a process need to be implemented so that team members with dual responsibilities will understand and know how to manage conflicting schedules and demands? Is it possible to work with the team members' day-to-day managers to coordinate efforts and prevent scheduling conflicts from occurring in the first place or at least to keep them to a minimum? If you anticipate the potential for conflict, do not hesitate to ask the sponsor for assistance and advice in preventing them.

The fact that conflict exists is not bad as long as it is effectively resolved. Effective or positive conflict resolution can result in:

- Exchange of ideas, resulting in creativity and innovation
- Clarification of inaccurate assumptions
- Increased respect and trust between team members
- Increased participation and a better ability to work together
- Increased understanding of what is important for the project as well as for each team member

Conflict that is allowed to fester can result in:

- Increased stress and anxiety
- Loss of respect and trust in team members
- Project progress being hindered
- Morale being lowered and teamwork becoming nonexistent

If there is a conflict, manage it. Remain calm, positive, and courteous. Focus on the issue, not the individual; on the present, not the past; and on constructive resolution without assigning blame. Determine the "right" conflict resolution approach to resolve conflict, each of which is effective in different situations. Confronting, collaborating, compromising, smoothing, forcing, and withdrawing are six basic approaches to conflict resolution:

- *Confronting or problem solving*: The most effective way to resolve a conflict is for the team members involved in the conflict to confront the problem head-on. Focus on the issues, evaluate the alternatives, and work with everyone on the team to decide on a solution that fixes the problem and resolves the conflict.

- *Collaborating*: All team members listen and discuss each other's viewpoints and perspectives. Using consensus techniques, the parties in conflict agree on a solution and commit to resolving the conflict.
- *Compromising*: The conflict is confronted, but the team members are unable to agree on a solution to resolve the conflict. This situation results in each team member negotiating with the other(s) and giving up something. Only use a compromise approach if confronting the problem is impossible or unsuccessful because the conflict may or may not be resolved.
- *Smoothing*: In an effort to downplay the conflict, emphasize the areas of agreement between the team members while de-emphasizing the differences. Smoothing is a temporary solution, but is ideal when tempers are high because the smoothing technique enables the team members to step back and reevaluate the conflict.
- *Forcing*: A person in authority pushes for acceptance of one team member's viewpoint about a solution over the other team member's viewpoint or the person in authority pushes for acceptance of his own viewpoint.
- *Withdrawing or avoiding*: One team member walks away from the conflict before the conflict is resolved, which can be counterproductive. Walking away could be a warning sign that something else is wrong.

Trying to resolve a problem using a conflict resolution approach such as confronting, collaborating, and compromising is best, but at times a project manager needs to make a command decision and use the forcing approach. For example, consider a situation in which two team members agree to disagree.

The two team members realize that reaching a consensus on a project issue is impossible, so each team member presented their mutually exclusive solution to the project manager. Confronted with two mutually exclusive solutions, the project manager needed to decide if it would be best to work with the team members using problem-solving and compromising approaches or to make a command decision. The command decision could be the selection of one team member's solution over the other team member's solution or the decision to implement a solution not recommended by either team member. Both of these options work only if the two team members trust and respect their project manager. In situations such as this, the project manager is required to use management, leadership, and interpersonal skills as well as power—legitimate, referent, and expert—to resolve the conflict.

IN REVIEW

- Building and maintaining a cohesive, collaborative team is an ongoing process requiring a project manager to continually use his or her management and leadership skills. Effective leaders focus on the vision, lead by example, and earn the respect and trust of the team while effective managers focus on the processes ensuring resources perform the work assigned; resolving issues; and providing communication updates to maintain control.

- Interpersonal skills are valuable assets that project managers as well as team members need to cultivate. Interpersonal skills include soft skills such as the ability to write, listen, and ask questions as well as the ability to influence, negotiate, and make decisions.

- Team members build relationships as they move through the five stages of team development: forming, storming, norming, performing, and adjourning. Successful project managers continually evaluate the developmental status of each team member and work with individual team members as they progress through the stages of team development.

- A project manager motivates and energizes a team by using a combination of tools and techniques such as team building, training, co-location, and recognition and rewards.

- Flat organizations tend to be more collaborative and compromising, which helps keep conflict to a minimum. Additionally, anticipating possible conflicts, resulting in resolving the conflict before it begins, tends to be easier in flat organizations. The best way to resolve conflict is to confront, manage, and resolve it.

STEP-BY-STEP INSTRUCTIONS

When developing and managing a team, the project manager should:

1. Determine the project team's stage of development:
   - Forming stage: The project is kicked off, the product guidelines are discussed, and team building begins.
   - Storming stage: The team members discuss project concerns and work through project conflicts.
   - Norming stage: The team starts to become productive and is open, honest, and communicative.
   - Performing stage: The team is productive, the team becomes self-managing, and team accomplishments are recognized.

- Adjourning stage: The work is completed, success is celebrated, and the project formally closed.
2. Determine approaches to motivate team members:
   - Develop and implement team building activities.
   - Provide training and coaching.
   - Consider co-location or a central meeting place for the team.
   - Develop and implement a rewards and recognition system.
3. Manage conflict:
   - Listen and acknowledge both sides.
   - If unable to defuse a conflict early, encourage discussion and confront the problem to determine a resolution to the conflict.
   - If impossible to resolve a conflict, encourage collaboration or compromise or a combination of both for a win-win solution.

SECTION 6

MANAGING THE EFFORT

All projects, regardless of how well thought-out and planned, require constant attention. Assumptions change, issues are raised, risk events occur, scope changes are requested, and deadlines are missed. Constant attention means the project manager determines if the project is progressing as planned, identifies potential problems, evaluates alternatives, implements appropriate controls and corrective actions, and forecasts new completion dates and final costs. Constant attention means obtaining the status of each team member's progress and reporting the project's overall status to the sponsor and stakeholders. Constant attention also means the project manager stays on top of project events, ensuring that the desired quality results are delivered on time and within budget. This section covers:

Chapter 20. Manage Project Issues and Change: Addresses issues, the impact of change requests on scope, schedule, and budget, and scope creep

Chapter 21. Monitor and Control Progress: Focuses on updating and evaluating the schedule and budget, monitoring risk and quality, and halting or cancelling a project

Chapter 22. Report the Status: Focuses on creating a status report and conducting effective status meetings

CHAPTER 20

MANAGE ISSUES AND CHANGE

Covered in this chapter:

- Managing issues, questions, and concerns
- Requesting changes to the scope, schedule, or budget
- Managing uncontrolled changes to the project deliverable

No matter how thorough the project planning is, issues and changes still occur: a stakeholder identifies a missed requirement; a business emergency causes the project's funding to be decreased; the project needs to be completed sooner than planned; or a potential risk event actually occurs. When the timeline is tight or project funds are limited, any change to the project's schedule or budget that is not properly managed can result in trouble, or even disaster, for the project. Continual changes can cause a project to never be completed. Without controls, the work planned can be modified without anyone understanding the impact on the final product or service, which can result in an unsatisfied sponsor. The project manager's responsibility is to understand the requested changes, issues, and potential risks and then to manage them accordingly, adjusting the project plan (scope, schedule, and budget) to keep the project on track.

MANAGE PROJECT ISSUES

Issues are questions or points of concern that can lead to changes to the project plan. Issues are discussed every day and at every status meeting. They arise on every project regardless of size. When an issue is identified, resolve it quickly. To begin managing an issue, clearly and concisely describe the issue, the significance, and the impact on the project. Not all issues result in a change or modification to the project scope, schedule, or budget.

For some projects, the issue resolution process might be very informal, with the project manager notifying the sponsor and then jointly crafting a decision with the sponsor as to the actions to be taken and the timeframe for resolution. The project manager then continues to keep the sponsor and stakeholders apprised of the status of the issue. The only documentation might be a few email messages and an entry in the project status report. Another option might be the creation of a very simple issue tracking log (Table 20.1). A simple issue tracking log provides a slightly more formal approach to tracking an issue. The issues are tracked from identification through resolution, thus ensuring nothing related to an issue is missed or forgotten.

Document the significance and impact of the issue on the project. Provide a brief description of the actions required to resolve the issue. Assign responsibility for issue resolution and a resolution date to the project manager, a team member, the sponsor, or another stakeholder. If the issue requires a change to the project scope, note that a change request is required. If the decision is to do nothing, indicate that the decision is to do nothing and the reasons(s) why.

For large projects, issues are assigned priorities, but for smaller projects with few issues, assigning a priority to each issue is rarely required. All issues tend to be top priority, and even through issues are assigned resolution dates, resolutions need to occur as quickly as possible to keep the project on track. If an issue cannot be resolved by the project team or project manager, contact the sponsor and ask for assistance. Consider the following story in which Sarah, the project manager, dealt with a major issue during a network infrastructure project.

Due to the age of the hardware and complaints by employees at the company, a project to overhaul and upgrade the network infrastructure was authorized. The scope of the project included new servers, switches, routers, firewalls, and related network software. The hardware and software were implemented and properly configured. Although the speed improved, communication problems continued. An investigation revealed the Ethernet cabling in the building could not support the higher speed and bandwidth capabilities required to support current internet searches, streaming videos, third-party hosted software, and graphic design business requirements. Upgrading the Ethernet cabling had not been identified as a project requirement and therefore was not included in the project plan.

Sarah, the project manager, evaluated the impact of the issue on the project and realized upgrading the Ethernet cabling was a missed requirement. Upgrading the Ethernet cabling, however, was a major initiative, a project in itself, and trying to make a change to the project now would have a negative impact on the budget and the completion date. Sarah also knew the sponsor and other stakeholders would not consider the project successful if the network response time was not improved. The issue was posted in the issue tracking log as an open issue (the third issue in Table 20.1). Because the issue impacted the project's scope, schedule, and budget, and a decision by management was needed to resolve the issue, the issue was assigned to the sponsor and the project manager.

Table 20.1. Issue Log: Network Upgrade Project

Project Name: Network Upgrade							
Date: August							
	Issue	Significance and Impact	Issue Date	Actions and Resolution	Assign to	Resolve by	Resolved
1	Security hardware equipment received damaged	A project delay; team unable to install security hardware equipment per plan; no impact on critical path	7/8	Contact vendor; ask vendor to overnight replacement	Joe, Team Member	7/8	7/9
2	Consultant responsible for configuring Cisco switches resigned; task started, but work not complete	Task on critical path; if configuring switches does not start by Thursday, project completion date will slip	7/15	Discuss replacement and timing requirements with project manager at technical consulting company	Sarah Project Mgr	7/21	7/20
3	Although network response improved with upgrade, still sluggish; investigation highlights cable backbone problem	Project will complete on time, but results will not be as expected	7/26	Upgrade of cabling requires change request Andrew to discuss possible actions with mgmt team Sarah to perform detailed assessment to support change request	Andrew, Sponsor Sarah, Project Mgr	8/22	Open

MANAGE PROJECT CHANGE REQUESTS

Not all changes are bad for a project. Some change requests can actually shorten the project timeline or reduce the cost. Nevertheless, change requests that shorten the timeline or reduce costs are the exception. The majority of change requests have an additional cost in either time or dollars.

Large projects in hierarchical organizations have a formal change control process with forms, approval processes, a change control board, and change orders. In flat organizations, many project managers and sponsors rely on a less formal communication process. Although the process is less formal, providing adequate control is still needed, which requires the project manager and sponsor to identify:

- *What* changes are considered significant enough to warrant a change request to be written and approved by the sponsor?
- *What* type of changes is the project manager authorized to approve? (These changes are normally minor changes that have minimal or no impact on the scope, schedule, or budget.)
- *Who* is able to initiate change requests?
- *How much* and *what type* of documentation is necessary?

Confirming *what* change was requested, even if it is only with an email, assists with clarifying the need and ensuring that the issue being solved is understood.

If the project has a signed contract with a vendor, a more formal change control process usually is required. If a specific change control process is required, the process should be outlined in the contract or statement of work and could be as simple as a written notification or a change order form, both of which are signed and considered to be amendments to the original contract or statement of work.

Not all changes can or should be performed. Some changes requests are *nice-to-have* additions that are not needed, but desired, and increase cost or time. Other change requests are requested too late in the project's life cycle and would impact the completion date, and still other change requests require a modification to the project objectives.

A change request needs to be assessed by the project manager to determine if the change is necessary or if other courses of action should be taken. Discuss the change request with the team and other people who might be impacted by the change:

- Determine if the change request is a nice-to-have or a requirement for project success.
- Evaluate the impact of the change on the project scope, schedule, and budget, keeping the triple constraints in balance.
- Determine if there are any potential product benefits or risks from accepting or declining the change request.

- Determine if there are any possible alternative solutions or other options.
- Evaluate the impact of the change on the quality of the final product or service

Discuss the change request with the sponsor and then jointly decide to approve, reject, or defer the change or to implement an alternative solution. If the change request is approved by the sponsor, update the project plan accordingly and communicate the change to the team members and stakeholders. If the change request is rejected or deferred, explain why to the appropriate people, including the person requesting the change (requester).

In the story about the Ethernet cabling upgrade not being included in the network infrastructure project plan, although the sponsor took responsibility for resolving the issue, Sarah, the project manager, performed the detailed assessment which included how the change in scope would impact the schedule and budget. Based on Sarah's assessment and the impact on the scope, schedule and budget, the sponsor, along with others in management, decided that the issue had been identified too late in the project life cycle to be included in the project. The sponsor and management thought authorizing a new project to upgrade the Ethernet cabling was better, thus enabling the current network infrastructure project to be completed on time. Sarah and the sponsor jointly informed the stakeholders that the requirement had been overlooked when the requirements had been gathered and that the missed requirement would be addressed with a new project. They also communicated management's awareness that until the new project was completed, the network infrastructure project objective pertaining to improving the network response time would not be met as previously expected.

Suggestion: Allow team members to make certain changes. Some projects permit "no change whatsoever" by the team members, but that is unrealistic if team members are accustomed to having autonomy and are creative, innovative, and take initiative. Innovative team members make their own decisions as to the best way to complete their assigned work because their project manager does not micromanage them. For a project with team members who are accustomed to making their own decisions, the project manager needs to explain to the team members what types of changes are acceptable and what types of changes must be approved. For example, a change is acceptable and does not need approval if it is under a certain dollar amount or the change will take less than X number of hours to complete.

Take the time to explain how to think about and evaluate the impact of a change on the project. Include in your discussion the importance of team members vetting ideas with other team members or the project manager. The better informed the team members are, the better the chance is for *gold plating* to not occur. Gold plating is a process in which a team member makes a change to a feature or functionality, thinking the change enhances the final product or service, without checking on the impact of that change. Gold plating can result in the need for redo work, which increases the cost and potentially the completion date, or can result in a feature or functionality being added that the sponsor is not interested in and is unwilling to pay for.

Similar to issue resolution, tracking change requests might be a very informal process, with the project manager discussing the request with the sponsor and then jointly making a decision with the sponsor to accept or reject the change request. The only documentation of a change request might be in emails and the status report.

An easy, slightly more formal but still informal, way to track change requests is to use a simple change control log (Table 20.2). A simple log provides a status of the change requests for the current project as well as a historical reference document for similar future projects. At a minimum, include the request, requestor, and requested date, the reason for the request, an assessment of the impact on the project, and the decision and associated date.

Table 20.2. Change Control Log: Network Upgrade Project

Project Name: Network Upgrade					
Date: August					
Change Request	**Reason**	**Requestor and Date**	**Impact on Scope, Schedule, and Budget**	**Decision and Date**	**Comments**
1 Upgrade IT cable backbone	Missed requirement: current cabling does not meet new hardware speed and bandwidth requirements	Sarah, Project Mgr 8/8	Major scope change To delay project completion 4– 6 weeks Cost unknown	Defer: new project authorized for cable upgrade 8/10	Waiting for cost estimate from cabling contractor
2 Sales application upgrade to current release	New release available	Nancy, Sales 8/10	Change requires 4 hours of work by application vendor at $150/hour No impact on project completion date	Accept 8/14	No impact on completion date and only 4 hours of work Sponsor approved request

CONTROL SCOPE CREEP

Adding features and functionality to a project without taking time to address the effects of the request on the scope, schedule and budget of the project, known as *scope creep*, is easy. Be careful when you hear, "It's just one little change. There's no need for a change request." That one little change can quickly turn into one more change, then another, and before anyone knows it, the scope has grown as well as the associated time and cost. A sponsor or key stakeholder saying "it's just one little change" also may still expect the project to meet the original schedule and budget. Consider the network infrastructure project again.

Nancy, a sales person for the business, decided that because changes were being made to the network this would be a good time to upgrade the sales application to the current software release. Because the change was only "one little change" Nancy's opinion was that an upgrade to the new release would be an easy, minor change and therefore a change request was unnecessary. If Sarah, the project manager, had agreed to the change without having an authorized change request, the result would have been scope creep. The right approach for Sarah to take is to state that a change request is required and then explain the reasons why following the change control process is important for the project's success.

In this story, Nancy, the sales person, agreed to follow the proper process for requesting a change. Sarah worked with Nancy to assess the impact of the software upgrade to the project's scope, schedule, and budget. The additional time and cost to the project was determined to be minimal and the sponsor approved the change.

IN REVIEW

- All projects have issues and change requests that need to be investigated and a determination made as to the impact on a project's scope, time, and cost. An issue might require a change request to affect a resolution.
- Issues and change requests need to be tracked and controlled, but the level of formality depends on the project and the organization. A project with one or two issues or change requests might decide to document an issue or change request in an email or in a status report while a project with a large number of issues or change requests might want to formalize the process by creating an issue or change request log and implementing formal sign-off processes.
- All change requests need to be approved by the sponsor before the project plan (scope, schedule, or budget) is modified.

- Scope creep can easily happen, particularly when issues and change control processes are informal.

STEP-BY-STEP INSTRUCTIONS

Follow these guidelines for issue management:
1. Determine how issues are to be documented.
2. Evaluate each issue by asking questions such as:
   - What impact does this issue have on the project scope, schedule, and budget?
   - How can this issue be resolved?
   - Is a change request required?
3. Assign the issue and a date for resolution to a team member.
4. Document the resolution and resolved date for historical and future projects.

Follow these guidelines for change requests:
1. Identify what is considered a change significant enough to warrant a sponsor's approval and who is able to initiate a change request.
2. Determine how change requests are to be documented, such as in a change request log, in written formal form, or in some other manner. Inform team members of the process.
3. Evaluate change requests by asking questions such as:
   - What is the impact of the change request on the project scope, schedule, and budget?
   - Are there any potential project benefits or risks?
   - Are there any impacts on quality?
   - What are the alternatives or options?
   - Is the request a nice-to-have or a requirement for project success?
4. Discuss the change request with the sponsor.
5. If the sponsor approves the change request, modify the scope, schedule, and budget accordingly and notify the team members and stakeholders.

CHAPTER 21

MONITOR AND CONTROL PROGRESS

Covered in this chapter:

- Updating the schedule and budget with actual data
- Reviewing and evaluating schedule and cost variances
- Monitoring potential project risks
- Performing quality reviews as deliverables are completed
- Halting, revamping, or canceling a project

A project manager and sponsor can agree that the scope, schedule, and budget require monitoring and that delivering a quality product or service is a top project priority, but how do they determine what needs to be monitored and controlled or how much administrative time should be spent capturing time and expenses? If an organization is not accustomed to creating formal reports or capturing and recording actual hour and cost-related data, too much control may end up becoming no control. If the project is not controlled, the lack of control can be the reason a problem is not identified, evaluated, and appropriate corrective action taken. Alternatively, if the project manager is not careful, the project's administrative overhead costs can become a burden, paperwork can be unbearable, and team members may become frustrated. Monitoring a project is easy, but determining the right approach to monitoring and controlling a project can be difficult and, as always with projects, there will be trade-offs to consider. Reasoned balance is the key to success.

MONITOR AND CONTROL THE SCHEDULE AND THE BUDGET

Monitoring and controlling requires balancing the needs of the project with the demands and needs of the organization. Start by focusing on what information is important to the organization and the stakeholder and what data and information are important for the success of the project. (Determining stakeholder requirements is discussed in Chapter 5.) With an understanding of the important data and information, the project manager and sponsor can start to determine what must be monitored and controlled and what must be communicated to others in the organization.

When monitoring and controlling a project, the project manager is reconfirming the project plan. The project manager is looking at how the team is performing against the scope (work), the schedule (time), and the budget (cost). Actual hour and cost-related data are captured and recorded by the team members, which enables the project manager to assess the project's performance or what has been accomplished by comparing:

- Work completed to planned work
- Actual hours to estimated hours
- Actual cost to the budget

Variances are then calculated, alternatives are contemplated, and corrective action is taken as quickly as practicable. The project manager works with the team members to monitor and control quality and continually evaluates the project for risks.

A problem arises for the project manager when the actual hour and cost data are not obtained in a timely manner or when information about potential problems is not identified quickly. Without the right data and information, monitoring and controlling the scope (work), schedule (time), budget (cost), quality, and risk becomes difficult, if not impossible. Many times, the level (deliverable, work package, or task) of actual hour and cost-related data required to properly monitor and control a project is a decision made by the project manager and sponsor during the planning process. Decisions as to how quality and risk are to be monitored and controlled also may have occurred during the planning process. Occasionally, these decisions need to be modified as the project progresses.

Factors that influence what data and information will be captured include project size, type of project, available historical information, industry studies and reports, and even the project's budget. For example, if benchmarking data, either from a prior project or an industry report, is available for comparison purposes, tracking the actual hours by key deliverable might be adequate to maintain control. If the project is a new initiative, capturing actual hours and cost data by task enables the accuracy of the planning effort to be evaluated and provides a baseline for a future similar project.

The approach for collecting and storing data varies by organization and project. Collecting and storing detailed data and other project information requires a degree of formality and adds administrative time to the project because determining who will be responsible for gathering the data, where and how the data will be stored, and when the data will be collected can be an involved and time-consuming process.

The Schedule

Missing planned dates due to the original task estimates being underestimated or a problem(s) arising for which there has been no resolution is a common occurence. For projects with short durations, conduct a **weekly** review of the project schedule. Identify any potential problems and resolve them as soon as possible so that the impact to the schedule is limited.

To properly conduct a review, actual hourly data needs to be captured. Some project managers capture the actual hours by task, but the more detail captured, the more administrative time is required to consolidate the data. Other project managers capture actual hours by work package or key deliverable level.

Update the project plan with actual hours by task (or work package or key deliverable) and compare actual hours to planned hours. The difference between the actual hours and planned hours is known as a *schedule variance* (Table 21.1). The schedule variance is calculated by subtracting the actual hours from the plan hours (variance = plan – actual). A variance is *favorable* (positive) if the actual hours are less than the planned hours or *unfavorable* (negative) if the actual hours are more than the planned hours. The project manager starts by focusing on the tasks that are behind schedule or the tasks that have an unfavorable schedule variance and evaluates possible alternatives and appropriate corrective actions as needed.

Table 21.1. Plan versus Actual Hours

	Plan	Actual	Variance	
Task A	100	90	10	Favorable
Task B	120	140	(20)	Unfavorable

After evaluating unfavorable schedule variances, the project manager should evaluate favorable schedule variances because favorable schedule variances sometimes mask future problems and usually indicate planning or estimating issues. For example, a team member states a 50-hour task has been completed in 30 hours, resulting in a 20-hour favorable schedule variance. Possibly the planned hours for the task were overestimated, but also possible is the team member misunderstood the acceptance criteria for the task and the task is therefore actually incomplete when reported complete.

Evaluating a project schedule and determining if corrective action is required is not always straightforward. Judgment calls are involved. Consider two different scenarios; each was resolved differently based on the facts and the opinion of an experienced project manager:

- A task is behind schedule with an unfavorable schedule variance of 5%. The project manager analyzes all of the tasks necessary to complete the deliverable and decides that no corrective action is necessary because other deliverable tasks are on or ahead of schedule and the task with the unfavorable schedule variance is not on the critical path. The project manager believes the deliverable will be able to be completed on time and the milestone completion date will be met.
- A number of tasks are behind schedule each with unfavorable schedule variances between 3% and 4%. The project manager analyzes the deliverable's tasks and is concerned that the tasks that are behind schedule could influence the tasks not yet started, jeopardizing the completion of the deliverable. The project manager decides corrective action is necessary to mitigate the risk of not meeting the milestone completion date.

In these two scenarios, the project manager's decision to take or not take corrective action was based on the impact of the variance to the overall deliverable and a milestone completion date and required the project manager to ask questions such as:

- Is the task on the critical path?
- If the task is not on the critical path, how much float is associated with the task?
- If completion of the task is delayed, will the critical path be impacted or changed?
- Is the task a high-risk task?
- Are other problems associated with the task?
- Are other tasks with problems associated with the same deliverable?

It is easy for a task to take more time than anticipated or to have a change request with a small increase in time be approved and the additional work and time to never be added to the project plan. At times, the project plan needs to be updated or replanned. For example, if the task that took longer than anticipated is on the critical path, revise the project plan because the completion date probability is impacted. If an approved change request adds more time, revise the project's scope and schedule accordingly.

The Budget

Monitoring and controlling the project budget is similar to monitoring and controlling the project schedule. For projects with short durations, monitoring and controlling the project budget should also be performed **weekly**. Compare the actual costs to the budget estimates, investigate cost variances, determine the impact, evaluate alternatives, and take corrective action. A budget forecast, or a projection based on what has occurred to date and what is expected in the future, is determined. The cost variance is *favorable* if the actual cost is less than the budgeted cost or *unfavorable* if the actual cost is more than the budgeted cost.

Project managers often assume that a favorable cost variance means the project is on track or an unfavorable cost variance means the project is in trouble. This is not always the situation. For example, Table 21.2 highlights a $900 unfavorable cost variance in Month 1 for supplies and materials. Because the project is a 4-month project, $300 was budgeted for each month (or $1200 for the entire project). Upon investigation, the project manager discovered that the organization's accountant was able to obtain a discount of $200 if all the supplies and materials were received and invoiced during Month 1 of the project. So instead of spending $1200 for all the supplies and materials, only $1000 was spent resulting in a Year-to-Date $200 favorable cost variance. In this instance, the cause of the unfavorable variance was a timing issue that masked an overall favorable variance.

Table 21.2. Budget versus Actual Costs

Category	Month 1			Year-to-Date		
	Budget	Actual	Variance	Budget	Actual	Variance
Supplies and Materials	300	1000	(900)	1200	1000	200
Consulting Services	2000	1800	200	7500	1800	5700

An investigation of the consulting services, which appears to have a favorable cost variance of $200 in Month 1, uncovered a potentially unfavorable cost variance of $300. The reason for the unfavorable cost variance was the contract with the consulting company stipulated that the consulting company was to be paid $500 per week. But the project manager knew that the consulting company had worked only 3 weeks, which meant they should have been paid $1500, not $1800. In this situation, the project manager needs to investigate why there is a discrepancy and determine if corrective action is required. If budget discrepancies cannot be easily solved, they can quickly become a serious issue. Ask for assistance from the sponsor, CFO, or another stakeholder familiar with the problem.

Just as the scope and schedule may need to be revised if there are changes in scope or time, so does the budget if there are changes to the anticipated costs. Revise as appropriate.

EVALUATE RISK

Risks need to be periodically monitored and evaluated for change in their likelihood because the occurrence of any risk event can potentially require a change in project direction. The ideal time to evaluate the status of potential risks is during a weekly review of the scope, schedule, and budget, which enables the project manager to see the status of the entire project at the same time. As a project progresses, some risks might disappear while others become prominent. Update the risk register, adding and deleting risks as appropriate.

PERFORM QUALITY REVIEWS

Just because work is being completed on schedule and costs are under control does not mean that the work is being completed according to project requirements. Waiting until a project is complete to discover nonconformance to requirements results in an unsatisfied sponsor and an unsuccessful project. Correcting a nonconforming final deliverable can cost enormous amounts of time and money to correct. If funds are limited, the correction may never occur.

Monitor work as it is performed. Review or inspect every deliverable to ensure that it conforms to requirements. If the project's quality approach consists of quality checklists, benchmarking standards, or quality metrics, use them to monitor work. If the project includes a formal quality plan with quality requirements or industry standards, follow it. Identify problems and implement the necessary corrective action promptly to ensure that subsequent work is completed properly with no or minimal impact on the overall project. If a quality problem impacts the project plan (scope, schedule, and budget), update the project plan.

Suggestion: Involve the sponsor and stakeholders in interim deliverable reviews. Keep the sponsor and appropriate stakeholders engaged in the project by asking them to assist with performing quality checks as the various work packages and interim project deliverables are completed. Confirm that the work package or interim project deliverable meets the requirements and passes the quality check. Discuss any discrepancies and determine a course of action to correct any problems. Follow up with a simple email recapping the discussion, including signing-off on the work package or deliverable if it does meet the requirements and passes the quality checks.

Despite everyone's best efforts, requirements will be missed or misunderstood. The sooner a misunderstanding or a problem with a work package or deliverable is discovered, the easier and less costly it is to correct, but be careful of scope creep. It is easy for nice-to-have features and functionality that are not requirements to creep into the evaluation of a project deliverable.

HALT, REVAMP, OR CANCEL A PROJECT

As a project's execution is being monitored, a decision to halt, revamp, or cancel the project may be required because:

- Milestones dates are continually missed.
- The team is working on a solution, but the solution is no longer needed.
- The solution chosen is discovered to not be the right solution for the need.
- The original project goal is different than the current goal due to change orders.
- Work has been added without assessing the impact of the change or obtaining approval.
- Cost of the project outweighs the potential benefits.
- The project manager is not the right person for the job.

A common occurrence with a troubled project is that no one wants to acknowledge that the project is in trouble or to be "the ogre who killed the project." As difficult as it may be, if a project is in trouble, someone needs to halt the project and ask questions, evaluate the project, and determine the cost impact. Expect conflicting opinions as to why the project is in trouble and what could have been done differently.

If a project is in trouble, the project manager must be open and honest. Do not hide the fact that the project might need to be revamped or even cancelled. Some stakeholders may want a project to continue, even if cancelling the project is better for the organization. Consider the following story about a medium-sized business and a new industry-specific software application.

Management decided that a software selection project was unnecessary. Their decision was based on the software vendor's guarantee that the software application would meet the needs of the business and that the business could be "up and running within six weeks." Additionally, a competitor was using the software application with apparent success.

Eight weeks into the project, the software application was far from operational, and the project team was questioning if the application's functionality even met the needs of the business. As the sponsor reviewed the overall project status, a decision was made to halt, and then cancel, the project because the software application was not the right software application for the business. Management then authorized a new project, a software selection project. The decision to cancel required courage because of the large amount of time and money sunk into the failed project.

If canceling a project is the best option for an organization, determine if there is a gradual way to close the project or if a "sudden death" approach is better. Follow a project close process and create a lessons learned report and store project files for future reference. These actions allow the organization to learn and therefore gain some benefit from the cancelled project.

Evaluating a cancelled project is just as, if not more, important as evaluating a successfully finished project. Conflicting opinions as to why a project was cancelled and what could have been done differently will be expressed. All comments should be evaluated and the recommendations documented.

If revamping the project is a possible option and the approach management decides to pursue, start by modifying the scope statement. Redefine the project description, objectives, and requirements. Agree on the deliverables and the new acceptance criteria. Modify the project scope, schedule, and budget and create a new project plan with new scope, schedule, and budget baselines. Even consider giving the project a new project name.

IN REVIEW

- For projects with short durations, on a weekly basis, update the schedule and budget with actual hourly and cost-related data. Review the results for any potential problems and take appropriate corrective action(s).
- Monitor potential risks and update the risk register on a periodic basis. Consider reviewing risk as the scope, schedule, and budget are updated.
- Review and inspect every deliverable as it is completed to ensure that the deliverable confirms to the requirements and acceptance criteria documented in the scope statement as well as in the change requests.
- Monitoring a project can result in the project being halted, evaluated, and then revamped or cancelled completely.

STEP-BY-STEP INSTRUCTIONS

Follow these guidelines to establish a monitor and control process:

1. Determine data and information requirements.
2. Determine the data collection and storage method:
   - Manual such as paper timesheets or interviews
   - Electronic such as Excel, a project management application, or an accounting system
3. Determine the frequency for monitoring and reporting. Recommend a weekly frequency for projects with short durations.
4. Update the project schedule with actual time data each week. Also:
   - Determine variances.
   - Focus on tasks that are behind or far ahead of schedule.
   - Evaluate alternatives.
   - Determine required corrective action.
   - Take corrective action.
   - Take additional appropriate action, including discussions with the sponsor.
5. Update the project budget with actual cost data each week. Also:
   - Determine variances.
   - Focus on variance discrepancies.
   - Investigate discrepancies.
   - Determine corrective action required.
   - Take corrective action to resolve discrepancies.
   - If discrepancies cannot be resolved, discuss the situation with the sponsor or CFO.
6. On a weekly basis, review potential risks and update the risk register, adding and deleting risks as appropriate.
7. Perform quality reviews of every deliverable as it is completed, ensuring that each deliverable confirms to:
   - Requirements and acceptance criteria documented in the scope statement
   - Change requests

CHAPTER 22

REPORT THE STATUS

Covered in this chapter:

- Reporting the progress of the project
- Planning and leading effective status meetings
- Managing the project using a project status report

Some project managers continually monitor and evaluate a project's progress, but never formally document the project's status. In other situations, the project manager may create formal project reports that meet the needs of the organization's management team, but the reports do not meet the monitor and control needs of the project manager and team members. The result may be that the *true* project status is in the project manager's head or in notes on scraps of paper. The sponsor or a stakeholder might say, "Just give me a quick update. Are we on track or not?" As long as the project *is* on track, an informal process works, but if a project is in trouble, forgetting or misinterpreting important information that has been communicated in an informal or verbal manner is very easy and can be very painful. As much as a project manager and sponsor need to determine the right balance of formal and informal controls, they also need to determine the right format for providing information about a project to the sponsor, stakeholders, and the project team.

REPORT THE PROGRESS

Performance reports are the documents, financial statements, project recaps, and presentations that assist with monitoring and controlling a project's progress. They can be in textual format, histograms, charts, tables, or PowerPoint presentations. Performance reports highlight for the project manager, sponsor, team members, and stakeholders how well the project is adhering to the project plan and any potential project problems that need to be resolved. They **are not** performance evaluations of the project team, the project manager, or individual members of the team.

Some organizations refer to performance reports as project management reports or project control reports. Other organizations just refer to performance reports by name, such as budget reports, schedule or cost variance reports, and forecast reports. Based on the organizational culture, each organization needs to decide what project performance reports.

A report that all projects should feature is a *status report*. A status report provides a snapshot of the project's progress at a given point in time. The report may be a newly created report or a number of different project reports assembled to create a status report. For some project managers working on a project in a flat organization with limited controls and informal communication methods, a status report is often the only project report necessary. A status report makes it possible for the project manager to see if the work is on schedule and if expenditures are within budget; if there are any warning signs or major problems that need addressing; and what, if any, steps are next.

The primary person needing a status report is the project manager. The status report is a:

- Monitoring and controlling tool that provides a point-in-time analysis of the project plan: the scope, time, and cost
- Communication tool used to discuss the project with the sponsor, team members, and stakeholders; advertise the project's successes; solicit help from the sponsor and stakeholders; and manage expectations

A project status report is used to help keep the project under control; to monitor the degree of uncertainty associated with the project; and to address and communicate issues as they arise. It highlights the project successes as well as the project problems. A project status report also becomes a historical record of the project's progress. A project status report should **not** be a report card used to judge the job performance of a project manager or the team members.

Too often, a project manager creates a status report based on the organization's project management methodology or in a format recommended or mandated by the sponsor. Under both of these circumstances, the status report format might not be a workable tool for the project manager. The ideal status report format is one that meets the needs of the project manager, sponsor (and others in management), team members, and stakeholders; does not add too much administrative overhead to the project; and as stated by a familiar saying "does not reinvent the wheel."

CONDUCT EFFECTIVE STATUS TEAM MEETINGS

For projects in which everyone, or just about everyone, spends 100% of their time working on the project, the project manager can determine the best day (normally not a Monday or Friday) and time (normally avoids the busiest times of day) to hold a status meeting, but when people have dual responsibilities or work virtually, getting key team members together for a status meeting can be difficult, if not nearly impossible. Orchestrating a status meeting under these circumstances requires the project manager to be organized, work efficiently, and involve the team members in the decision process.

One of the best ways to be organized and work efficiently is to keep status meetings short and focused. *Short* might mean no more than an hour while *organized* means creating a standard agenda format, even if it is only an informal agenda that is posted on the whiteboard. Follow the same format at every meeting. Communicate all additions to the agenda to the team ahead of time. A status meeting agenda should include an update on the scope, schedule, and budget as well as discussions on issues, change requests, potential risks, and any follow-up action items. Consider adding a time to each agenda item, such as "10 minutes is allotted to discuss each work package," so that the meeting can remain short, focused, and be finished within one hour.

Adding set times to the agenda helps keep the meeting from wandering off topic into a gab session, but having set times is also important to ensure that everyone attending the meeting has a chance to speak. In an effort to stick to the agenda and keep the meeting short and focused, it is possible to overlooking an important issue. Be sure to ask "Is there anything else that needs to be discussed?" and to include time in the agenda for the "extras" needing discussion. If a detailed conversation is necessary pertaining to a particular task, issue, or some other project-related topic, schedule a separate meeting that includes only the team members impacted by or involved with the task, issue, or project topic. Consider including the meeting on an action item list.

By the end of the meeting, a new status report will be created (or almost created). Status meeting notes are in writing, but the notes should be limited, with heavy reliance placed on the accuracy of the status report. End the meeting by confirming what was discussed and the action items with associated dates that the team is responsible for completing or resolving.

CREATE A STATUS REPORT

The "best" status report should not take an enormous amount of time to create. The report can be textual (Table 22.1) or graphical and feature visual aids such as pie and bar charts. If the status report is graphical, the report indicates the percentage of the project that is complete or uses colors, such as green to indicate the

Table 22.1. Textual Status Report Template

Project Name:	
Prepared by:	
Week Ending:	
Project Description:	

Project Status:

Overall Status	
Work	
Schedule	
Budget	

Key Deliverables and Milestones:

Key Deliverables and Milestones	Planned End	Actual End	Forecasted	Comments

Issues:

Description	Action

Summary and Forecast
Accomplishments This Week:

Plans for Next Week:

Late Tasks:

project is on track; red to indicate the project is in trouble; or yellow to warn that there is minor trouble or the potential for trouble. Some status reports include a combination of text and graphics.

Status reports focus on the triple constraints, scope, time, and cost and are easy to read and understand. They are kept simple, not too long or complex, and are based on what has already occurred. Although there is no set format, a status report might have:

- Project name, prepared by, week ending, and a project description
- An overview of project status
- The key deliverables and milestones
- Issues
- A summary and forecast of accomplishments this week, planned for next week, and late tasks

Including the project description in a status report is optional, but the project description can assist with managing expectations, including managing scope creep. The project description included in the status report should be the same project description or subset of the project description found in the project scope statement.

The overview section of the project status is subjective and if not carefully defined can be misunderstood because even if overview comments are based on reality, the overview section reflects the opinions of the project manager and the team members. The "right" overview section is a high-level summary that answers questions such as: "Will the project be completed on time?" Responses to this question could be *yes* or *no, on target, in trouble,* or *warning, potential trouble* with no supporting detail for the reader.

A status report may have additional information that is required by the sponsor or organization. For example, the status report could include a budget report, a quality section (particularly if there is formal quality plan), a list of unapproved change requests, and a list of potential risks. There are many different approaches and formats for status reports. The "right" status report is the one that works for the organization and for the project. Consider a scenario that walks through how a project manager created a status report and minimized administrative overhead time.

A Scenario: Creating a Project Status Report

A business decided to open their first satellite office for five staff people. Office space was selected and a four-month network infrastructure and communication project was assigned to a project manager, Andrew. With the assistance of the sponsor, Andrew and the core team created a project plan. Andrew and the sponsor agreed to plan and capture level of effort numbers at the task level, but to manage or monitor and control the project's scope and time at the work package and key deliverable level. Direct expenses were budgeted by task, but actual cost details would be captured at the work package level. Indirect expenses and direct salary related information were excluded from the project's budget.

During the planning process, Gantt charts were created at the task level and at a summarized level. The summarized Gantt chart included the key deliverables, work packages, and milestones. A risk register was created with two risks: the potential for delayed receipt of equipment and the potential for receipt of damaged equipment. The project manager and sponsor decided to be more formal than some other projects that had occurred within the organization. Andrew was to create an issue log and a change request log, even if no issues or change requests occurred. One reason to be more formal and create issue and change request logs was because the project was to be a prototype for future office openings. The project manager and sponsor thought that the additional formal documentation would simplify planning the next office opening.

The sponsor requested a formal weekly report be created of the project's status and wanted to know about any potential expense problems, but the sponsor was neutral as to the status report format used by the project team. Because the organization did not have a standard format, Andrew decided to use a generic status report template (see Table 22.1) and modify it to meet the needs of the project. Andrew was not interested in rekeying information into a template, so he decided to leverage other project-related reports for the status report by including them as attachments. Additionally, he did not want to create multiple reports for the various stakeholders, but knew he needed to keep all stakeholders informed. For example, some stakeholders expressed an interest in only knowing if the project was on track while others, including the sponsor, were interested in more detail.

Andrew decided to create a one-page summary status report for all stakeholders, including the team members and sponsor. The summary overview included the project status, accomplishments this week, plans for next week, and late tasks. Andrew decided to use three categories when describing the overall status. In an effort to eliminate any confusion as to what each category meant, written definitions were included on the report:

- *On target:* No known issues exist, but risks still exist and something could go wrong.
- *Minor trouble:* An issue has been identified and a risk exists that could impact the project, but the team is working to resolve the issue and is monitoring the risk.
- *Trouble:* An issue has been identified that will impact the scope, completion date, or budget.

Andrew also decided to add three attachments to the one-page summary status report. Each attachment contained pertinent detailed information for the team members and the sponsor:

- *Key deliverables and milestones:* Because Andrew had successfully used a summarized Gantt chart to manage a prior project and he thought the chart had been instrumental in keeping the team focused on the big picture, he decided to use a similar approach for this project. Andrew had assigned responsibility for key deliverables and work packages to the various team members, so he modified the chart slightly to include an owner column and added the team members' names to the key deliverables and work packages.
- *Issues:* Andrew had decided that because the project timeline was short, all issues had the same priority and needed to be addressed immediately.
- *Expenses:* The sponsor wanted to be kept aware of potential expense problems. Even though a weekly budget report was not a section in the generic status report template, Andrew decided to include the budget report as the third attachment.

Because Andrew, the core team, and the other team members had dual responsibilities, finding a time to meet weekly proved to be a challenge. They decided to hold weekly status meetings on Tuesday mornings, but agreed that the meeting needed to be focused and kept to one hour. Additionally, they agreed to provide actual time worked and cost from the prior week to Andrew on Monday before noon. The process was to be kept simple. An email was to be sent to Andrew with the actual hours by work package, noting if the hours were on target or not. This email reporting process enabled Andrew to update the project plan, compare actual versus plan numbers, and print out a new plan (Table 22.2). The Gantt chart could also be updated.

A typical weekly meeting started with Andrew confirming the agenda and providing a quick status of his activities during the past week. A team member volunteered to take meeting notes and post them in the shared project folder stored on the company network. Then, using the summarized Gantt charts (prior week and current week) and having the current plan available for reference, each team member provided an informal verbal update on their assigned work package(s) or key deliverable. The Gantt chart enabled everyone on the team to visually identify potential problem areas immediately and focus on resolving them. Issues were discussed, if needed, and the issue log was updated. Potential risks were reviewed. Actual versus budget costs were discussed, as needed. If necessary, potential change requests were discussed. Normally, task detail was

Table 22.2. Plan versus Actual Hours: Satellite Office Project

Project Name: Satellite Office Network and Communication
Date: End of Week 3

		Plan		Actual		Week 3 Hours			Cumulative Hours		
	Week	S	F	S	F	P	A	V	P	A	V
	Owner										
Consultant Hired	Scott	6/4	6/15	6/4	6/15	8	6	2	16	16	0
Hardware	Paul										
Facility Readiness Assessment		6/11	6/22	6/11	6/22	6	5	1	10	10	0
Hardware Plan		6/18	7/13	6/18		4	4	0	24	4	20
Hardware Design		7/9	8/3						24		24
Hardware Ordered		7/9	8/3						8		8
Server Implementation		8/13	9/21						90		90
Workstation Implementation		9/3	9/21						25		25
Other Hardware Implementation		9/3	9/21						24		24
Cabling	Wayne										
...	...	...	...	...	...	...	...	...	...	...	...
...	...	...	...	...	...	...	...	...	...	...	...

S, Start; F, Finish; P, Plan; A, Actual; V, Variance.

not discussed at the status meeting, but if a detailed conversation was required, a separate meeting was scheduled. The goal was for everyone to provide and obtain an update on the project's status, focus on the exceptions and issues, and at the same time to be respectful of everyone's time.

Week three's meeting included a discussion about the project's first issue. The preferred telephone and internet service provider had informed the project manager that they could not meet the target date for establishing telephone and internet connectivity. The team discussed the unexpected nature of this issue and the possible alternatives. The issue was logged and responsibility was assigned to a team member. Because resolution of the issue could impact other project deliverables and the risk had not been identified earlier, the risk was added to the risk register.

At the end of the status meeting, meeting notes were added to the project's documentation file and the project manager completed the creation of a status report that consisted of four pages:

- Project Status Report (Table 22.3)
- Summarized Gantt chart (Table 22.4)
- Issue Log (Table 22.5)
- Budget Report (Table 22.6)

The weekly status report was forwarded to the sponsor and the summary page was forwarded to other applicable stakeholders. A copy of the entire weekly status report was posted in the shared project folder stored on company network. Because the team had a project workroom, Andrew took the time to post the summarized Gantt chart on the wall to provide a quick, easy visual reminder of the project status.

Two key points are highlighted in this scenario:

- The team members collaborated and decided on the best way for them to provide actual time worked and cost from the prior week.
- A weekly status meeting was held and a status report, a formal written document, was created for documentation and reference purposes as well as to communicate with everyone pertinent to the project. How formal or informal the report was depended on the team and the project. In this scenario, the project manager leveraged other project documents in an effort to minimize administrative time, which resulted in an efficient approach.

As a project is monitored and controlled, communicating and collaborating on a project's status is necessary for project success. Be innovative. Decide on a reporting format that works for the team members as well as the organization. For most projects, the reporting format that works best for the team is a combination of informal and formal communication. Although the project manager is responsible for monitoring and controlling the project, having the team assist with determining a process for reporting the status of a project is a good practice.

There are a number of reasons why engaging the team members is a good practice. Two are related to obtaining team member support:

- The project manager is responsible for looking at the big picture and needs time and cost information so that an analysis of actual versus plan can occur, but if a process is implemented that the team members are unable or unwilling to support, the project manager will not have accurate data and information.
- By asking team members for input to the status reporting process, guidelines for the project are developed by the entire team. They work together to determine the best way for the team to function.

Table 22.3. Project Status Report: Satellite Office Project

Project Name:	Satellite Office Network and Communication
Prepared by:	Andrew
Week Ending:	Week 3
Project Description:	Plan, order, and install network and communication infrastructure for the first satellite office. Project includes computer hardware, software, telephones and internet service, and cabling. Project will become the prototype for future satellite offices.

Project Status:

Overall Status	On Target
Work	Minor Trouble
Schedule	Minor Trouble
Budget	On Target

Summary and Forecast
Accomplishments This Week:

Communication plan complete
Started planning hardware, cabling, and software

Plans for Next Week:

Continue planning hardware and software
Complete cabling plan

Late Tasks:

Issue 1: Phone and internet order not placed

Project Status Key:
On Target: There are no known issues, but risks still exist and something could go wrong
Minor Trouble: An issue has been identified and a risk exists that could impact the project, but working to resolve it.
Trouble: An issue has been identified that will impact the scope, completion date, or budget.

Attached:
Summarized Gantt Chart
Issue Log
Budget Report

Table 22.4. Summarized Gantt Chart: Satellite Office Project

Project Name: Satellite Office Network and Communication
Date: End of Week 3

	Owner	Week 1	2	3	4	5	6	7	8	9	10	11	12	13	14	15	16	17	18	19	20	21	Comments
Consultant Hired	Scott																						
Hardware	Paul																						
Facility Readiness Assessment																							
Hardware Plan																							
Hardware Design																							
Hardware Ordered																							
Server Implementation																							
Workstation Implementation																							
Other Hardware Implementation																							
Cabling	Wayne																						
Cabling Plan																							
Cabling Bids and Ordering																							
Cabling Installed																							
Software	Dana																						
Software Plan																							
Software Ordered																							
Software Implementation																							
Communication	Vic																						
Phone System Planned																							
Phone and Internet Order																							Issue 1
Internet Connectivity Established																							Issue 1
Training	Lauren																						
Documentation	Ann																						

Table 22.5. Issue Log: Satellite Office Project

Project Name: Satellite Office Network and Communication
Date: Week 3

	Issue	Significance and Impact	Issue Date	Actions and Resolution	Assign to	Resolve by	Date Resolved
1	Preferred phone and internet provider requires 6 weeks from signing of contract to service being activated	Plan anticipates a 4-week notice A 2-week delay could impact testing of cable installation, but will not impact hardware installation effort	5/1	Discuss impact of delay with vendor Decide by 5/3 if preferred phone and internet provider will be used or if project team will use their second choice	Karl	5/3	—
2							

Table 22.6. Budget Report: Satellite Office Project

Project Name: Satellite Office Network and Communication							
Date: Week 3							
	Week 3			**Cumulative**			
Category	**Budget**	**Actual**	**Variance**	**Budget**	**Actual**	**Variance**	
Consulting	$5,000	$1,000	$4,000	$20,000	$1,000	$19,000	
Hardware	$0	$0	$0	$25,000	$0	$25,000	
Software	$0	$0	$0	$6,000	$0	$6,000	
Communication	$0	$0	$0	$7,500	$0	$7,500	
Training	$0	$0	$0	$3,000	$0	$3,000	
Miscellaneous	$200	$150	$50	$3,200	$500	$2,700	
TOTAL	$5,200	$1,150	$4,050	$64,700	$1,500	$63,200	

Do not forget to include the sponsor in the project reporting discussion. The sponsor is a member of the team. The sponsor's reporting needs as well as the needs of the team members who are working on the project tasks need to be met.

If there is a required organizational status report format or if management requires a certain type of status report that does not meet the needs of the team, talk to the sponsor. Ask the sponsor for assistance with determining the right reporting solution so that the needs of everyone are met. The sponsor wants the project to be successful and he or she understands the team members need to have the right tools to monitor and control the project. The sponsor also understands that creating reports takes time and costs money and that this time and the associated costs need to be included in the project plan.

Some project managers, sponsors, and team members tend to forget that status reporting and status meetings are monitoring and controlling techniques. Creating a written, formal status report and holding status meetings to discuss the project are only two methods for reporting status. The project manager and team also need to determine how the day-to-day informal communications about project activities will occur. It is the combination of formal status reporting and informal communication and collaboration that assist with ensuring that the project is on track.

The person responsible for monitoring and controlling a project is the project manager, but for the project manager to be successful, having support from the project team is imperative. Without obtaining accurate data from the project team and having the "right" information in a format that can be used, ensuring project success will be difficult for the project manager.

Can creation of a status report be bypassed? Yes. If a project is very small, the project manager and sponsor may decide that a formal, written status report is unnecessary—but the project still needs to be monitored and controlled, which means the status of the project still needs to be communicated and discussed. The concern is that without a written status report, the entire status reporting process will be informal and over time, informal information will be lost and forgotten.

Suggestion: Keep project manager notes. Just as every project is unique and different, so are project managers. When making decisions about monitoring, controlling, and reporting, every project manager needs to determine the best approach for him or her and the best approach for the project. During the planning of a project, the project manager and sponsor discuss how to perform the monitoring, controlling, and reporting processes. A project manager and sponsor in a flat organization do not want to waste time or create excessive overhead. Compromise is often required because rarely is enough time available to document in detail all the work performed.

Project managers are constantly being asked questions that need to be answered quickly, which requires having project information readily available. Consider keeping a summary document such as a summarized Gantt chart with comments next to each work package and key deliverable or a journal with you at all times. The key point is to be prepared to answer questions at all times—you never know when a sponsor, team member, or stakeholder will ask a question. A quick, factually correct response is always better than "I need to check my notes. Let me get back to you."

IN REVIEW

- Monitoring and controlling a project are the formal and informal processes that occur daily during the execution of a project.
- Performance reports are the documents, financial statements, charts, and presentations for the project manager, sponsor, team members, and stakeholders that assist with monitoring and controlling the project. Performance reports may be referred to as project management reports or project control reports.
- The primary person needing a status report is the project manager. The project manager uses the status report to manage the work being performed by the team and to discuss the project with the sponsor, team members, and other stakeholders.
- A status report is a type of performance report that should be created for all projects. A status report is normally a formal written document that provides a snapshot of the project's progress as of a point in time and becomes a historical record of a project's progress. The report can be textual, graphical, or a combination of both.

- Just as a project manager and sponsor need to determine the "right" level of formal and informal control, they also need to determine the "right" level of data and information to include in a status report. At a minimum, a status report should include an overview of the project status, a summary and forecast of activity, the status of key deliverables and milestones, and the status of issues.
- The frequency of project status meetings varies by project size and type and organization. When managing a smaller project, at a minimum, consider holding a weekly status meeting and creating an updated formally written status report.
- Status meetings should be held on the same day and at the same time each week; be less than one hour; and have an agenda.

STEP-BY-STEP INSTRUCTIONS

Follow these guidelines for status reporting:

1. The project manager and team members discuss and develop formal and informal guidelines for communicating and collaborating on a project's status.
2. The project manager and sponsor determine the project's required project performance or management reports and include input from team members in the decision process.
3. Decide on status report frequency and format and, at a minimum, include in the format:
   - Project name, prepared by, week ending, and a project description
   - Overview of project status
   - Key deliverables and milestones
   - Issues
   - Summary and forecast of accomplishments this week, planned for next week, and late tasks
4. Decide on the time and frequency for the status meeting and create a standard status meeting agenda.

SECTION 7

CLOSING THE PROJECT

All projects have a close, an end. The work is completed and the project manager and team are ready to move on to another endeavor, whether to another project or back to day-to-day operations. Before this transition can occur, the project manager and sponsor verify that work has been accomplished as delineated in the scope statement and in subsequent change requests. Everyone reflects on what worked, what did not work, and ways to improve. The project manager collects and archives pertinent documents for future use, produces a final report, and communicates project experiences to others in the organization. The project manager and sponsor then thank the team members for their contributions and celebrate the project's completion. This section covers:

Chapter 23. The Closeout: Focuses on the administrative close of the project, including evaluating the project's performance, identifying the lessons learned, and archiving project documentation; migrating the final product or service to operations (if appropriate); and celebrating the project's completion

CHAPTER 23

THE CLOSEOUT

Covered in this chapter:

- Accepting the final product or service
- Evaluating the project and vendor
- Determining and evaluating the lessons learned
- Creating a final project report
- Archiving project documentation
- Celebrating the project completion and releasing the team

The close phase is the last phase of the project life cycle. Some organizations have elaborate checklists to close a project, but in flat organizations with informal controls, using elaborate checklists can be overkill. Just because an organization is flat, however, does not mean the close phase should be skipped. Properly closing the project ensures a completed project meets its objectives, all deliverables are complete, and the sponsor is satisfied with the final results. It also includes recapping project performance, documenting lessons learned, archiving project documentation for future reference, and before the team members are released from the project having a celebration thanking everyone involved for their hard work.

ACCEPT THE FINAL DELIVERABLE

Accepting the final product or service—the deliverable—sounds easy and uncomplicated, but there can be intervening tasks that a project manager and the team members may need take into account before the official acceptance occurs. Consider a project in which a marketing product was created by the project team and delivered to the sponsor. The sponsor agreed the deliverable met the requirements, accepted the marketing product, and declared the project complete. There were no problems, no outside vendors were involved, and there was no need to migrate tasks or processes to operations. But, what if the final product or service needs to be migrated to operations for future marketing campaigns? Or, what if a vendor had been used to augment the project team and the vendor is responsible for the final product or service? Or, what if the sponsor had found problems with the final product, which resulted in the product not meeting the requirements? Before a project team can close a project, they:

- Confirm, if applicable, the final product or service provided by a vendor or consultant meets contractual requirements
- Confirm the final product or service meets acceptance criteria outlined in the scope statement and subsequent change documents
- Migrate, if applicable, the final product or service to operations or production

Acceptance of a Vendor Deliverable

The formal acceptance of a vendor's product or service, the deliverable, and the agreement that the terms of the contract have been met closes a vendor's contract. The timing for acceptance depends on the project and the vendor. Acceptance can occur at the end of the project or it can occur during the project's execution when the product or service is delivered. Review the contract or statement of work for instructions on closing the contract and accepting a product or service.

Some contracts require written notification of acceptance. Some organizations, even if not required, send a letter to the vendor formally acknowledging acceptance and stating that the contract is closed while others consider the contract closed with the final payment. Still others find that a closeout meeting with an informal conversation is more appropriate. A closeout meeting is a walkthrough of the contract and statement of work to ensure nothing has been missed. The closeout meeting also provides both parties with a forum for discussing their relationship, which may be important if the vendor is a preferred vendor or if the organization would like the vendor to be a preferred vendor. Regardless of the method, be sure to close the project and the related contract with the vendor.

Acceptance of a Project Deliverable

Before a project is officially closed, the sponsor needs to accept or reject the final product or service—the deliverable. Sponsor acceptance or rejection of the deliverable begins with the project manager validating that the final product or service meets the requirements and acceptance criteria outlined in the scope statement and modified through change requests. If any discrepancies are noted, they are identified and an action plan with resolution dates is created. After the discrepancies are resolved, the project manager verifies that the deliverable confirms to the acceptance criteria and meets with the sponsor to verify the sponsor's satisfaction and acceptance of the final product or service.

In theory, a formal acceptance form should be signed by the sponsor, just like the scope statement that started the project. Many large projects within hierarchical organizations have formal acceptance documents. For smaller projects, if the sponsor is satisfied, a formal sign-off may not occur nor even be necessary, but recapping the meeting with the sponsor in writing to confirm what was discussed is always a good practice.

Suggestion: Use an acceptance questionnaire. Writing a few sentences outlining the acceptance criteria for the scope statement at the beginning of a project is usually an easy task. Also possible at the end of the project is a sponsor to state, "I meant acceptance to mean ...." In effect, an authority, the sponsor, has "moved the goal post"—changed the acceptance standards—resulting in the project no longer being complete because the sponsor's desired quality product or service has not been delivered or achieved. Fairness and morale issues aside, a project manager can take preemptive steps to mitigate the impact of changing sponsor or stakeholder standards. Depending on the size of your project, consider creating an acceptance questionnaire based on the sponsor's expressed and implied needs and expectations at the same time as the scope statement is written. The questionnaire might only have a few questions, but using a simple, brief questionnaire can assist with mitigating (not necessarily eliminating) new acceptance criteria being proposed at the end of the project.

Migration to Operations

If the final deliverable is migrated into operations (or production), the close phase includes a formal handoff to the operational staff. This formal handoff might be included in the project plan, particularly if tasks are associated with the transfer. A potential task could be the creation of an operational instructions manual. Project team members are involved in the handoff and assist with the transfer of knowledge and training. Once the migration is complete, operational staff are responsible for the deliverable and all questions are to be directed to the operational staff. Closing a project is extremely important when the deliverable is migrated into operations (or production) because without a formal close, the project may never end. Consider a story about the implementation of a software package.

The application was tested, the operational staff were trained, a list of follow-up action items was created, and the application was "moved into production." Everyone, including the project manager, Beth, was released from the project. A few minor follow-up items remained on the action item list, so the sponsor considered the project to be uncompleted and did not want to officially close the project. Six months later the action item list had grown, and the project manager, Beth, was splitting time between the "project" and her day-to-day operational responsibilities. A review of the action item list revealed many items that were never part of the original scope. Instead, the items were actually enhancements to operational processes around the software package.

What happened in this story is common when a project does not have an official close. To prevent a situation such as this, officially close the project, but create an action plan, assigning the project manager the responsibility of following up on the open action item's list. Make it clear that no more items can be added to the open items on the list and allocate adequate time for the project manager to resolve the items on the list. Alternatively, assign the action plan to the person who is responsible for the day-to-day operations of the project, which cuts all ties between the project manager and the project. The project manager will still be available to assist with questions, but will not be responsible for resolving the open items.

PERFORM THE ADMINISTRATIVE CLOSE

Once the final product or service is accepted (or accepted and transferred to operations), start the *administrative close*, which consists of evaluating the project and vendors; collecting and evaluating the lessons learned; writing a final report, if applicable; and collecting and archiving project documents. Cancelled projects also need to perform an administrative close process.

Perform Evaluations

One of the first administrative close actions is to evaluate the project and any vendors used on the project. The goal is to compare the original project request to the final deliverable. The information gathered during this evaluation process can assist with evaluating the lessons learned and writing the final report.

Project evaluation. At the end of the project, determine how well the project execution performed against the project plan (scope, schedule, and budget) and any subsequent change requests. A reason for performing an evaluation is so the project manager, sponsor, and team members can see what was planned and executed properly and determine if there are any areas for improvement. Another reason for performing an evaluation is for historical purposes. If the project plan is to be used as a template for a similar project in the future, the next project manager will have a starting point with valid historical information and suggestions for improving the project plan. Evaluate the project's overall performance by asking questions such as:

Scope:
- Was all work accomplished as assigned and agreed?
- Were all objectives met?
- Did the deliverable meet the requirements? If not, why not?
- How many change orders were received and approved? Why were these requirements omitted from the original requirements-gathering process and scope statement?

Schedule (Time):
- Was the project completed on time? If not, why not?

Budget (Cost):
- What was the cost to complete the project?
- Were all payments to third-party vendors accounted for?
- Was the cost within the budget constraints? If not, why not?

Document the project evaluation for future reference.

Vendor evaluation. A vendor had been hired because a service was needed for the project. As the project comes to an end, evaluate the vendor. Just as the project manager, sponsor, and core team evaluate how well the project performed against the triple constraints—scope, time, and cost—compare the vendor's performance to the signed contract or statement of work. Ask questions such as:

- Did the vendor adhere to the schedule?
- Did the vendor keep us informed about the status of the project in a timely manner?
- Did the vendor meet our acceptance criteria?
- Were the roles and responsibilities clear and understood?

Ask the same questions as when evaluating the project for adherence to the scope, schedule, and budget, but ask additional questions such as:

- Was the vendor competent and knowledgeable?
- Was the vendor professional and positive or was the vendor difficult and inflexible?
- Was the vendor open to suggestions? If a suggestion was not appropriate or could not be accommodated due to cost, did the vendor offer alternative recommendations?
- How did the vendor's project management processes compare to our standards?
- Did the vendor's personality fit with our culture?

Then ask the most important question:

- Would we hire the vendor again or recommend the vendor to another organization?

Document the vendor evaluation for future reference.

Collect and Evaluate the Lessons Learned

If nothing is evaluated, nothing is learned. Projects are learning experiences for the project manager, sponsor, team members, and the stakeholders. Every project team performs some tasks well, makes mistakes on others, and could have performed some tasks better. Capturing the lessons learned helps the people who worked on the project to learn as well as provides insight for future projects. The lessons learned help answer questions such as: "If we were going to start the project today, what should we do differently?" and "What would we do the same way?" Two types of lessons are learned from every project:

- The lessons learned about the project itself
- The lessons learned about the organization's project management methodology

Project lessons learned. Some organizations have elaborate processes for gathering lessons learned, but in a flat organization with informal controls, a brainstorming session with the project manager, sponsor, team members, and key stakeholders is an effective way to create a lessons learned document. If possible, have someone not involved or closely connected with the project facilitate the session. If holding a brainstorming session is impossible, collect information by email, telephone, or a quick survey and recap the information in a lessons learned document. Although creating a lessons learned document at the end of the project is imperative, conducting brainstorming sessions to capture lessons can occur at anytime during the project. Some project managers and sponsors prefer to brainstorm after each project phase or after the planning session and then brainstorm again when the project is complete. Keep a lessons learned brainstorming session simple; ask for positive and negative feedback; and document the comments (Table 23.1). Ask questions in three categories:

- What worked?
- What did not work?
- Are there ways to improve?

Table 23.1. Lessons Learned: Satellite Office Project

Project Name:	Satellite Office Network and Communication Infrastructure
Prepared by:	Project Manager
Date:	End of Project

What Worked
Assigning the work packages to the core team members with expertise in the area resulted in the duration and level of effort estimates being accurate.

The status meeting format and using a summarized Gantt chart to manage and communicate kept meetings and team members focused.

What Did Not Work
Team members with dual responsibilities were overcommitted even before the project started. In a few cases, their tasks were completed late.

The supply vendor used was late with the delivery of the cabling supplies.

Ways to Improve
Consider using PERT to estimate work package duration when no one has expertise in level of effort for the task.

As each question is brainstormed, consider addressing each project life cycle phase (initiating, planning, execution, and monitoring and controlling). Ask questions to assist with the brainstorming such as:

- Were the right people involved in the project?
- Was the work defined at the right level?
- Were the task durations over- or underestimated?
- Were the right project management tools and techniques used?
- What changes should be made to the status reporting format?
- Could the vendor contract negotiation process been improved?
- Did the quality checklist require "too many controls?"

Comments recorded in the lessons learned document assist with future projects, but they can also be used when discussing the organization's project management methodology lessons learned.

Project management methodology lessons learned. If an organization is new to project management or uses many informal processes and procedures, evaluate the organization's project management methodology to determine how well it is working for the organization. Determine if any processes and controls could be improved or if any processes or controls need to be eliminated from the organization's methodology. Start the lessons learned evaluation by reviewing the organization's written project guidelines and informal procedures. If there are no guidelines or procedures, determine which project management processes and controls are considered important to the organization. Consider starting with:

- The creation of the scope statement
- The project plan
- The formal and informal status reporting processes

Then brainstorm using the same categories as used for the project lessons learned:

- What worked?
- What did not work?
- Are there ways to improve?

Focus on the project management methodology, not the project. For example, *what worked* might be the use of a Microsoft® Word scope statement template. Even though the template was modified based on the project, the template provided a starting point, was easy to use, and ensured major points were not missed. Also review the project lessons learned comments to *what did not work.* Determine if any of the comments relate to the project management methodology being followed by the organization. For example, a comment to *what did not work* might be, "Each week's status report followed a different format. It was hard to compare one week to the next." Did this comment result from not having a standard format, a template, to use as a starting point or could it be that the project manager was inconsistent? Discuss comments about *are there ways to improve?* For the status report comment, ask: "What changes should be made to improve the status reporting format?" Improve does not mean developing formal processes and procedures. Improve can be changes to informal processes and procedures. After gathering and evaluating the lessons learned comments, create an action plan or implement changes to the project management methodology immediately. Too often, gathering and evaluating occurs, but nothing is changed.

Is holding two separate lessons learned sessions—one for the project and one for the project management methodology—necessary? No. If only one session is held, carefully analyze each comment to determine if it concerns a lesson learned about the project (a comment someone managing a similar project might be interested in knowing) or about an enhancement needed in the organization's project management methodology or both. Another idea is to periodically hold a lessons learned brainstorming session that consists of team members who have worked on three or four different projects. *Periodically* could mean after *X* number of projects or after the organization's annual strategic planning is complete. Discuss what worked, what did not work, and ways to improve. Possibly, some team members will make the same comments about what works well and what needs improvement, but there very well could be new ideas that surface that will benefit all of the organization's projects.

Suggestion: Use surveys for lessons learned. In an effort to be better organized for a brainstorming session, send a survey to all attendees—team members, sponsor, and stakeholders soliciting feedback prior to holding the brainstorming session. The survey can focus on areas of concern for the project manager or sponsor, such as the project communication process, estimating the time required, and volunteer involvement, or a quality control process. Ask specific project-related questions or general questions such as what worked well, what did not work, and what are ways to improve? To encourage team member and stakeholder honesty, keep individual surveys and results anonymous, but use the aggregated results from the survey as a starting point for the brainstorming sessions.

Write the Final Report

A separate formal written final report may not be necessary, particularly if the project and the vendor were evaluated and the lessons learned were documented. However, some sponsors or organizations prefer (or require) a final written report so that pertinent information is consolidated in a single document. The report might be used as a reference point for the next similar project; to provide information about a cancelled project; or, if funding was received, as the final report for the funding source. Consider including:

Organization:
- What was effective about the project's organization?
- Who were the project manager and sponsor?

Project Success:
- Was the project successful? If so, how and why was project success measured?
- How did the project's overall performance compare to the scope statement?
- If the project was cancelled, what were the reasons?

Migration to Operations:
- Was there an open item action plan?
- Were there any difficulties with the migration?

Lessons Learned:
- What worked?
- What did not work?
- Are there ways to improve?

Location of Project Documents:
- Where are the project documents archived?

Collect and Archive Project Documents

Historical project plans and project-related documentation are valuable resources for a project manager who is planning a future project. Having a project plan (scope, schedule, and budget) with actual numbers, even if the project is not identical to the project being planned, is a great starting point for estimating a future project. Knowing what issues occurred during a past project assists with avoiding future problems and risks. Information about a vendor enables a project manager to see how the vendor performed and if the vendor should be used again. Documents to consider archiving include:

- Scope statement
- Project plan (scope, schedule, and budget)
- Planning work papers and other documents
- Status reports and meeting notes
- Risk register and issue logs
- Vendor contracts and correspondence
- Evaluations, lessons learned, and final project reports

ANNOUNCE, CELEBRATE, AND RELEASE THE TEAM

With the final deliverable accepted and the administrative paperwork completed (or almost complete), the project has come to an end. The last actions are to announce the completion; celebrate, even if the project was not successful; and release the team.

Announce the End

During a project's close, communication still needs to occur with the stakeholders to ensure they are aware of the project's status. One way to inform stakeholders of the project's close is to announce that the project is complete in a similar manner to the project's start announcement. If the project's start announcement was a formal presentation, announce the close with a formal presentation. If the project's start announcement was by an email, announce the close with an email. The point is to officially inform the stakeholders and any other people that might be impacted by the project completion.

Be innovative and creative when thinking about ways to announce the project completion. For example, consider:

- Creating a video and posting it on the organization's website
- Highlighting the project in a newsletter, particularly if it impacts clients or customers
- Posting an announcement in the lobby or a building entranceway of the organization

Celebrate the Completion

During the kick-off meeting, the sponsor explained the objectives and the importance of the project to the organization and answered questions. At the end of the project, a similar event occurs, but this time the sponsor reflects on the project and, regardless of the project's success or failure, acknowledges and thanks everyone who participated and supported the project; they celebrate.

How an organization celebrates, acknowledges, and thanks everyone varies. Celebration does not necessarily mean a gigantic party-type gala. By the time a project is completed, some team members may be working on another initiative or working full time in a day-to-day operational role. Additionally, funds for celebrating may be limited.

Relatively simple effective ideas to help celebrate and thank the team members are posting their pictures on the organization's website with a thank-you message; including their pictures and highlighting team and individual efforts in videos and newsletters; having a simple low-cost team luncheon, pizza gathering, or reception right after work; presenting certificates of thanks; and giving token gifts such as a tee-shirt or gift card. Another idea is to combine the announcement about the project's completion with a thank you to the team members. Celebration for some team members just means they want to know they are appreciated. A personal thank you or a handwritten thank-you note may be all that is needed for them.

Release the Project Team

Some team members might have been released prior to the celebration and are now working only on their day-to-day operational tasks. Other team members might be assisting the project manager with administrative close activities or resolving product- or service-related discrepancy items. Once all administrative work is complete and issues are resolved, there should be no more project tasks. The project is complete. The very last act is to release all of the team members from the project, including the project manager.

IN REVIEW

- The close phase is the last phase of the project life cycle. The close phase consists of accepting the product or service, transferring the product or service to operations, closing the contract with the vendor, evaluating the project, and celebrating the project's completion.
- The project manager verifies the final product or service meets the requirements and acceptance criteria and then presents the deliverable to the sponsor and requests acceptance. If the deliverable is acceptable to the sponsor, the project close phase continues. If not, an action plan is created to address open items.
- The project's overall performance is evaluated based on compliance with the project's plan (scope, schedule, and budget), the scope statement, and subsequent change requests.
- A vendor's overall performance is evaluated based on compliance with the contract and statement of work.
- An important document, the lessons learned document for the project, in which the project team memorializes what worked, what did not work, and ways the project could have been improved, is created during the close process.
- Another document, the lessons learned document for the organization's project management methodology, might be created. This document is as important as the lessons learned document for the project, particularly for organizations that are new to project management.
- Project documentation is archived to serve as a valuable reference source for future projects.
- The project's success is celebrated and all team members and stakeholders are thanked for their participation and support.

STEP-BY-STEP INSTRUCTIONS

To close a project, follow these guidelines:

1. Verify that all work has been completed including:
   - Confirmation by the project manager that the deliverable meets the acceptance criteria in the scope statement and subsequent change requests
   - Creation of an action plan for any discrepancies or open items
   - Verification of acceptability of the deliverable and sign-off by the sponsor

2. Transfer or migrate the final product or service to operations (or production). Ensure that knowledge transfer and training occur.
3. Verify that the vendor's contract and statement of work are complete.
4. Perform an administrative close if the product or service is acceptable, which includes:
   - Evaluating the project's overall performance
   - Evaluating the vendor's overall performance (if a vendor was used)
   - Collecting and evaluating project and project management methodology lessons learned
   - Creating a recap or final report (if necessary)
   - Archiving project documentation
5. Communicate the project's completion to all stakeholders and any other appropriate people
6. Celebrate the project's success. Thank the team members and everyone who participated and supported the project.
7. Release the project team members.

CONCLUSION

People working in flat organizations are accustomed to a culture of creativity, flexibility, adaptability, and collaboration. They are comfortable working in an environment with limited controls and informal processes with minimal bureaucracy. When a decision is made to introduce and start following a project management methodology either for a single project or for all of an organization's projects, it is possible for staff to become frustrated. The reason is that project management is, by its nature, formal and controlling, with processes, tools, and techniques meant to provide structure to tasks aimed at achieving a defined goal—a very different approach from a casual culture.

The goal of this book is to assist people working within flat organizations to think through what they need to do to be successful when planning and managing a project—how to modify an approach so that it fits their needs and organizational culture. This book has focused on three critical activities: the first key activity is the defining of the project outcome and the recording of that definition in a scope statement (or project definition); the second activity is to plan what needs to be done and to create a project plan documenting what needs to occur to accomplish the outcome; and the third activity is to "work the plan" and successfully deliver the outcome with the aid of a status report. Subjects that support these key activities have been offered starting with providing the reader an understanding of the fundamentals of project management; then walking the reader through the entire project life cycle, from management aligning a project to the organization's strategy, to creating a project plan; and finally completing the project. Theory has been imparted; instruction has been given; and examples, visual aids, tools, and techniques have been provided so that readers can determine what is applicable to them and what fits and works within their organization.

The cultural differences between hierarchical and flat organizations and the project environment are discussed throughout the book. Are there and can there be cultural similarities between hierarchical and flat organizations? Of course, there can be and there are similarities, but there are a number of characteristics that tend to be different. These differences influence the planning of the project scope, time, and cost, the second key activity, and the process and controls for monitoring and controlling the project's execution, the third key activity.

Five characteristics of flat organizations that can impact an organization's project management methodology and the projects within the organization are identified and discussed in this book. The first characteristic is that rarely are staff able to be devoted to working on a project full time, resulting in the staff needing to juggle their day-to-day operational responsibilities with their project responsibilities, dubbed *dual responsibilities*. A second characteristic is that due to the limited number of staff, flat organizations often need to rely on third-party vendors and consultants to augment their staffs, but that costs money and typically includes a contract. Many flat organizations have limited funds, a third characteristic, which necessitates splitting these funds between their day-to-day operational needs and a project's needs. This characteristic can result in a much-needed project being postponed or even cancelled when money is tight. A fourth characteristic is the tendency for communication to be informal with minimal formal documentation, which can result in resistance when trying to implement a project management approach that relies on formal written communication methods. A fifth characteristic is lack of training and inexperience. The majority of people working within flat organizations are not trained or experienced in project management. Consequentially, assignment to a project team is a new experience for many people.

When focusing on the key activities, a project manager needs to work with the sponsor and team members to determine and maintain the right balance between formality and informality so that the benefits associated with a successful project are reaped without destroying the culture of the organization. *Right balance* means ensuring the project management approach implemented does not take on a life of its own, but rather blends with the culture and fades into the organizational background. Decisions are made jointly as to what works and what does not work for the organization. At first, management and staff can find project management to be overwhelming.

WHERE TO BEGIN

A common question asked by people working on their first project is, "If we do nothing else, what processes or controls should we implement first?" Focus on the three critical activities: defining the final project outcome, planning what needs to be done to accomplish the outcome, and then working the plan.

For some projects, the project information pertaining to the three activities might be recorded on only three sheets of paper—one for each of the key activities—while other projects will require more documentation due to the type or size of the project and the requirements of an organization's management:

1. ***Define*** the outcome, the deliverable: The first element of success is to define just what the project is to do for the organization and why. The introduction to this book starts with a quote by Yogi Berra: "If you don't know where you're going, you might end up some place else." Achieving an *undefined* goal—the "not knowing where you're going"—only happens by luck.

Focus on understanding the wants, needs, and expectations of the final deliverable. Create a scope statement (or project definition) that defines what the project will and will not accomplish. This scope statement document assists with determining the work being required of the team and is used as the starting point for creating a project plan. As the project is being defined, ensure the project is small enough to be manageable, enabling the product or service to be delivered within a reasonable timeframe. *Reasonable* is subjective, but if it appears that the project is going to take too long to deliver something, it might be too big. Analyze the project and, if possible, create a smaller project or a series of projects. Many big, complex projects are really a collection of a number of smaller projects. Projects of a modest scale tend to be simpler and easier to plan, manage, and execute, increasing the chances for project success.

2. ***Plan*** what needs to be done: The second element of success is to create a plan to do what has been defined—the deliverable. Although creating a plan sounds intuitive, some organizations hear the word *plan* and immediately think of a gigantic formal document that takes forever to create. They, therefore, skip this step and "wing it" hoping the project is successful. What tends to be forgotten is that a plan is a method or an approach for doing something—it can be as formal or informal as needed by the circumstances.

Create a project plan that outlines the project work (scope) and determines the schedule (time) and budget (cost). Planning can be tedious and require careful thought, but usually planning is not difficult. No matter how hard a team tries to create an accurate and realistic plan, it is also possible for a task to be missed or the level of effort for a task to be over- or underestimated, particularly when team members have dual responsibilities. A good plan prepared promptly that appears to be realistic is better than no plan or a perfect plan that is prepared too late to be beneficial to the project. Planning mistakes commonly occur, but with training and experience, mistakes tend to be reduced and planning mistakes can be remedied when working the plan.

3. ***Work the plan***: The third element of success is to execute the project by working the plan and monitoring and controlling the work with the aid of a status report. *Working the plan* means focusing on the work required for a particular task and performing the work. Strive to complete the task by the planned date and at the planned budgeted cost. Any adjustments needed to make the project successful should be made along the way.

When working the plan, the project manager and sponsor discuss and agree on how formal or informal the monitoring and controlling of the project will be including how to deal with issues, potential risks, and change requests. Working the plan also includes discussing how to report the project status. Although this report should be a formal written document, it should not be an administrative burden. The report needs to be a working document that supports the needs of the project manager, project team, sponsor, and other stakeholders. Successful project managers and sponsors add or revise processes and controls as required. If a process, control, tool, or technique does not work for you, the organization, or the project, evaluate to determine why not, and if need be, change or discard it. If there is no reason to implement a process or control, do not implement it. Just because a process or control is mentioned in this book, or in any other source, does not mean it must be put into practice in your organization or on your project. Keep project management processes and controls as simple as possible and ensure that anything that is implemented fits your organization's culture.

A FEW LAST COMMENTS

Project management is "not the end-all and be-all" solution. Implementing a project management approach does not mean a project will be successful, but the likelihood that it will be successful is improved.

Leaders within flat organizations intuitively realize that the inflexible and controlling formal project management methodologies used by many hierarchical organizations do not fit their culture. Leaders clearly understand that staff are their "number one" asset and too much control can destroy the morale and motivation of the staff. They realize that the success of a project and the success of a project management approach is a team effort requiring the support of everyone within the organization. Management and staff jointly work hard to implement project management concepts within the organization, but they also impose boundaries and limits so that flexibility, openness, collaboration, and an ability to respond quickly are maintained and formal processes and controls do not dominate. All in the organization understand that following project management processes can ensure project success, but all must also work hard so that the creativity, innovation, and culture of the organization are not destroyed.

Leaders also realize project management is not easy. There will be obstacles and challenges, and implementing a project management approach, either for a single project or all projects within the organization, requires change. Rarely does change occur smoothly. There will be bumps in the road, but even with the bumps people can successfully plan, manage, and execute projects.

At its heart, the goal of this book is to assist people to be successful when planning and managing a project by focusing on defining the final project outcome, planning what needs to be done to accomplish the outcome, and then working the plan. The book provides ideas to help ensure that work is productive, is efficient, and work goals are met by offering guidelines and suggestions for adapting project management processes and controls to flat organizations. Use the book to help your organization succeed. It is now time to get to work!

GLOSSARY

Acceptance criteria. Standards and conditions that must be met in order for a final product or service to be found satisfactory by a sponsor.

Actual cost. The direct and indirect expenditures incurred to complete the work for a task or work package during a given time period.

Analogous estimating (top-down estimating). An approximation method that uses the actual costs and durations of previous projects as the basis for estimating a current project.

Baseline. The scope, schedule (time), and budget (cost) plans that are the basis from which actual performance is compared to determine project variances.

Bottom-up estimating. An approximation method used to determine duration and cost by planning at the individual task or work package level and summing up the tasks or levels.

Brainstorming. A data-collecting technique that gathers people together in groups to identify and spontaneously discuss their ideas about potential risks, ideas, or solutions.

Budget. The amount of money allocated to a project to perform the work and deliver the final product or service based on the scope and schedule.

Change request. A request to expand or reduce project scope or some other aspect of a project plan.

Closing. A project life cycle process (also phase); all work is complete, the final product or service is accepted, and the project is formally ended.

Co-location. Project team members situated close to one another to improve communication, working relationships, and productivity.

Constraints. Factors that will, or could, limit the way a project can be planned or managed.

Contingency reserve. The extra time and money added to a project plan to respond to the potential expected and unexpected opportunities and difficulties of a project.

Contract. A mutually binding agreement that obligates the seller to provide a specified product or service and obligates the buyer to pay for the product or service.

Core team. Team members who are integral to a project's success, are involved in more than one project life cycle phase, and who perform a significant amount of the project work.

Cost. The actual expenses a project has incurred or has paid for resources, such as equipment, materials, salaries, and vendors.

Cost of quality. Total expenses for implementing a quality initiative; includes all costs associated with preventing as well as fixing quality problems.

Crashing. A schedule-compressing technique that decreases project duration by analyzing the critical path and then determining if the duration of a task can be shortened or reduced by adding additional resources.

Critical path. The sequence of tasks that requires the longest duration to complete with no slack or extra time and sets the minimum length of time required to complete a project.

Critical Path Method (CPM). A technique that uses a project's network diagram to analyze each task's relationship to another and each task's duration to determine the minimum length of time required to complete the project.

Critical tasks. Tasks on the critical path.

Decomposition. Each deliverable is broken down into smaller, more manageable deliverables until the lowest realistic level is achieved.

Decision matrix. Tools that assist with ranking potential projects or outcomes based on predetermined criteria.

Deliverable. All products, services, and documents that the team produces as a result of a project.

Delphi technique. An anonymous information-gathering technique used to collect opinions and ideas and then reach consensus.

Description. Prose briefly explaining a project's purpose and the work to be performed.

Descoping. Reducing the scope of a project by removing features and functionality from the agreed-upon product or service.

Dual responsibilities. Day-to-day operational duties and project duties that are assigned to one person.

Duration. Lapse time needed to complete each task, work package, deliverable, phase, or project.

Early start (ES). The earliest date a task can begin.

Estimate. A rough calculation; a best guess of a project level of effort, duration, cost, and resource requirements.

Estimating worksheet. A table, spreadsheet, or Word document used to collect and memorialize for each task or work package the duration, level of effort, and staff and other resource needs; may also include costs and known risk(s).

Exclusions. The features and functionality not included in a project.

Executing. A project life cycle process (and phase); the necessary work to be performed by team members to create a product or service.

Expert judgment. Opinions and advice provided based on knowledge of a particular area or based on experience.

Fast tracking. A compressing technique that shortens the critical path by overlapping or performing work in parallel instead of sequentially.

Fish bone diagram. A cause-and-effect diagram approach used to evaluate quality problems and to determine the cause.

Fixed-price contract. Service or product provided for a specific price from a vendor.

Float (slack). The amount of time a task can slip without delaying a project's completion date; the difference between the early start and the late start (or the difference between the early finish and the late finish).

Forecast. An expenditure projection based on what has occurred to date and what is expected in the future.

Functional organizational structure. An organizational structure in which a functional (department) manager is responsible for the day-to-day operational tasks and related project tasks and staff (team members) may be assigned from to another department (e.g., accounting) to support specific needs.

Gantt chart. A bar chart of schedule information with dates across the horizontal axis and tasks (or deliverables and milestones) listed down the vertical axis; task durations are shown as horizontal bars under the appropriate dates.

Guidelines. Recommendations that allow for the use of judgment and discretion.

Histogram. A bar chart that organizes a group of data points into user-specified ranges to provide an easy-to-interpret visual diagram.

Initiating. A project life cycle process (and phase); the project is started, the final product or service delivered is clarified, and stakeholders are defined.

Interest. A subjective expression of a person's attention to and concern about a project's success or failure; an expression of the significance of a project to an individual.

Issues. Questions or points of concern that can lead to project changes.

Lag. The time delay between the start or finish of one activity and the start or finish of another activity.

Late finish (LF). The latest date a task can finish and still allow a project to be completed on time.

Late start (LS). The latest date a task can start and still allow a project to be completed on time.

Lead. The time overlap between the start or finish of one task and the start or finish of other tasks.

Level of effort. Amount of time required to complete a task.

Lessons learned. Experiences of the team that provide insight for future projects.

Logical relationship table. A columnar table used to identify the relationships between tasks by linking a task to its predecessor.

Matrix organizational structure. An organizational structure that is a blend of functional and project reporting structures using a dotted or broken line relationship; the staff (team members) reports to a project manager and a functional manager (see Dual responsibilities).

Milestones. Important project checkpoints that mark the start or finish of a significant task or group of tasks or the completion of a major deliverable.

Monitoring and controlling. A project life cycle process that consists of tracking, analyzing, adjusting, and reporting a project's progress.

Network diagram. A graphical flow of the tasks that must be accomplished to complete a project; shows the sequence of the tasks and their duration, interdependencies, and interrelationships; a common networking technique is the precedence diagramming method (PDM).

Objective. Statements expressed in terms of scope, time, and cost that describe what a project is trying to achieve.

Operations. Tasks that are repeatable, cyclical, and ongoing; best thought of as "business as usual."

Overlapping projects. Two or more projects that partly occur at the same time.

Parametric estimating. An approximation method that uses mathematical parameters to predict project costs.

Performance reports. Documents, financial statements, project recaps, and presentations that assist with monitoring and controlling a project's progress.

Phases. A clearly distinguishable period or stage in a project's process or project work breakdown structure.

Planning. A project life cycle process (and phase) defining the scope, objectives, deliverables, and course of action for a project.

PMBOK® Guide. *A Guide to the Project Management Body of Knowledge* is the Project Management Institute's international project management standards.

Portfolio. A collection of programs and projects that are linked together because they support the overall strategic objectives of an organization.

Power. Refers to the amount of influence a stakeholder has in decision-making.

Precedence Diagramming Method (PDM). The most commonly used network-diagramming method that shows tasks as boxes and uses lines with arrows to connect them.

Predecessor task. A task that occurs before another task in a project.

PRINCE2®. PRojects IN Controlled Environments is a generic project management methodology that is the standard in the U.K. and over 50 other countries.

Probability. The likelihood that the risk will occur.

Probability-impact matrix. A tool to assist with assigning risk by plotting the probability (the likelihood that an event or circumstance will occur) and impact (the effect a risk will have on the scope, schedule, and budget of each risk).

Product requirements (service). The feature and functionality requirements of a final product or service.

Program. A group of interrelated projects with a common objective that by managing them together accrues a benefit to an organization.

Program Evaluation and Review Technique (PERT). A three-point estimating method that uses probability to determine the duration estimates for project phases and tasks.

Project. Temporary work that has a clearly defined beginning and end that results in the creation of a unique and specific product or service.

Project charter (project authorization form). A document written by the sponsor (or management) that formally authorizes a project.

Project life cycle. The four phases or logical divisions of work that together to describe the chronology aspects of a project: initiating, planning, executing, and closing; project life cycle also consists of five processes: initiating, planning, executing, closing, and monitoring and controlling.

Project management. An established approach for planning, managing, and controlling resources to achieve a particular goal within a specified timeframe and budget.

Project management methodology. An established approach for planning, managing, and controlling a project; the objective of project management is to facilitate the delivery of a quality product or service within a specified timeframe and budget.

Project management plan. A formal, approved document that defines how a project is executed, monitored, and controlled; the document is composed of one or more subsidiary management plans and other planning documents.

Project manager. A person assigned responsibility and authority by management to ensure the work is successfully completed on time and on budget.

Project organizational structure. An organizational structure in which the staff (team members) and a project manager are assigned exclusively to a project.

Project plan. The combination of the scope (work), schedule (time), and budget (cost) baselines.

Project requirements. The business and project-related management requirements of a project.

Power-interest grid. Stakeholders grouped based on their level of authority or power and their level of concern or interest in a project's outcome.

Project tracking report. A document used to assist with monitoring and managing potential and current projects.

RACI. An acronym for Responsible, Accountable, Consulted, and Informed; a more complex RAM (see Responsibility Assignment Matrix) in which each task or work package is assigned to a team member.

Resources. Staff, equipment, third party services, supplies, commodities, material, and funds needed to complete a project.

Resource histogram. A bar chart that shows the amount of time a person or group will be working over a period of time to ensure a person or group is not overcommitted or underutilized.

Responsibility Assignment Matrix (RAM). A communication tool that assists with ensuring that all tasks or work packages are assigned to team members or a group of team members.

Requirements. Something wanted, needed, or expected to satisfy a condition, contract, or standard expressed by management, the sponsor, or other stakeholders.

Requirements document. A document that memorializes the product (or service) and project requirements.

Risk. The unknown, unplanned, and unexpected events, but also the known but unexpected events, that have a positive or negative effect on a project's outcome.

Risk register. A document that provides details about all project risks, including the category, causes, probability of occurring, impacts, proposed responses, and status.

Schedule. The dates for starting and ending the work and the hours required to create the final product or service and manage a project.

Scope. The work that will or will not be performed to deliver a specific product or service.

Scope creep. The uncontrolled addition of features and functionality without an increase in time or cost.

Scope statement (project definition or project initiation document). A formal, signed document that provides an official description of a project and defines the project objectives, requirements, deliverables, exclusions, acceptance criteria, and sign-offs.

Sequential projects. Two or more projects that occur consecutively or one after the other.

SMART. An acronym for Specific, Measurable, Attainable, Realistic, and Timely; defines the characteristics of a properly written objective.

Sponsor (project sponsor or champion). A business leader assigned by management as the primary point person for an approved project; a person responsible for the approval and acceptance of the key deliverables.

Stakeholders. A person or group that can affect or be affected by a project; a person or group who has an involvement, an interest, or a degree of commitment to a project's outcome.

Stakeholder list (stakeholder register). Captures each person's expectations as well as other pertinent stakeholder information.

Statement of Work (SOW). A part of a contract (or an amendment) to a contract that authorizes work and defines the final deliverable.

Status report. Provides a snapshot of a project's progress at a point in time.

Successor task. A task that occurs after another task in a project.

Suggestions. Ideas to be considered.

Sunk cost. An expense that has been incurred and cannot be recovered.

Tasks (activities). The manageable and executable pieces of work that roll up to work packages and have a time, cost, and resource requirement.

Team members. Anyone who contributes or has some role in a project in assisting with achieving project goals and contributing to the overall success of a project.

Techniques. A procedure or method employed by a team member.

Template. A predefined document format used to collect, organizes, and present data and information.

Time. How long a project phase, work package, or task will take measured in duration and level of effort.

Trigger. An event or signal that a risk event is likely to happen.

Triple constraints (the project triangle). The constraints around which all projects are built: scope, time, and cost; if any one of these constraints changes, at least one of the other constraints changes or quality is impacted.

Tools. A tangible that team members use to perform work.

Quality. A subjective expression of how close a project's product or service fulfills its requirements.

Variance analysis. A method of scrutinizing the differences between actual cost and budget; also actual time and planned time.

Work Breakdown Structure (WBS). A hierarchical breakdown that organizes and defines all work to be completed by a project.

Work package. Composed of the tasks, the deliverables, at the lowest level of the work breakdown structure.

INDEX